LIFE IN CHRIST

Register This New Book

Benefits of Registering*

- ✓ FREE accidental **loss replacement**
- ✓ FREE **audiobook** – *Pilgrim's Progress*, audiobook edition
- ✓ FREE information about new titles and other **freebies**

www.anekopress.com/new-book-registration

*See our website for requirements and limitations.

LIFE IN CHRIST

Lessons from Our Lord's Miracles and Parables

The Miracles of Our Lord
Volume 9

Charles H. Spurgeon

We love hearing from our readers. Please contact us at www.anekopress.com/questions-comments with any questions, comments, or suggestions.

Life in Christ, Vol. 9
© 2023 by Aneko Press
All rights reserved. First edition 1891.
Revisions copyright 2023

Scripture quotations are from The Authorized (King James) Version. Rights in the Authorized Version in the United Kingdom are vested in the Crown. Reproduced by permission of the Crown's patentee, Cambridge University Press.

Cover Design: Natalia Hawthorne
Cover Painting: Matt Philleo
Editors: Ruth Clark and J. Martin

Aneko Press

www.anekopress.com

Aneko Press, Life Sentence Publishing, and our logos are trademarks of
Life Sentence Publishing, Inc.
203 E. Birch Street
P.O. Box 652
Abbotsford, WI 54405
RELIGION / Christian Life / Spiritual Growth
Paperback ISBN: 979-8-88936-256-2
eBook ISBN: 979-8-88936-257-9
10 9 8 7 6 5 4 3 2 1
Available where books are sold

Contents

Chapter 1

A Great Bargain

*Again, the kingdom of heaven is like unto a merchant man,
seeking goodly pearls: who, when he had found one pearl
of great price, went and sold all that he had, and bought it.*
(Matthew 13:45-46)

A merchantman endeavors to trade so as to make a profit. Whether he deals in pearls or in grain, he does not hope to obtain riches by labor. He leaves that to those who eat their bread by the sweat of their face. He tries to get his by the sweat of his brain. He is dependent not so much upon labor as upon knowledge, upon skill, upon the advantage which superior acquaintance with the article which he deals in gives to him. Now, this merchantman is, at the very commencement, in some measure a picture of the seeker after Christ.

Christ and his salvation are not to be earned; they are not to be procured as the result of labor. But Christ is to be had by knowledge. What does the Scripture say? *By his knowledge shall my righteous servant justify many* (Isaiah 53:11); that is, through their knowing Christ they become justified. This is, indeed, another way of putting the system of salvation which is stated thus: *How shall [I] hear without a preacher?* (Romans 10:14). The work begins with hearing the preacher; then it goes on to believing what they hear, and through believing they are saved.

This is virtually knowledge – the knowledge communicated by God's messenger or by God's Word – the knowledge heard, the knowledge believed. So men come to the knowledge of him whom to know is life eternal, for when a man knows Christ and understands him so that he gives his heart to him, then is he saved. Inasmuch, then, as the merchantman seeks his advantage by superior knowledge, he becomes a type of the man who gets saved through obtaining the knowledge of the glory of God in the face of Jesus Christ.

I shall not, however, enlarge upon this analogy, but will proceed at once to speak of the merchantman in this parable, for here we have a good emblem of many who lay hold on Christ and find him to be their all in all. Let us watch this merchantman while he is doing four things: first, *seeking*; then *finding*; then *selling out*; and fourthly, *buying again*.

First, then, we shall watch him while he is seeking. *The kingdom of heaven is like unto a merchant man, seeking goodly pearls.* It is different from the man we read of just now who, by accident, discovered a treasure while he was in the field. He was looking for something else and came upon the treasure. That is the man whom God, in infinite sovereignty, saves, though he was up to this time indifferent and careless. This is a person of a nobler sort. He is of a higher grade of mind – of altogether different mental constitution. He is seeking goodly pearls – something good – not exactly seeking the one pearl of great price, for at first, he does not know about it; but still, he is seeking pearls, and he comes upon one pearl in consequence of his seeking.

Now, notice about him, as a seeker, that *he has his mind aroused and engaged.* He is thinking about something – thinking about pearls. His heart is occupied with his business. His energies are thrown into it. All his thoughts are in the direction of precious stones. Oh, that we could wake men up to exercise the faculty of thinking, and then to direct, to regulate, and to control their thoughts! But thinking is an occupation that a great many persons altogether dislike. They are frivolous. We cannot get them to think about anything.

Why is it that people are so passionately fond of reading novels, and so seldom read the true histories which are quite as interesting, and far more capable of affording pleasure and pastime? It is because the minds of men are frivolous. An idle tale – a silly story of a love-sick maid – will engross them by the hour together; but anything that is solid and worth knowing seems to have small charm for their shallow brains.

Many minds never get on the wing at all. Not a few men work so hard with their hands, and suffer such fatigue from bodily labor, that they are scarcely able to think much; while there are others who squander their time and consume their lives in idleness, until they are utterly disqualified for any vigorous thought. They are lazy and sluggish. They have the dry rot in their very souls. Their brains do not work. They seem to live in one everlasting lethargy and daydream.

Oh, that men were wise, that they were thoughtful! Happy would be the preacher who knew that he was addressing himself to a thoroughly intelligent, thoughtful congregation. We should expect, then, that the handfuls of good seed would drop into the furrows readily and bring forth an abundant harvest. This merchantman's mind was aroused. He had something before him.

Equally evident is it that *he had a fixed definite object*. He had given himself to pearl hunting, and pearl hunting was to be the one object of his life. If you had met him and said, "What are you seeking?" he would have answered in a moment, "I am seeking good pearls; have you any to sell me?" He would have been sure to have the answer ready at hand. But ask many a man whom you meet with, "Sir, what are you living for?" and he would, perhaps, tell you what his trade or what his profession is; but if you pressed him with the question, "What is the main object of life?" he would not like to say that he was living only to enjoy himself – seeking his own pleasure. He would hardly like to say that he was living to grasp and grab and get a fortune. He would hardly know how to answer you.

Many young men are in this condition: they do not have a definite object. Now, you will not make a good captain if you do not know the port you are sailing for. You will make a poor life of it, young man, if you go out as an apprentice, and then afterwards out as a master, with no definite aim and end. Say to yourself, "I can only live for two things. I can live for God, or I can live for the devil; which now am I going to do?" Get your mind well fixed and firmly resolved as to which it shall be.

I will put it to you as boldly and openly as even Elijah did when he said, *If the Lord be God, follow him: but if Baal, then follow him* (1 Kings 18:21). If the world, if the flesh, if the devil be worth serving, go follow the career of a sensualist and say so. Let yourself know what you are about. But if God be worth serving, and your soul worth the saving, go in for that; but do not sneak through this world really seeking yourself, and yet not having the courage to say to yourself, "Self, you are living for yourself." Do have a definite and distinct object or else your vital energies will be wasted, and your most industrious days will be recklessly squandered.

This merchantman, in the next place, had *an object that was not at all commonplace.* Other people might go in for bricks and stones, or for grain, or for timber. He went in for pearls. He was a merchantman seeking pearls, and those the best he could pick up. He did not go in for common sea pearls, or pearls such as you may get in a Scotch river, but he went in for goodly pearls. He took a high aim, as far as that line of action was concerned. He went into a fine business. I would to God that many who have not found Christ nevertheless had sufficient common sense, sprinkled over with grace, to say, "I will go in for something good. My life shall not be an inferior one."

> Lives of great men all remind us
> We may make our lives sublime.

It bodes well for a young man when he has such an aspiration as this within him: "My life, too, shall be sublime. I will not seek ordinary or lowly objects; I will not cultivate any depraved or groveling tastes. I will seek something that I can commend to my own conscience – something that will bear reflection when I come to die – something that will carry the sterling mark when I have to value it in another world."

O young merchantman, if you are about to start in business, I recommend you this business of seeking goodly pearls. Seek truth, seek honor, seek moderation, seek peace, seek love, seek that which will make you good and true and right. I will tell you immediately where you may find these, but for the present it may suffice me to infuse a commendable ambition for everything that is honest and of good repute, and an eager desire with your heart for that which your conscience commends.

He went thus, to seek pearls, and *he sought them with diligence.* The merchantman was seeking goodly pearls. He did not open a shop, and say, "Pearls bought here if anybody likes to bring them," but he went forth in search of them. How far he traveled I do not know; but the Oriental trader frequently goes immense distances. You may meet a Nijni Novgorod in the south of Russia, with traders who have been all around the globe seeking what they want – men who do not always travel by railway, but who will walk any distance to obtain the very article on which they have set their minds, and in which they deal.

Distance seems with them to be no object. Ah, and when a man has got a noble object before him, and says, "Before I die, I will accomplish something that shall be right and true and beneficial to my fellow man," he will face hardships that would baffle his fellows. I pray God that he may have the perseverance to carry that out, and that he may say, "Is there anything right to be learned? I will learn it, let it cost me what it may of care and toil, of headaches and heartaches, of buying experience and burning the midnight oil. If there is anything to be done that is good and true, I will do it at any hazard, for I am seeking goodly pearls."

And as the man was seeking, so he was *using discrimination at the same time.* When we are very diligent and full of desire, we are in imminent danger of being easily deceived; but this man seeking goodly pearls was not like a lady unacquainted with the nature of pearls, but he was a merchantman who knew a pearl when he saw it. He knew the character of pearls and the value of pearls; he could tell which were cloudy, and which had a soft radiance, and which were of the highest quality. Indeed, he could tell a genuine pearl from an imitation one. He was a merchantman seeking goodly pearls.

Yes, dear friend, and I pray God that if he put into the heart of any brother here to live for the right and for the true, he would give you great discrimination, for there are many shams in the world, and you may readily grasp that which appears to be substantial goodness, and it may turn out to be a shadow. Seek not pearls alone, but seek goodly pearls. Go in for the good; yes, cast your soul around to find the best.

Evidently this merchant *went into the business with comparatively moderate expectations.* He was seeking pearls. They must be of a tolerable size, and pure. He evidently expected to buy a good many of them. It was what he was seeking, seeking goodly "pearls" (in the plural). He had not reckoned that he would be fortunate enough to light upon one huge pearl that would be worth an emperor's ransom. That he had not looked for, though he did feel a desire that way. If anybody had said, "Would you like to find a big pearl?" he would have said, "That I would, infinitely better than to find a number of little ones." He hardly hoped for it, and therefore he did-not seek it; but still, he was ready enough to have it if it came his way. And so, my dear friends, I am speaking of a class of persons – and I hope there may be representatives of them here – who want everything they can get that is good and true.

You want to be moderate in all things; you want to have an spotless character. I recollect that was my own desire, when first I thought of the life that lay beyond me. Before I knew the Lord I used to think, "O that I might be kept from dishonesty, that I might be preserved from falsehood, that I might be kept from a malicious spirit, that I might be right-hearted and true." Those were the pearls that I wanted. I did not know just then that I could find something that would include all these minor pearls and a good deal more. Still, it is well when such a desire as that is in the heart, especially of any young man. I wish it were in the heart of the old, if up until now they have never found the pearl of great price.

Thus have I shown you the man while he is seeking. I wonder whether he has come in here tonight and is sitting among this assembly. Perhaps it is not a man at all, but a woman, a merchant woman. They can do trading well. Lydia, that seller of purple, was, no doubt, an admirable tradeswoman, and in the divine trade of which we are now speaking there is no difference. Well, you do not know the Lord yet, dear friends, but you do want to seek everything that is excellent. So far so good.

Let us go a stage further, then, and look at this man's findings. He was buying pearls everywhere. Where he went, he asked people if they had any pearls. He went down the back streets, into the slums of big cities, and found the Jews in those old days, living in the dirtiest corners of the city. He wanted to know whether they had any pearls. It was pearls of a morning, pearls at midday, pearls at night. If under his window at night anybody had cried, "Pearls!" he would have been downstairs in an instant to get them. He was going hard after pearls; and so it came to pass that he lit upon a pearl that he had never hoped to see. It was more than he expected.

Ah, I pray God that some here, whose hearts are honestly seeking after that which is right, may find Christ, who has in him more of the spirit of moderation, uprightness, truth, and philanthropy than will be found anywhere else. Oh, that they might find him who is the truth, and whose doctrine is perfect holiness and everlasting life. It will be more than they ever expected to find, but when they do find it, how glad they will be.

Certainly this man was in the way of finding a fine pearl if anybody was. He was seeking *goodly pearls,* not *the one* pearl; but he was in the pearl line, and so he was likely to discover the best pearl if anybody discovered it. "Being in the way, the Lord met with him," says one of old. Oh, if you have desired that which is right and true and good, I trust that the Lord Jesus will manifest himself to you, and that you will say, "This is the very thing I sought for; I have longed and yearned for it, and here it is."

This find was to this merchantman *a remarkable one.* He did not find goodly pearls; he found what was much better: one pearl; and to him that one pearl contained all the little pearls that he had formerly been seeking after. Tell it, and let all men know it, that all that is good beneath the moon – all that is true, all that is right, all that is loving, all that is philanthropic, all that is of good report, commendable before God and praiseworthy among men, is to be found in the teaching of the Lord Jesus Christ, and will be given to us, and effected in us when we submit ourselves to him, and make him our all in all. He who is a Christian, if he be perfectly a Christian, has all good things in one. If there be anything that is to be praised and extolled by philosopher or sage, you shall find it in the example of the Master, and he will give us grace to exhibit it in ourselves.

So this man *found all in one.* What the value of that pearl was, I do not know. The estimate of its value is not given. We only know that he thought it was worth all that he had, and he went away and sold all that he had that he might buy it. And he evidently thought it was worth all the other pearls he had ever been seeking for, because if he spent his all upon that one pearl, it would be clear that he must have abandoned from this point on the searching after smaller pearls, since he had no capital left. But he thought the one pearl of more account than all other pearls, and worth more than all that he had.

Yes, I warrant you that he thought it worth a great deal more than all that he possessed. He would not have sold all that he had in stock to buy it if he had not the notion that it was worth ten times the price then, and that when he had paid it all he would have made his fortune, and would be rich beyond a miser's dream, for that is how traders in such things are sure to fetch their bargains. Well, when a man finds Christ, I cannot tell you how much he values him, but this I know, that all the world besides seems as nothing to a Christian when he has once found his Lord and Master. "Oh, what a Christ have I!" says he. But he cannot tell how dear – how inconceivably precious – the Christ of God is to his soul.

Concerning this find we must observe next that the man having found it was *resolved that he would have it*. Having found the pearl of great price, he did not question whether he should buy it or not. If he had not gone out honestly to seek pearls, he would have objected to the price; but being intent upon pearl-finding, he no sooner found this than he said, "I must have that. I can let the little pearls go if you like, but I must have that." And it is a grand thing when the Lord brings the human mind to this. "I see that in Christ there is everything I want – pardon for my sin, cleansing for my nature, grace to maintain my character and to make me perfectly fit for heaven. There is all in Christ that I want, and I must have him. I *must* have him. It comes to this – at any price and whatever it may cost me – I must and I will have him."

Now, although the parable does not say it in so many words, it is perfectly clear that the person with whom he was dealing was willing to sell. When he had found one pearl of great price, he bought it, which he could not have done if the other person had not been ready to sell it. Albeit the Lord in his mercy does not sell his grace, but gives it freely, the manner in which he disposes of it is here described under the figure of speech of "selling." If you want Christ, you may have him, if you are willing to come to the terms which God lays down. Of this I shall have to speak presently. If you desire this pearl of great price, there is no reason in the world why that pearl should not be yours.

If now you have found him, who is *the chiefest among ten thousand* (Song of Solomon 5:10) and *altogether lovely* (Song of Solomon 5:16), and you value him so that you cannot be happy without him, he will become at once your portion. If, having heard of Christ, your desire is toward him as all your soul can need, and you are ready to say, "I will not leave this house of prayer until Christ is mine," there is no obstacle

8

to your possessing this priceless asset. Yes, God, even the Father, is willing that you should have his only begotten Son to be your pearl henceforth and forevermore.

Having thus described the seeker, and described the finder, we must go on to describe him selling out. He sold out all that he had. It had taken him a long time to get it together, and I have no doubt he had much pleasure in the accumulation; but now he has great pleasure in selling. "Buy my farm," he says to one man. "Come buy it."

"I don't know that I want to buy farms," says the other. "It is nothing; it is nothing."

"Nevertheless, let us come to terms. I want money, and I must have money." And away went the furniture down in the house, one article after another.

They must all go; clear them all out. There was a rapid sale. He must have money. They must *go*; everything must go for that pearl. Though he did not tell anybody his motive, that pearl was on his brain and on his heart, and all must go. He is more glad to get rid of his possessions than ever he was to obtain them. Away they shall go at the best price they will fetch, but go they must, for he must have the pearl. Well now, Jesus Christ is to be had, but there is a great deal that a man must give up if he is ever to call Christ his own.

"What, then," says one, "what am I to give up?" Well, there must be a selling off of a whole mass of *old prejudices.* Sometimes when the truth as it is in Jesus comes to a man's mind, he repels it because it is so different from what he has learned ever since he was a child, and the notion is that you had better follow the religion of your parents. If you had been a Hottentot, you would have worshipped a fetish. If you had been born in Hindustan, you must have worshipped Juggernaut, according to that theory. But it is a great mercy when a man says, "Now I understand that Jesus the Son of God has died in the room and place and stead of sinners that believe in him, and I am simply to believe in him and I shall be saved.

On my believing I shall receive a new nature and be born again by the Holy Spirit, and henceforth I shall become the disciple and the servant of Christ. "Now," says the man, "I will do it. It is contrary to what I have always been told. I have been led to think that it was my good works which would save me. I have heard that the grace was in the sacraments, but at length I perceive that God teaches in his Word that salvation is by faith in Jesus Christ, and I will have it. I will sell my prejudices off. Away they shall go."

Next to that you must sell off *your righteousness*. It will not fetch much, but I daresay you will think it is a fine thing. Up to this time you have been very good, and your own esteem of yourself is that as touching the commandments – *All these have I kept from my youth up* (Luke 18:21). And what with a good deal of churchgoing, or attendance at the meetinghouse, and a few extra prayers on a Christmas Day and on Good Friday, and just a little dose of sacraments, you feel yourself in a tolerably good condition.

Now, friend, that old moth-eaten righteousness of yours that you are so proud of you must sell off and get rid of, for no man can be saved by the righteousness of Christ while he puts any trust in his own righteousness. Sell it all off, every rag of it. And supposing that nobody will buy it, at any rate you must part with it. Assuredly it is not worth putting among the filthiest of rags, for it is worse than they are.

And everything else that you have before now thought fit to boast of – come, you must get rid of it. You know so much. Well, you had better sell off what you know, for unless a man becomes as a little child, he cannot enter the kingdom of heaven. You are somebody; you imagine you are not cast in a common mold, for you have a great strength of will, and can force your own way to heaven. You will have to get rid of that little conceit, for that strength of yours will be your weakness. It is only when we are weak in ourselves that we can ever be strong in Christ. Are you content to do so? Will you sell off all the old prejudices and all the old righteousnesses? Going, gone! Will you let them go, or have you got a reserve price? Let them go, for they are rubbish and dung, and the sooner they are gone the better, for then you can buy the pearl, but not until then.

Alas, and there are some men that will have to give up a good deal of what they call pleasure, *sinful pleasure*. No pleasure which is honest, which is really beneficial to us, need ever be denied to us.

> Religion never was designed
> To make our pleasures less.

It makes them vastly more. But any pleasure that smacks of sin is to be done away with. Come, can you sell all that off? That mixing in loose company, anything approaching lewdness, anything that has to do with the gratification of the vile passions of the flesh – come, for the Lord's sake, can you give it up? Well, if you cannot, of course you cannot have the pearl. If you must have the world, you cannot have Christ; if you can find pleasure in the haunts of sin, you are of your father the devil, and his works you do. But come out from it; give it all up; cast it behind you. These things must be sold off if we are to have the pearl.

And then, sometimes, in some cases, men have to give up a good deal of the honors and the satisfactions of life that arise from the esteem of their fellow creatures. Has it come to this: "If I become a Christian, they will ridicule me"? Well now, can you not put up with a little bad repute for Christ? "But if I am an earnest Christian, then I shall have to encounter all sorts of slander." Be it so, and can you not give up the applause of men for the sake of Christ? Come and let the dogs tear your character to shreds, so long as you are right before him, and your motive is pure. "Alas, but I know what it is. I shall get the cold shoulder in society if I become a thoroughly earnest Christian. There is Lady So-and-so, for whom I have very great respect, whose good opinion I would not forfeit on any account, and she will not recognize me anymore." Very well, can you put the whole lot of it into the scale and say, "I sell it all off; let it all go, that I may have the pearl"? That man is not worthy of Christ who would be ashamed to stand in the stocks with him, or go with him to prison and to death. We must so love him that we count reproach for his sake to be an honor, even as Moses counted the reproach of Christ as greater riches than all the treasures of Egypt.

"Well, you have taken enough surely." Yes, but this pearl hunter sold all that he had, and you have got a little left. You have got some prospects. If you become a Christian your old uncle will cut you out of his will. You know very well that if you shall go to hear the gospel at such and such a place, you are very likely to be turned out of your situation. "But we *must* live," says somebody. This is not at all clear to my mind. I do know that we must die, but as to "must live," I do not feel quite so certain about it.

It is infinitely better to die than ever to do a dishonorable thing. If Jesus Christ be our Master, we must be content to let the fairest prospect go, and all things that seem to reveal themselves for our success in this life must be secondary in our account. We must seek first the kingdom of God and his righteousness. Alas, and sometimes love that has been longed for must go for the Lord's sake.

Company that has been delightful must be forsaken for the Lord's sake, and if all this be done, even still it is not enough. He that has Christ must give to Christ himself and all that he has. I would doubt whether I was a follower of Christ if I had not in my very soul given up to him all that I am and all that I have, to be forever his. He has bought us with a price, and it is not surely suitable for us to give him one arm, and one eye, and one foot, and half a heart. He that is a true Christian is a Christian through and through. Whatever he possesses of talent, whatever of substance he owns, he looks upon nothing as being his own, but as all belonging to his Master, and he is prepared to use all for his Master's glory, and to part with it all if it were needful for the maintenance of his Master's kingdom. The merchantman sold all that he had.

I think I see you drawback. "This – this is too hard a line." Very well; if you do not want to buy the pearl, you see – that is to say, if you do not want to make your fortune, for that buying of the pearl was the making of the man's fortune – if you do not think the pearl is worth it, pray do not have it. It is not possible to estimate the intrinsic value, the real worth of Christ. We do not cast pearls before swine. If you do not want him, there are plenty who do. He need not come begging of you that you will be his customer. God forbid you should refuse, but if you do not want him, then He will not override your decision.

But this man went and sold all that he had. I tell you he was glad to sell it. He counted that the man who bought his property was doing him a favor. "Take it," he said. "There, I will let you have it under price if you will only let me have the money. I so much want to get money, so that I can buy something worth much more." He was not sad to see his personal possessions go. Instead, he said to himself, "I really would be obliged to anybody who will take off me that stock on the spur of the moment." So if you really want Christ, instead of needing him to urge you to dispose of these poor effects which I have described, you will be eager to be rid of them so that Christ may be yours. May the Spirit of God work in you such a high resolve.

Now, the last thing is the buying. He had sold all that he had, and then he pays over the shekels – pays them over so that he may have the pearl, and he gets the pearl. It was a considerate purchase – a deliberate bargain. He did not see the pearl and then in a hurry go and sell his goods and guess at the value of it. No, but he had looked at it, for he was a seeker of pearls. He knew a pearl when he saw it, though I dare say he did not tell the seller all that he had seen in it. He said to himself, "That is a wonderful pearl. If I can get the money – my little stock won't fetch above five hundred pounds – but if I can get it for that, I am a made man." And so he thought it over.

It did not need much thinking over. Oh, if a soul did but know Christ, he would not think twice before he would have him. If men were not such fools – if they had but light from heaven to see the value of my Lord and Master, instead of our standing here and having to beg and persuade and find out new words of commendation, I think they would only say, "Tell us about him. We will have him. What does he ask of us? What can we do for him? What can we submit to as long as we may but be sure of him who forgives all sin, who gives immediate and perfect salvation to all who trust him? So long as we may have the Christ of whom it is written, *He that believeth on [him] hath everlasting life* (John 3:36), we shall be content." It was a well-considered purchase.

And it was an *immediate purchase.* He did not go home and say, "I shall think about this." No, but he knew that pearl and he said, "If I let that slip through my fingers, I shall never see the likes of it again. If anybody else gets that bargain, then I shall have lost the one opportunity of my life." And so he does but take time enough to go and sell his farm off, and the little land he had, and the little property he had. He was back quickly with his money, only afraid somebody might have slipped in between and offered another thousand or two more than he was able to raise, and that thus he might lose the pearl.

So, dear friends, he that comes to Christ correctly may well deliberate about it, but the end of his deliberation ought to be very speedy. "If he is to be had, let me have him. Oh, if I can know my sins are forgiven, let me know it. Oh, if by any means I can have peace with God – if I can become a child of God and an heir of heaven – if my eternal happiness can be secured, oh, let it be secured! How is it done? Come, tell me at once. I wish not to leave my seat until I have found that which you speak of." It was a deliberate bargain – an immediate bargain.

And then it was a *joyful one*. I am sure his eyes twinkled as he handed over his money. I would like to have a picture of his face when at last he had gotten his pearl. Now, that which he had been all over the world for, he had gotten, only something a great deal better. He had gotten his pearl, and I dare say he was ready to jump for joy to think that he had gotten ready with his money. Ah, when a soul gets Christ, it is

> Happy day, happy day,
>   For he has washed my sins away.

It is the beginning of delight to a soul when he can say, "Jesus is mine; I know he is. Grace has enabled me to lay hold upon him."

And oh, what an *enriching purchase* it was which the man had made. When he had once gotten the pearl instead of his property, he thought to himself, "Why, I have gotten a hundred times more property now than I had. Though I have given up that bit of land, I can buy half a province now, if I like, with this pearl which I have obtained." So, brothers and sisters, if you have ever given up anything for Christ, I am sure that the Lord Jesus Christ has made you very ample amends for it.

Some years ago, a person rather eccentrically advertised for persons who had been losers by obedience to the divine command – that if anyone who had lost anything through love for Christ would make an appeal to him, he would make it up. The odd advertisement appeared for some months in one of our religious periodicals. But the oddest thing is that nobody ever answered it. I would have thought that somebody would have tried and made out a case; but nobody did. They cannot make out such a case: they are no losers by Christ. "But," say some, "the martyrs were, were they not?" Well, they are up there; ask them. They will tell you as you look at them with their ruby crowns, all brilliant in the light of God, as they stand

> Fairest of the sons light,
>   Midst the bright ones, doubly bright,

14

that they counted it their honor that they should be permitted to lay down their lives for Jesus' sake. Oh, there is no losing when you deal with him. You will make 500 percent over this exchange; be sure of that. No, it shall be 1,000 percent, for "no man," says he, "shall lose house and lands for my sake that shall not receive in this world a hundredfold, and in the world to come, life everlasting."

This was a *final purchase*. The merchantman, according to the parable, never went buying pearls anymore. "No, no" said he. "I have bought a pearl of great price, and now I will go out of the business." And when a man once finds Christ, ah, then he seeks nothing more. If Jesus Christ be mine, more than all in him I find. He does not want a secondary object. His desires all stay at home and satisfy themselves with the fullness that is in Christ Jesus. He went out of the pearl-hunting line, for he had found all the pearls he would ever want. And it was *a purchase he never regretted*. The parable does not say that he came back to the seller and said, "There, take your pearl, and let me have my house and lands again." No, it was done. The great transaction was done. He never wished to have it undone. With his pearl of immense worth he was a rich man, worthy to be the rival of princes, and he felt that it was enough. Oh, blessed are they who can say, "It is enough," and can rejoice and bless and magnify the Lord.

> Now rest, my long-divided heart;
>   Fix'd on this blissful centre, rest:
> With ashes who would grudge to part,
>   When call'd on angels' bread to feast?

Let me, however, just put in one word of caveat. Take care, dear merchant brothers, that when you buy a pearl, you buy a good one – that it is the pearl of great price, because I have known noble spirits whom I have admired and felt ready to weep over; men that have been heroic in the pursuit of that which seemed to them perfectly true, and have made a sacrifice of all that they have for it, and yet they have been deceived. They have grasped antichrist instead of Christ and welcomed the lie of hell which came to them in the garb of the angel of light. Be sure that you get Christ and his truth as you find it revealed in Scripture, and revealed a second time in your own heart by the Holy Spirit, for whatever is short of Christ will prove a cheat and deceive you.

Some years ago, one of the largest pearls that was ever found passed into the hands of a Russian. It was a very large pearl indeed – as large as an egg, and of a pear shape. He purchased it, the party who had it being ignorant of its value. He was a man of substance, and he kept it, and prepared a house which, though shabby on the exterior, was sumptuously furnished within; and he would take his guests into an inner chamber which, when it was unlocked, contained a table of marble, in the center of which was a box which had to be unlocked with myriad keys and the reading of an alphabet, and so forth, and at last he produced this pearl, and he was very cautious about ever permitting it to depart from his hand, for it was of immense value.

The emperor of Russia bid an enormous price for it, and promised him honor and rank besides, but he would not part with it. It happened, however, that the possessor of this pearl was implicated – whether truthfully or not I cannot tell – in a conspiracy and had to leave his home at Saint Petersburg. He took with him nothing but his pearl, and came to Paris sufficiently rich in the possession of that pearl. On a certain day the duke of Brunswick, who was his only rival in such matters, came with some others to see the pearl.

The owner unlocked it with great care and much deliberation, and when he had opened it, he was observed to turn suddenly pale. It seemed as if he had been stricken with death. Unhappy man! His pearl had suddenly become clouded, as pearls sometimes do. It had been taken with some disease which happens to pearls, if I may so express it. In a short time it would turn to powder; it had ceased to be of any value whatever, and he had come down from being a millionaire to being a pauper. Yet he had bought a good pearl notwithstanding.

There is only one pearl that never can be clouded, and will last right on throughout eternity, and that is the Son of God, *who only hath immortality* (1 Timothy 6:16). If you get him, you have a hope divine which never can fail you; but if you get a hope in priests or a hope connected with sacramentarianism, or any other hope but that of which Christ is top and bottom, beginning and end, you may make what sacrifice you will, but your brightest prospects will end in the bitterest disappointment. The Lord grant that none of us may ever be thus balked from our life confidence, that no such blank bewilderment may ever fall on our spirits.

Hearken to me, ye that follow after righteousness, ye that seek the Lord (Isaiah 51:1). The voice of Jesus is heard in this parable of the kingdom describing and directing the *seekers*. Such persons comprise no small fraction of an assembly like the present. It would indeed be strange if seekers were not always largely represented here and in every stage of anxious inquiry. I am sure some of you have seen the pearl you want sparkling before your eyes. I wonder how many of you have resolved to sell all you have to buy it.

But who among you all have actually made the pearl your own, and rejoice in its possession? That such of you will go on your way rejoicing there is no doubt, but will you not return and give glory to God? Shall we not have the happiness of greeting you here in the fellowship of the kingdom of his grace? The Lord grant it may be so for Jesus' sake. Amen.

Chapter 2

Early and Late

For the kingdom of heaven is like unto a man that is an householder, which went out early in the morning to hire labourers into his vineyard. And he went out about the third hour, and saw others standing idle in the market-place. Again he went out about the sixth and ninth hour, and did likewise. And about the eleventh hour he went out, and found others standing idle, and saith unto them, Why stand ye here all the day idle? (Matthew 20:1, 3, 5-6)

We have frequently observed that we do not think it right to neglect the connection of Scripture. We have no right to tear passages of Scripture from their context and make them to mean what they were not intended to teach; and therefore I have in the reading given you, according to my ability, what I think to be the immediate design of the present parable. It is a rebuke to those who fall into a legal spirit and begin calculating as to what their reward ought to be in a kingdom where the legal spirit is entirely out of place, since its reward is not of debt but of grace. I think I may now, without any violation of propriety, dwell upon one very distinct fact in connection with the parable. It is not right to violate the drift of the parable, but having already observed it and made it as clear as we can, we believe that we are now authorized to make use of one of the main circumstances mentioned in it.

This morning I intend to call your attention to the fact that the laborers were hired at different periods of the day, by which, no doubt, we are taught that God sends his servants into his vineyard at different times and seasons; that some are called in early youth, and others are not led to enter into the service of the Master until declining years have brought them almost to the evening of life.

I must, however, ask you to remember that *they were all called,* by the mention of which the Savior would teach us that no man comes into the kingdom of heaven by himself. Without exception, every laborer for Jesus has been called in one sense or another, and he would not have come without being called. They are all called. If a man were what he should be, he would need no pressing and no invitation to come to the gospel of Christ.

But since human nature is perverted, and men put bitter for sweet and sweet for bitter, darkness for light and light for darkness, man needs to be called by the outward word; he needs to be invited, persuaded, and entreated; he needs – to use the strong expression of the apostle Paul – *as though God did beseech [him] by us* – that we should pray him in Christ's stead to be reconciled to God. No, further than this, although some men come to work in a legal spirit in the vineyard through this common call of the gospel, yet no man in spirit and in truth comes to Christ without a further call, namely, the effective call of God's Holy Spirit.

The general call is given by the minister; it is all that he can give. If the preacher attempts to give the particular call as some of my hyper-Calvinistic brethren do, confining the gospel command to a certain character, and trying to be themselves the discoverers of God's elect, and to make that particular which is always universal; if the preacher acts thus, and virtually endeavors to give the particular call, he makes a sorry mess of it, and usually fails altogether to preach the gospel of glad tidings to the sons of men. But when man is content to do what he can do, namely, preach the commandment to believe on the Lord Jesus Christ, and that God *commandeth all men every where to repent* (Acts 17:30), then there comes with the general call to the chosen of God a particular and special call which none but the Holy Spirit can give, but which he gives so effectively that all who hear it become willing in the day of God's power, and turn with full purpose of heart unto the Lord.

In what sense is it true that many are called but few are chosen, if none are to be called by the preaching of the Word but those who are chosen? There are two callings: the one is general to all who hear of Jesus, and many who are thus called are not chosen; the other is personal and unique to the elect, for *whom he did predestinate, them he also called* (Romans 8:30).

To return to our point – all in the vineyard are in some sense called. There is not a solitary exception to this rule in the entire Christian church. The doctrine of free will has not a single specimen to show to prove itself. There is not a sheep in all the flock that came back to the shepherd unsought; there is not a single piece of money which leaped again into the woman's purse after she swept the house to find it: no, I will go further, and say there is not even a single prodigal son in the entire family who did ever say, *I will arise and go to my Father,* until first the Father's grace, veiling itself in the afflicting providence of a mighty famine, had taught the prodigal the miserable results of sin, as he fed the swine, and *would fain have filled his belly with the husks that the swine did eat* (Luke 15:16), but could not do so.

I want you to notice another fact before I come to the subject now in hand, and that is, that *all those who are called are said to have been hired.* Of course, in a parable, no word is to be construed harshly; we are to give the meaning according to the drift; but still I think we may say that there is this likeness between hiring a servant and the engagement of a soul to Christ, that henceforth a man hired has no right to serve another; he serves the master who has hired him. When a soul is called by grace into the service of the Lord Jesus Christ, he cries, "O Lord, other lords have had dominion over me, but now you only will I serve." He plucks off the yoke of sin, its pleasure, its custom, and he puts upon him that yoke of which the Master says it is easy, and he bears that burden which Jesus tells us is light.

A hired servant must not work for another; he works for his master, and so a man who is called by grace lives not for any sinister object or motive, but for his Master only. A hired servant, again, does not work on his own account, for he is not his own master; *and ye are not your own, for ye are bought with a price* (1 Corinthians 6:19-20). Henceforth, though he calls no man "Master" on earth, yet he remembers that one is his Master in heaven, to whom all his service is due.

21

There is a compact between the hired man and his master, and there is a solemn compact of spirit between the true believer and his Lord. We have devoted ourselves to his service, we have given up all liberty of self-will, and henceforth our will is at the government of our Lord, and all our powers and passions are to be, we hope will be, through God's grace, obedient to him who has hired us into the vineyard.

Now the word *hired* was used in order to bring in the idea of reward. It was used to suit Peter's view of the case; it was used in order that his legal question of *what shall we have therefore?* (Matthew 19:27) might be clearly brought out, and its folly shown in the light of that sovereign grace which does as it wills with his own. Yet for all that, believers are hired in an evangelical sense; they do not serve God for nothing; they shall not work without a reward. *The wages of sin is death; but the gift of God is eternal life* (Romans 6:23). We shall have our reward for what we do for the Master, and though it be not wages in the sense of debt, yet truly I say unto you, there shall not be a single truehearted worker for God who shall not receive from his Master most blessed wages of grace in the day when he comes to take account of his servants.

Now to the point. *The master calls these hired servants of his at different hours of the day;* and, in the second place, *distinguishing grace shines forth in each case,* and is illustrated and made more manifest in its varieties of glorious compassion and loving-kindness by the different hours at which the chosen ones are called.

All are not called by grace at the same time. Some, according to the parable, are called *early in the morning.* Three times happy are these! The earliest period at which a child may be called by grace it would be difficult for us positively to define, because children are not all of the same age mentally when they are of the same age physically, and even in the matter of mental development we dare not limit the Holy One of Israel as to the chosen period of operation. As far as our observation goes, grace works upon some little ones at the very dawn of moral consciousness. There are, no doubt, precocious children, whose intellect and affections are very much developed and very deeply sanctified even as early as two or three years of age. Such children usually are intended by the Master to be taken home at once.

There are interesting biographies around, which prove that holiness may bloom and ripen in the youngest heart; and many anecdotes are treasured up in such collections as James Janeway's *A Token for Children* of children whom I might call infants with strict propriety, out of whose mouth God ordained praise, and did, through them, silence the Enemy and the avenger. Little babblers, whose tongues it would have been supposed could only have talked about toys, have been able to speak with an apparent profundity of knowledge of spiritual, and especially of heavenly, things.

It is certain that some have effected their day's work for the Master in their mother's arms; they have spoken of the Savior in tones which have melted a mother's heart and gone to a father's conscience, and then they have been taken home. "Whom the gods love die young," said the heathen, and doubtless it is no small privilege to be so soon admitted into glory. Only shown on earth, and then snatched away to heaven, too precious to be left below. Precious child, how dear were you to the good God who sent you here and then took you home! Fair rosebud! Yet in the perfection of your young beauty taken to be worn by the Savior on his bosom, how can we mourn your translation to the skies?

No bitter tears for thee be shed,
Blossom of being seen and gone!
With flowers alone we strew thy bed,
O blest departed one!
Whose all of life, a rosy ray,
Blush'd into dawn and pass'd away.

Early in the morning would also include those who have passed the first hour of the day, but who have not yet wasted the second opening hour. I mean those hopeful lads and girls who perhaps would rather I should call them youths – those who have reached their teens, have overleaped infancy and childhood, and are growing up in the heyday and vigor of youth. They are youngsters still more at home in the playground than in the workplace, and fitter, as Satan tells them, to be sporting in the marketplace than busy in the vineyard. Such as these, to the praise of divine love, are often hired by the householder.

It is worthwhile to warn some of our brethren who seem to be

23

exceedingly doubtful of boyish and girlish devoutness – to warn them against indulging harsh and suspicious doubts. We have said, and I think those who have watched our membership carefully will have said it too, that among all the slips and falls which have caused us sorrow, we have had but little sorrow from those who were added to us as boys or girls.

There are those preaching the gospel this day with acceptance and power whom these hands baptized into Jesus Christ very early in their boyhood, and there are among us honored servants of God who have served this church well, who, while they were still at school, were joyful followers of the Lord Jesus Christ. With our earliest understandings some of us got an understanding of the things of the kingdom; our Bible was our child's primer, our spelling book, the guide of our youth, and the joy of our earliest years.

We thank God that there are Timothys still among us, and those not few and far between; and young Samuels, who, being brought as infants to the Lord's house, have from that day forth worn the linen ephod and served after their manner as priests unto God, serving him with all their hearts. Happy are those who are called *early in the morning*! They have unique reasons for blessing and praising God.

> Grace is a plant, where'er it grows,
>   Of pure and heavenly root;
> But fairest in the youngest shows,
>   And yields the sweetest fruit.

Let us spend a minute in thinking of their happy condition who are saved in boyhood. Early in the morning the dew still twinkles on the leaves, the maiden blush of dawn remains and reveals an opening beauty, which is lost to those who rise not to see the birth of day. There is a beauty about early devoutness which is indescribably charming and unutterably lovely in freshness and radiance. We observe in childhood an artless simplicity, a childlike confidence, which is seen nowhere else.

There may be less of knowing but there is more of loving; there may be less of reasoning, but there is more of simply believing upon the authority of revelation; there may be less of deep-rootedness, but there is certainly more of perfume, beauty, and emerald vegetation. If I must choose that part of the Christian life in which there is the most joy, next to the land of Beulah, which I must set first and foremost by reason of its lying so near to Canaan, I think I would prefer that tract of Christian experience which lies toward the sunrising, which is sown with radiant pearls of love, and cheered with the delicious music of the birds of hope.

Early in the morning, when we have just risen from slumber, work is easy; our occupation in the vineyard is a cheerful exercise rather than a toil such as those find it who bear the burden and heat of the day. The young Christian is not oppressed with the cares and troubles of the world as others are; he has nothing else to do but serve his God. He is free from the embarrassments which surround so many of us and prevent our doing good when we would consecrate ourselves wholly to it. The lad has nothing to think of but his Lord. There are his books and his lessons, but he can be fervent of spirit in the midst of them. There are the companions of his childhood, but in innocence and simplicity he may be of service to them and to God through them.

Give me, I say, if I would have a promising time to work for Jesus, give me the blessed morning hours, when my heart is bounding lightest and joy's pure sunbeams tremble on my path; when my glowing breast lacks no fervency, and my happy spirit wears no chain of care.

One would prefer early conversion because such persons have not learned to stand idle in the marketplace. A fellow, you know, who has been for hours standing with his hands in his pockets, talking with drunken men and so on, is not worth much at the eleventh hour; no, even by the middle of the day it has become so natural to him to prop the walls, that he is not likely to take to work very readily. Begin early with your souls, break in the colts while they are young, and they are likely to take well to the collar. There are no workers like those who commenced work while they were still children. What a promise of a long day there is for young believers; the sun has just risen, and it has to travel to its zenith and descend again. There is ample room and threshold enough, though none to spare. If God in his providence permits it so to happen, that the youngster yonder has twelve hours' work before him, what may he not accomplish?

For a grand and glorious life early devoutness, if not essential, is certainly a very great advantage. To give those first days to Jesus will spare us many sad regrets, will prevent us from acquiring many evil habits, and will enable us to achieve good success through the Holy Spirit's blessing. It is well to begin to fly while yet the wings are strong, for if we live long in sin, the wings may be broken and then they will flap wearily through the rest of our days, even when grace shall call us. Let it be the desire of parents here to have their children converted as children! And oh! may God cast that desire into the hearts of some of you young people who are here this morning, so that before you reach twenty-one years of age, before you are called men, you may be perfect men in Christ Jesus, so that while you are yet children you may be children of God. May you *as newborn babes, [receive] the sincere milk of the word* (1 Peter 2:2), and the Lord grant *that [you] may grow thereby.* Happy, happy, happy souls, whom the Master thus by distinguishing grace brings *early in the morning*!

The householder went out again *at the third hour.* This may represent the period in which we have mounted above being children and youths and are entitled to be called men. Suppose we settle the first hour as extending over the earliest seven or eight years of age; then the second hour runs on from that to twenty-one or thereabouts; and then we have a good length of time between twenty and thirty and onwards to reckon as the third, and fourth, and fifth hours. There are some whom divine grace renews at the third hour. This is late! Twenty-one is grievously late, when you consider how much of early joy is now impossible, how much of sinful habit has now been acquired, and how many opportunities for usefulness have now gone past recall.

A quarter of the day has flown away forever when we reach the third hour. It is the best quarter of the day, too, that has gone past recall. The first meal of the day is over – that blessed breaking of the fast with Christ is possible no more. A very precious meal is that, when the Savior gives us the morning portion, the manna which melts when the sun is up. Blessed is the child's feeding upon Jesus. Truly I remember when I was awakened like Elijah from under the juniper tree and fed on such dainty food that to this day the flavor abides with me. The man of twenty-one has lost that first meal, breakfast is all over; Christ will say to him as he will to some others, *Come and dine* (John 21:12), and that is precious; but the daintiest meal is over, and the first early enjoyment, the first early rapture can never be known.

I have no doubt there are many here who think that to be converted at twenty-one is very soon; but why twenty-one years given to Satan? Why a fourth of man's existence devoted to evil? Besides, it may not be a fourth, it may be one-half; no, in how many cases it is the whole of life. The sun goes down before it is yet noon, and the idler in the marketplace has no hope of ever being a worker in the vineyard. Death who comes when God wills, and gives us no notice, may cut down the flower before it has fully opened. *In the morning [it is] like grass which groweth up. . . . in the evening it is cut down, and withereth* (Psalm 90:5-6). It is late, it is sadly late! It is a sad thing to have lost those bright days in which the mind was least engaged, in which it was the most susceptible to forming godly habits. It is a sad thing to have learned so much of sin as one may have learned by twenty-one, a sad thing to have seen so much of iniquity, to have treasured up in one's memory so much of defilement.

Twenty years with God, and one might have been in such a time a good scholar in the kingdom; but twenty years in the world, and one begins to be like scarlet that has been lying in the dye until it is stained through and through. *It is late, but we thank God that it is not too late.* No, it is not too late even for the grandest of purposes. Not only is this period of life not too late for salvation, but it is also not too late to do much for Jesus Christ.

Some of us, when we were twenty-one, had finished five years of Christian ministry, and had been the means of bringing many souls to the cross of Christ; but if others are led by grace to begin then, why, there is a good period still remaining if God in providence spares our lives. The young man is now in all his strength and vigor, his bones are full of marrow, and his heart is full of fire. He ought to have acquired a good degree of education and be prepared to acquire more.

Now he is just in the time when he should work. His plans of life are not settled as yet; he is not married yet, probably; as yet there are no children around him to have been injured by his ill example; he has an opportunity of rearing up a household in the fear of God. He is commencing business; he has an opportunity of so conducting that business that there may never need to be a time when he shall have to change direction and steer another course. He may, if called by God's grace at twenty-one, begin an honorable career in which there need not be an angle or a curve, but straight to the harbor's mouth he may steer and mark upon the sea of life one shining furrow which shall reach in a direct line from the present moment straight to the lights of heaven, and which he shall reach with his sail full and a priceless cargo on board to the praise of the glory of divine grace. It is late, it is very late in some respects, but oh! it is not too late to serve the Master well, and to win a crown of great reward, the gift of love divine.

There is an abundance of work to do for us who are in this third, fourth, and fifth hour of the day. In fact, I suppose the church must look to us for its most active work. After this period and the next, a man frequently becomes rather a recipient from the church than a donor to it in the matter of activity. Its fresh blood, its energy, its warmth of heart, its ready action must to a great extent come from the young men who are converted. Oh, you of twenty-one, I would to God that you were all born from heaven! You maidens, in your early beauty may the Master in his infinite mercy bring you in! Oh, could you know the sweetness of his love, you would not need persuading! Could you understand the joy of true religion, you would not need pleading!

There is more holy mirth enjoyed in secret with the Lord Jesus Christ than in all the merriment the world can yield. One ounce of Christ's love is better than a ton of the world's flatteries. The world offers bubbles with fair hues, bright to look upon, but vanishing at a breath; but Christ gives real treasure, enduring as eternity. The world's gold is all vile money; it glitters, but it is not precious. There may be less glitter about the things of God, but there is a solid joy and lasting pleasure which none but Zion's children know. May the Master come this morning to your hearts, and by my simple words may he call you at the third hour of the day into the vineyard.

The Master's grace was not exhausted, and therefore *he went out at the sixth hour.* We find him going into the market at high noon. Half the day was over. Who is going to employ a man, and give him a whole day's wages when twelve o'clock has come? He will not do too much if you hire him at six; what will he do if you engage him at twelve? Half a day's work! That is a poor thing to seek or to offer. The Master, however, seeks and accepts it. He promises, *Whatsoever is right I will give you* (Matthew 20:4); and there are some found who at the sixth hour enter into the vineyard and being saved by grace, begin their work for Jesus. This may represent the period of life in which man is supposed to be in his prime – when he is past forty and onward. *This is sadly late, very sadly late.*

It is sadly late in a great many respects, not only because there is so little time left, but also because so very much of energy, and zeal, and force, which should have been given to God, has been wasted, and has to some extent been used to fight against God. Forty years of hardness of heart! That is a long time for divine patience. Forty years of sin! That is a long season for conscience to mourn over. *Forty years long was I grieved with this generation,* said God (Psalm 95:10). In the wilderness they hardened their hearts all that time; and he swore in his wrath that they would not enter into his rest. What a blessing for you who are forty and unconverted, that he has not sworn so terrible an oath concerning you, that still his long-suffering lingers, still his patience bears with you, still does he say to you, *Son, go work to day in my vineyard* (Matthew 21:28). It is sadly late, because it has become so much more than natural for you to walk in the way of sin. You will have so much to contend with in the future, as the result of the past.

Turning the ship of the soul around is not such easy work as turning a vessel by her helm; only a divine hand can steer a soul upon the course of grace. You will need much grace to conquer those corruptions which have had forty years to take root in. You have a tenant in your house who is in possession, and you will find that possession to be nine points of the law; it will be a hard ejectment for you to effect, so hard indeed, that only a *stronger than he* can cast him out. To your dying day, the recollection of evil things which you heard during these forty years of being unconverted will stick by you; you will hear the echoes of an old song just when you are trying to pray, and some deed which you regret and mourn over will come to check you just when you are about to say, *Abba, Father,* with an unstammering tongue.

It is late, it is very, very late, this sixth hour, *but it is not too late.* It is not too late for some of the richest enjoyments; you can yet dine with Jesus; he can yet manifest himself unto you, as he does not do unto the world; you can have still much time to serve him in. It is not too late yet to be distinguished among his servants.

Take John Newton's life. He was called in the middle of the day, but John Newton left his mark in God's vineyard, a mark that will never be forgotten. I suppose Paul could not have been much less than of that age when he was called by sovereign grace; no, most of the apostles were probably very little short of this age when mercy met with them; still they did a glorious day's work. If saved by grace in middle life, my brother, you must work harder, you must let the time past suffice you to have worked the will of the flesh, and now you must redeem the time, because the days are evil. Why, a man converted at forty should do a double-quick march to heaven; there should not be a moment lost now.

Work the engine at high pressure and give two strokes for every one stroke that might be given by younger men and younger minds. Seek in the divine strength to do twice as much in the time, since you have only half the time to do a life's work in. Crowns for Christ, I know you wish to win them; then be up and doing, beloved. You are saved by grace, and by grace alone. You want to honor Christ, because of his free love for you; cannot you endeavor to honor him as much in the remnant which remains as others do in the whole length of their life? You may by zeal, and prudence, and discretion, and perfect consecration still serve the Master well.

The householder *went out at the ninth hour,* at three o'clock in the afternoon. Nobody thinks of engaging day laborers at three o'clock in the afternoon. A day's work to be done from three until six! It shows you that this gospel hiring is nothing like a legal hiring; it must be all of grace, or else a man would not think of doing such a thing. Well now, three o'clock in the afternoon, that is from sixty to seventy. The prime of life has gone. *It is late, it is sadly late, very sadly late.* It is late because all the powers of the man are weak now. His memory begins to fail; he thinks his judgment to be better than ever it was, but probably that is only his own opinion. Most of the faculties lose their edge in old age. He has acquired experience, but still there is no fool like an old fool; and a man who has not been taught by divine grace learns very little of any value in the school of providence.

Sixty thousand years would not make a man wise if grace did not teach him. Now think of it; is it not late? Here is the man: if he be converted now, what is there left of him? He is just a candle end. He may give a little light, but it is almost like a snuff burning in the socket. All those sixty years, seventy years have been spent, where? Cover it all up. Let us go backward as Noah's sons did, and cover it all up; and oh, may almighty grace cover it too! The fact is terribly appalling – sixty, seventy years spent in the service of Satan! Oh, what good the man might have done! Had he but served his God as he served the world, what good he might have done! He has made a fortune, has he! How rich he might have been in faith by this time. He has built a house! Yes, but how he might have helped to build the church.

The man has been playing at houses of cards; he has been like boys by the seashore building castles of sand, which must all come down, and must come down very soon too, for I hear the surges of the dread tide of death; it is rolling in even now. Those teeth which have fallen out, those pains and rheumatics, and so on, all show that this is not his rest. The tabernacle is beginning to crumble around the man, and the warning is loud which reminds him that he must soon be gone, and leave his wealth and his house; and so if this be all, in the end it will turn out that he has done nothing; he has piled up shadows, heaped together thick clay, and that is all he has done, when he might, if he had believed in Jesus, have done so much for God and for the souls of men.

What evil habits he has acquired! What can you ever make of this man? If he be saved, it will be so as by fire. He is called, and he shall enter heaven, but oh! how little can he do for the Master, and what strong corruptions will he have to wrestle with, and what an inward conflict even until he gets to heaven! It is late, it is very late, but oh! blessed be God! *It is not too late.* We have had within these walls persons who have long passed the prime of their days, who have come forward and said, "We will cast in our lot with you because the Lord is with you." We have heard their joyous story of how the old man has become a babe, and how he that was gray with years has been born again into the kingdom of Christ. It is not too late. Did the devil say so?

The gate is shutting; I can hear it grating on the hinges, but it is not shut! The sun is going down, but he is not lost beneath the horizon yet; and if the Master calls you, only run the faster because it is so; and when you are saved, serve him with all your might and muscle, because you have so little time to glorify him here on earth, and short space in which to show your sense of deep indebtedness to his surpassing love.

The day is nearly over, *it has come to the eleventh hour* – five o'clock! The men have been looking at their watches to see whether it will not soon be six o'clock; they are longing to hear the clock strike; they hope the day's work will soon end. See; the Master goes out into the marketplace among those hulking fellows who are still loitering there, and he moves toward some and asks them, "*Why stand ye here all the day idle?* Go and work! And whatsoever is right I will give you" (Matthew 20:6-7). At the eleventh hour they come in – half-ashamed to come, I am sure, hardly liking the others to see them; ashamed to begin work so late. Still they did steal in somewhere; and there were generous laborers who looked over the tops of the vines, and said to them, "Glad to see you, friends! Glad to see you, however late."

There were a few, I dare say, among the laborers, at least there are if this be the vineyard, who would even stop their work and begin to sing and praise God to think that their fellows had been brought in at the eleventh hour. Now the eleventh hour must be looked upon as any period of life which is past seventy years; how late it may extend I cannot tell.

There is an authentic instance of a man converted to God at the age of a hundred and four, during the last Irish revival, who walked some distance to make a confession of his faith in Jesus Christ; and I recollect a case of one converted in America by a sermon which he had heard, I think, eighty-one years previously. He was fifteen when he heard Mr. Flavell at the end of a discourse, instead of pronouncing the blessing, say, "I cannot bless you. How can I bless those who do not love the Lord Jesus Christ? *If any man love not the Lord Jesus Christ, let him be Anathema Maranatha*" (1 Corinthians 16:22); and eighty-one years or more afterwards that solemn sentence came to the man's recollection when he was living in America, and God blessed it to his conversion.

There have been some to whom the eleventh hour has been the very hour of death; some, I say, but how many or how few is not for me to know. There is one instance we know in Scripture; it was the dying thief. There is but one. God, however, in his abundant mercy, can do as he wills to the praise of the glory of his grace, and at the eleventh hour he can call his chosen.

It is very late, it is very, very, very late, it is sorrowfully late, *it is sadly late, but it is not too late;* and if the Master calls you, then come – even though a hundred years of sin should make your feet heavy to you, so that your steps are painfully limping. If he calls you, it is late but not too late, and therefore come. Have you ever thought of how the thief worked for his Lord? It was not a fine place for working, hanging on a cross dying, just at the eleventh hour; but he did a good deal of work in the few minutes. Observe what he did. First, he confessed Christ – he acknowledged him to be Lord, and confessed him before men. In the second place, he justified Christ – *This man has done nothing amiss* (Luke 23:41). In the next place, he worshipped the Lord Jesus, calling him *Lord*. He even began to preach, for he rebuked his fellow sinner; he told him that he should not revile one who was so unrighteously condemned. He offered a petition which has become a very model of prayer – *Lord, remember me when thou comest into thy kingdom* (Luke 23:42).

At any rate, I wish I could say of myself what I can say of the thief: *he did all he could.* I cannot say that of myself, and I am afraid I cannot say it of any of you. I do not know anything the thief could have done on the cross which he did not do. As soon as ever he was called, he seems to have worked in the vineyard to the utmost extent of his ability; and so let me say to you, if you should be called at the eleventh hour, my dear friend, though you be well stricken in years and aged, yet for Jesus Christ's sake out of great love for all the great things which he has done for you, go your way and praise him with all your might.

My time has gone, and I wanted to have shown that distinguishing *grace shone gloriously in every instance.* Those called in the early morning have delightful reason for admiring sovereign grace, for they are spared the ills and sins of life. I must content myself, however, by repeating concerning them the lines of Ralph Erskine:

> In heavenly choirs a question rose,
>   That stirred up strife will never close;
> What rank of all the ransomed race,
>   Owes highest praise to sovereign grace.
>
> Babes thither caught from womb and breast,
>   Claimed right to sing above the rest;
> Because they found the happy shore,
>   They never saw nor sought before.

What distinguishing grace is that which called us when we were young! Herein is electing love. *When Israel was a child, then I loved him, and called my son out of Egypt* (Hosea 1:1). Some of us in time and in eternity will have to utter a special song of thankfulness to the love which took us in our days of folly and simplicity, and conducted us into the family of God. It was not because we were better disposed children than others, or because there was naturally anything good about us; we were willful, rash, and high-minded; proud, wayward, and disobedient as other children are, and yet mercy separated us from the rest, and we shall never cease to adore its sovereignty.

Look at the grace which calls the man at the age of twenty, when the passions are hot, when there is strong temptation to plunge into the vices and the so-called pleasures of life. To be delivered from the charms of sin, when the world's cheek is ruddy, when it wears its best attire, and to be taught to prefer the reproach of Christ to all the riches of Egypt – this is mighty grace for which God shall have our sweetest song.

To be called of the Lord at forty, in the prime of life – this is a wonderful instance of divine power, for worldliness is hard to overcome, and worldliness is the sin of middle age. With a family around you, with much business, with the world eating into you as does a canker, it is a wonder that God should in his mercy have visited you then, and made you a converted soul. You are a miracle of grace, and you will have to feel it and to praise God for it in time and eternity.

Sixty again. *Can the Ethiopian change his skin, or the leopard his spots? If so, then may ye also do good, that are accustomed to do evil* (Jeremiah 13:23). And yet you have learned, you have had a blessed schoolmaster who sweetly taught you, and you have learned to do well. Though your vessel had begun to rot in the waters of the Black Sea of sin, you have gotten a new owner, and you will run up a new flag, and you will sail around the Cape of Good Hope to the Islands of the Blessed, in the Land of the Hereafter.

But what shall I say of you that are called when you are aged? Ah, you will have to love much, for you have had much forgiven. I do not know that you may be in thankfulness a bit behind those of us who are called in our early youth; we have much to bless God for, and so have you. We are at one extreme and you are at the other; we would love much because we have been spared much sinning, and you must love much because you have been delivered from much sinning.

Not to go through the fire is a theme for song; but to travel the flame and not be burned, to walk the furnace and to be delivered from its vehement fire, oh! how should you find words with which to express your gratitude! Called early or called late, called at midday or called at early noon, let us together, since we have been called by grace alone, ascribe it all to the Lord Jesus; and moved by the mighty constraints of his love, let us work with body, soul, and spirit – work for him until we can work no longer, and then praise him in the rest of glory.

I pray you, brethren, permit no idleness to creep over you. If you have sought to extend the Redeemer's kingdom, do it more. Give more, talk more of Christ, pray more, labor more! I often receive the kind advice, "Do less." I cannot do less. Do less? Why, better rot altogether than live the inglorious life of doing less than our utmost for God. We shall none of us, I am afraid, kill ourselves with working too hard for Jesus. It would be such a blessed act of suicide that if there be a sin that is forgivable, it would certainly be that. I am not afraid that you are likely to perpetrate such an enormity.

Work for the Master! Labor for the Master! We must spend and be spent and wear ourselves out for him! Make no reserve for the flesh to fulfill the lusts of it! And oh, how happy shall we be, if we may be privileged to finish the work, and hear him say, *Well done, thou good and faithful servant: . . . enter thou into the joy of thy lord* (Matthew 25:21). May the Lord bless you for His name's sake. Amen.

Chapter 3

The First Last, and the Last First

But many that are first shall be last; and the last shall be first. (Matthew 19:30)

So the last shall be first, and the first last. (Matthew 20:16)

W e must be saved if we would serve the Lord. We cannot serve God in an unsaved condition. *They that are in the flesh cannot please God* (Romans 8:8). It is vain for them to attempt service while they are still at enmity against God. The Lord does not want enemies to wait upon him, nor slaves to grace his throne. We must be saved first, and salvation is all of grace. *By grace are ye saved through faith* (Ephesians 2:8). After we are saved, and as the result of salvation, we serve. Saved – we serve. He that is saved becomes a child of God, and then he renders a childlike service in his Father's house. That service is also all of grace. He serves not under the law of the old commandment, *This do, and thou shalt live* (Luke 10:28), for he is not under the law, but under grace.

Therefore, sin shall not have dominion over him, but grace shall have dominion over him; and he shall seek to serve the Lord and please him all the days of his life. When we are saved, we must never forget that we are saved so that we may serve; we are made free from sin so that we may become servants to God. David says, *O Lord, truly I am thy servant;*

I am thy servant, and the son of thine handmaid: thou hast loosed my bonds (Psalm 116:16). Because our bonds are loosed, we are under new bonds – bonds of love, which bind us to the service of the Most High.

Now, when we come thus to be servants, we must not forget that we are saved men and women, for if we begin to imagine that while we serve, we are working to win life by our merits, then we shall get upon legal ground, and a child of God on legal ground is going back; he is departing from his true standing before God. Still remember, *Ye are not under the law, but under grace* (Romans 6:14). But if you begin to forget your indebtedness to your Savior, not only for eternal life, but also for everything you are, and have, and do, then you will be like the Galatians, who began in the Spirit, but sought to be made perfect by the flesh. You will be like the young man whose question we have just read: *What lack I yet?* (Matthew 19:20). You will be like Peter, who puts in a sort of claim for reward: *Behold, we have forsaken all, and followed thee; what shall we have therefore?* (Matthew 19:27). You will be like the men who had worked in the vineyard from early morning, and who murmured because the penny was given to those who had only worked for a single hour.

Christ will not have his servants under bondage to a legal spirit. Wherever he spies it out, he strikes it on the head, for both the service and the reward are all of grace. The service itself is given to us by God, and God rewards the service which he himself has given. We might almost speak of this as an eccentricity of grace. God gives us good works, and then rewards us for the works which he himself has given. So all is of grace from first to last, and must never be viewed with a legal eye. Into this subject I want on this occasion to conduct you.

I dare say that you have heard sermons from this text, but have probably not heard preaching from it in its connection. I like to take the text as it stands, and get from it a bit of exposition for my own heart, which I may pass on to you; for, remember, although the text away from its connection may be true, yet it is not the truth that God there intended to teach us, and it suits us to look around us to see what comes before the text, and what comes after, in order that we may catch the exact meaning of the Holy Spirit in giving the words.

I shall begin by dwelling upon this remark: In the service of our Lord free grace is manifested. It may not strike you as being upon the surface of the text, but it lies on the very surface of the whole connection. In the service of our Lord free grace is manifested. Think that over.

It must be so, in the first place, because, although it is rewarded, *all our service is already due to God.* Under the law we are bound to love the Lord with all our heart, and with all our soul, and with all our mind, and with all our strength. There can be nothing beyond that. All that we can do we are already bound to do, under the law. Works of supererogation (performing more than is required by duty, obligation, or need) must be impossible, since the law recognizes all holiness and condemns every form of sin.

When we have done all, we are unprofitable servants, we have done no more than it was our duty to do. Therefore, brethren, if there be a service to which we are called, and for which a reward is promised, it must be a service of grace. It cannot be any other. Under the gospel, the same thing is true: All that we can do is already due. *Know ye not that . . . ye are not your own? For ye are bought with a price.* There is no faculty, there is no capacity, there is no possibility of your nature which is not redeemed, and which does not belong to Christ by virtue of the ransom price which he has paid for it. You will gladly and gratefully acknowledge the obligation to do all that lies in you for him who loved you, and bought you with his precious blood.

> Could my zeal no respite know,
> Could my tears for ever flow.

Surely, they are all due to my Lord already in repentance and gratitude. All the zeal of missionaries, all the patience of martyrs, all the faith of confessors, all the holiness of godly men is Christ's by right, and therefore there can be no reward for them, seeing that they are his due already. If there be a service for which a reward is given to us, it is a service granted to us of grace, that we may receive grace thereby.

But next, there is this reflection – *all our service is in itself unacceptable.* When all comes to all, it is still, in and of itself, a thing so shabby and poor, so imperfect and defiled, that it could not claim any reward. Job was made to feel this in the day of his humiliation. He said, *If I say, I am perfect, it shall also prove me perverse. Though I were perfect, yet would I not know my soul: I would despise my life* (Job 9:20-21). If it were possible for us to stand before God in any merit of our own, we feel so certain that we have come short of the glory of God and that in many things we have offended, that we would tear off our righteousness from us, and throw it away as filthy rags, even the best of it.

I count all things but loss, says Paul, *that I may win Christ, and be found in him, not having mine own righteousness, which is of the law, but that which is through the faith of Christ, the righteousness which is of God by faith* (Philippians 3:8-9). If, then, we are so conscious of our failures, and shortcomings, and transgressions, and if we have to cry for mercy even on our holy things, and to confess sin in them, how can we suppose that any reward that may be given can be otherwise than of grace, seeing that the whole service itself must be of grace?

Think again. *The ability to serve God is the gift of God's grace.* I refer not only to mental ability, but also to the capacity that men of substance have to help the cause of God by their generous gifts. It is God who gives the power to get wealth, as it is he who gives the brain to think, and the mouth to speak. *What hast thou that thou didst not receive?* (1 Corinthians 4:7). If any present here are serving God with gifts and graces, I am sure that they must acknowledge that these were given to them. They did not win them themselves. Or, if some of them be acquirements, still the power to acquire them was given to them by him from whom comes every good gift and every perfect gift. Thus the ability to serve God is the gift of grace.

Beloved, *the call to serve God in any special way is also of grace.* If we are called to the ministry, remember how Paul puts it: *Unto me, who am less than the least of all saints, is this grace given, that I should preach among the Gentiles the unsearchable riches of Christ* (Ephesians 3:8). If our kings put upon their coins *"Dei gratia"* – kings, by the grace of God – well, well, let them say so; but we can put it on our lives: "Sunday school teachers, by the grace of God"; "Street preachers, by the grace of God"; "Students in the college, by the grace of God"; "Preachers of the gospel, by the grace of God." It is God who calls us to our several sacred employments. Our ordination, if it be an ordination at all, is from that Great Shepherd and Bishop of souls, who went up into a mountain, and called unto him whom he would, and made them to be his first messengers.

Before he left them, he gave them that Great Commission which is still binding upon all his followers: *Go ye into all the world, and preach the gospel to every creature* (Mark 16:15). It is of grace that we are put into any sphere of service; and what a grace it is to be permitted to do anything for him! His shoes' latchets we are not worthy to untie; his shoes we are not worthy to bear. Though it be a servant's work, it is a monarch's work to do anything for Christ. Blessed be his name, if he will let me be anywhere in his service, though it were but as a helper in the kitchen! The kitchen is in the palace, and Christ's kitchen maids are maids of honor. He that serves God, reigns. To serve him on earth is to be glorified. To serve him in heaven will be a part of our endless glory. Surely this, then, is by grace.

Still further, *every opportunity of serving God is a gift of grace.* I am sure that when I have been shut out from the pulpit by sickness, I have thought it a great grace from God to be permitted to climb into the pulpit once more. When one's hand has been unable to hold a pen, we count it a grace to be able to write again some loving words that may be a blessing to men. I think that it is God's grace that puts in your way people to whom you may speak privately. It is God's grace that brings those children to the Sunday school to you, so that you may teach them. If we were wide awake, we would see, all day long, opportunities of usefulness, and we would be saying, "Blessed be God who puts me by providence where I can be of some little service to him, and bring forth some fruit to his praise!" It is all of grace; these providential openings, and the spirit and the power to avail ourselves of them, come as gifts from God.

Another thing I know: when you have the call to a work, and the opportunity, still *it is a gift of grace to be in a right state of mind to do your Lord's service.* Do you never feel sluggish and dull? Would you not *always* be so if his Spirit did not invigorate you? Are you not sometimes frostbitten, so that your soul seems like a great iceberg? Would the waters ever flow unless the Spirit came with melting power? Do you not thank God, dear brother, that you have had gracious occasions in which the Lord has made you like Naphtali, *a hind let loose* (Genesis 49:21)? When you have given forth goodly words, from whom has come the unction? from where the power? You have spoken; ah, that is a poor thing! But God has spoken through you; ah, that is a grand thing! Is not that wholly the work of grace?

Every tear of sympathy that the preacher sheds when he is wooing men to Christ, every heartthrob and all the anguish of his soul when he would willingly compel them to come in, the whole bearing and behavior of a grace-taught minister or teacher – all this is of grace, and unto God must be the glory of it. It is not under law that we are working, for law provides no strength, no tone, no savor. It is grace that makes us work, for it gives us the strength with which to work. *God hath spoken once; twice have I heard this, that power belongeth unto God. Also unto thee, O Lord, belongeth mercy: for thou renderest to every man according to his work* (Psalm 62:11-12). You give him strength proportioned to his need, and the guidance necessary because of the difficulties of his task. Here is grace. Is it not so?

You will be sure to join with me in the next point without a single objection: *success in holy service is wholly of the Lord.* If we were so wicked as to attribute to ourselves the sowing, and to ourselves the watering apart from grace, then we dare not attribute to ourselves the increase. *I have planted,* said Paul; *Apollos watered; but God gave the increase* (1 Corinthians 3:6). Would a single persuasion of ours prevail with man's hard heart if the Holy Spirit did not convince him of sin and make him repent? Would the preaching of the gospel in our poor way ever enlighten a single eye if Jesus Christ were not seen in his own light? Could we comfort the brokenhearted, could we proclaim liberty to the captives, and the opening of the prison to them that are bound if the Spirit of God were not upon us?

Why, if we did make the proclamation, would it not fall flat to the ground apart from the work of God, who does all things through us and by us? We are laborers together with him. We lift our hand, and God lifts his. We speak, and he speaks. We would willingly lay hold of men's hearts, and he does lay hold upon them. We would weep them to Christ, and he brings them weeping to Christ and saves them to eternal life. Blessed be his name! After many years of prophesying in his name, dare any of us say that we have made the dry bones to live? After having long given the invitation, do we say that we have persuaded one to come to the wedding feast apart from the Lord's divine working? Do we take any of the glory of a saved soul to ourselves? It would be treason; it would be blasphemy. We dare not commit such a sin. Our work, if it succeeds at all, if it is worth calling good work, is all of grace.

And if, my dear friends, any of you are called to suffer for Christ's sake, *the honor of suffering is a special gift*. If you have been reviled, if you have lost position, if you have suffered those moderate martyrdoms which are possible in a free country like this, then *unto you it is given in the behalf of Christ, not only to believe on him, but also to suffer for his sake* (Philippians 1:29). *Rejoice, and be exceeding glad: for great is your reward in heaven: for so persecuted they the prophets which were before you* (Matthew 5:12). But take no credit to yourself. You are elevated to the rank of your companions of suffering; it is your King who brought you there. You have his gracious permission to pass through great tribulation, and that would be nothing to you if you had not washed your robes, and made them white in the blood of the Lamb.

You owe your patience, your courage, your steadfastness, all to the Spirit of God. You had long since been carried away by the fear of man, which brings a snare; you had long since been a traitor to the truth, and to your Lord, if he had left you. It is your duty to be faithful. When you are faithful, it is not in yourself that you are so. He works all our works in us, and he must have the praise of them. *Work out your own salvation with fear and trembling* (Philippians 2:12). Work it out to the very full. Be thorough with it. *For it is God which worketh in you both to will and to do of his good pleasure* (Philippians 2:13). *Be ye stedfast, unmoveable, always abounding in the work of the Lord* (1 Corinthians 15:58). God will reward you; but your steadfastness, your diligence, your patience, all these are the work of the grace of God, and you know it. If you indeed possess them, you ascribe them all to him.

Now then, we have established this, I think, beyond all contradiction, among spiritual men – that in the service of the Lord free grace is magnified.

So we take another step, and we say, as our second topic, therefore, the Lord has his own way of measuring what we do. You see that in the case of these persons who had toiled in the vineyard; their master measured their work after his own fashion. He did not go by the regular pay-way of so much an hour; but inasmuch as it was all of grace, this great householder made the reward to be after his own measure, a penny for one hour and a penny for twelve hours. He made the last equal to the first. So shall it be: *The last shall be first, and the first last.*

This is because we are dealing here not with a legal paymaster, but with a God of grace, who measures our service, which itself is all of grace, by his own measurement, and not by ours.

He will reward every worker, but not as we judge. He will do no man any injustice, even in the omnipotence of his grace. He will be able to say to every worker, *Friend, I do thee no wrong* (Matthew 20:13). He will do no wrong to any one of his servants, whomever they may be; rest assured of that. But still he will reply, *Is it not lawful for me to do what I will with mine own?* (Matthew 20:15), and he will reward his workers in his own royal yet gracious way.

So then, *he will not reward us according to the time spent, or surface covered.* Some may be Christians for thirty or forty years, and may never be among the first. It is not the length of your service, good as that is, that will be God's gain. There may be some who shall come to Christ and go home to heaven in a single year, and yet shall bring great honor to their Master. It is not the length of time in which you are engaged in the Lord's service. Neither is it the space that is apparently covered. Some seem to do a great deal, skimming over a wide surface, but that is not how the Master measures: neither by the hour, nor yet by the acre. That might be a legal way of measurement, but his gracious way of measurement is not so.

And *he will not measure out the reward according to our ability,* whether it be mental ability, ability of substance, or ability of opportunity, for some of us might come in for a large share, and others might come in for a very little, if this were the rule. But this is not the way the Master measures. If to one man he gives the gift of speech, to another the great gift of diving deeply into the meaning of his Word, and to another experience, and so on, the reward to the persons holding these various gifts will not be in proportion to the gifts they have, but will be quite according to another rule.

The reward will not be according to the judgment of men. A brother has served God in his way, and his brethren think much of him, and appoint him to an office. He is a deacon, or an elder, or perhaps he becomes a pastor. It is a high reward to be allowed thus to increase our opportunities of usefulness; but we shall not at last be rewarded according to the height of office. That is not the standard in this kingdom where Christ rules.

Above all, *no man shall be measured by his own judgment*; if it were so, I know some friends who would have a very grand reward. They are free from sin; they are perfect, they say; but their Master knows, if they do not, whether that is true or not. Another says, "I have done this, and I have done that." But it is not what you say that you have done that will gauge your Master's reward to you. There are some that speak very loudly of what they have accomplished. I do not think that their brethren, for the most part, think more of them for thinking so much of themselves.

I believe that those who have lower opinions of their own capacity and usefulness are much more honored in the presence of the saints of God. No, our self-judgment, our tall talk, our loud profession, and so forth, will not be the measure by which we shall be rewarded, or else those who said, *[We] have borne the burden and heat of the day* (Matthew 20:12), would have had twopence, at least, if not threepence, or, perhaps, even a shilling, in proportion to those poor creatures whom the master made equal to them, though they had only come in at the eleventh hour.

Our reward will not be according to the impression made among men. We may have made our mark upon our age, and neighborhood, and surroundings. Some men's names will go down to posterity; others have no fame at all. It will be found of some men that their lives are written and emblazoned everywhere. Others will live in the little circle of their family, but not beyond that narrow range. But God will not measure that way. The godly housewife, with four or five children trained for God in her cottage, may be reckoned of God among the first; and the able speaker, in his pulpit, who has thousands hanging on his lips, may be reckoned of God among the last. God has his own ways of measuring up men's works.

But let me add that *we shall not be rewarded even according to our success.* To some men success is meted out in large measure; that success which really is not their own, but is the fruit of other men's labors. A man preaches the gospel with many tears for years and sees little fruit. He dies. Another man, of earnest spirit, follows him, and gathers in the old man's sheaves. The former man planted; the other man entered into his labors. To whom shall the reward be given? The success is not due to him who seems to have achieved it. You remember the old Roman Catholic legend, which contains a great truth.

There was a brother who preached very mightily, and who had won many souls to Christ; and it was revealed to him one night, in a dream, that in heaven he would have no reward for all that he had done. He asked to whom the reward would go, and an angel told him that it would go to an old man who used to sit on the pulpit stairs and pray for him. Well, it may be so, though it is more likely that both would share their Master's praise. We shall not be rewarded, however, simply according to our apparent success.

Neither shall we be put down as one of the last because of nonsuccess. God intends that some men shall never succeed, according to the rule of success that pertains among men, for he sent even his servant Isaiah to go and make the people's hearts hard, and their ears dull of hearing; and he sent Jeremiah to weep over a nation to whom his tears brought no repentance and no reformation. He may send you, like Noah, to preach for 120 years, and never get a soul beside your own family into the ark. But if you are faithful, that is well pleasing in his sight. Here lies the good pleasure of God.

I do not suppose that it will happen that you are to do all the plowing and all the sowing, and that there should never be an armful of sheaves for you in all your life; though, if it should be thus, and you shall have been at the end found faithful to the commission that your God has given to you, truly, I say unto you, you shall have your reward; but the reward is not measured out according to man's rule of success.

Let me tell you what I think is a rule with God. It is a many-branched kind of rule. Some men stand first because of their strong *desire*. Oh, they would have saved the people if they could; they would have persuaded men to be Christians if they could; they would have laid down their lives to do it. They preached their very hearts out in their desire for their hearers' salvation. Their souls ran over at their lips while they talked with men. God knows their desires, and he takes the will for the deed, and *so the last shall be first.*

God also measures *proportions.* The brother never had more than one talent, but he did as much with it as some with ten; yet it did not seem to come to much in his eyes. He was always mourning because he was so little. He thought that he was like one of those coral insects at the bottom of the sea, just making a little bit of coral which never came above the waves; but it was part of a great whole that would afterwards rise into a fairy island of the sea. Our Lord will measure not according to what a man does not have, but according to what a man has.

And here is one who has little to commend him except his *spirit*. He waits upon God. He is very gracious. He trembles at God's Word. He speaks with his whole heart very reverently, very tenderly, desiring always to be silent if God would have him be silent, and only to speak when God would move him to speak. His delight is to do the Lord's will and nothing but the Lord's will, and he is quite content to be nothing. Indeed, he cries for that –

> Oh, to be nothing, nothing,
>   Only to lie at his feet!

Now, God may put that man among the first; whereas the self-contained man, who does work for God sincerely, may, nevertheless, have to go into the back rank and be among the last.

Here is one again, who, whatever he does, does it with *thoroughness*. He does not attempt many things, but he does one thing. It is all that he can do, and he throws his whole soul into it, and works at it like some Eastern artist working on a cameo for a prince. All his life is put into that little bit of a thing; and, it may be, that our great King will count him first, while another who did much in a sloppy, stained style, and was thought to have done a great deal, will have all his work rejected, for it has not measured up to the Prince's mark, and he will not adorn his palace therewith.

I think, dear friends, that God will measure our work very much by our *thought of him* in it. If we did it all *to* him; if we did it all *for* him; if he was always in our mind in the doing of it, and we did not think of our friends, nor of our own reputation, then God would be more likely to honor us, for he will put those who think much of him among the first, and others among the last. *Them that honour me,* says the Lord, *I will honour* (1 Samuel 2:30).

And especially, again, God would be more likely to honor us if all that we do is baptized with *love*. Why, see that woman who brought her alabaster box, and broke it, and poured the precious ointment of spikenard upon Christ's head! She is put among the first, and Christ makes honorable mention of her wherever the gospel is preached. Some that did much have to go among the last, for they did not have such love as she had.

Some work for God with great *faith,* and the Lord loves to see us working in faith. To do a great deal of work with a great deal of unbelief is to do very little after all; for if a prayer that is unbelieving does not prosper, then preaching or teaching that is unbelieving is not likely to do so either. Put faith into your work, and, maybe, you will be among the first.

I am sure that God measures much of our work according to the *prayer* we spend over it. Oh yes, it was a fine sermon! You could tell how the preacher had worked at it; you could see how he had polished up that phrase, and how he had cut that sentence into diced pieces to make it strong; but you could also see that he had never prayed over it. A sermon that is prayed over is worth ten thousand that are merely prepared, or copied, or that spring out of a man's mind without being effected by the Holy Spirit in his heart. Oh, to pray down the sermon, and then to pray up the sermon, and pray it all over, resting upon God alone!

God will often look upon our work in *giving,* not according to how much we give, but I think that the Lord's rule is to take notice of *how much we have left.* That woman who gave all her living gave more than all the rich men gave, because she had nothing left. It was but two mites that make a farthing; but then it was all her living, and so she goes into the front rank. My lord has given a thousand pounds, and we are very much obliged to him. He must go into the back rank, for all that, for he has so much left.

And then, it may be, that they will take the first place *who did not get any reward* for what they did. Our Lord tells us that when we are making a feast, we should call in the blind and the lame. Why? *For,* he says, *they cannot recompense thee* (Luke 14:14). He speaks of the Pharisees again, and says, *Verily I say unto you, they have their reward* (Matthew 6:5). You will not be paid twice. If you have done something for Christ – for instance, defended the faith – and you are denounced for it, and betrayed for it, very well, you have not had your pay for it. There remains the recompense for unrewarded services.

It is a grand thing when, by the grace of God, you have something standing in God's Book, not of law, but of grace. You helped a poor man, and he was not grateful. Oh, be so thankful that he was not grateful, because, if he had been grateful, you would have had your reward, maybe! When those you relieve are very kind afterwards, and speak well of you, and do you some good service in return, it is very nice; of course it is. Well, but you are paid. But those who have done good and suffered for it; who, for the best thing that they did have had the worst return; who have rendered kindness, and have only received unkindness as the result, it may be that the Lord will say of them, "These were last, but they shall be first"; whereas many that stood first in men's esteem, and in the gratitude they received, will have to go last.

Now, my time almost fails me, but you must bear with me on my third topic, for here is the practical part of free grace in our service.

Accordingly, we have instruction as to our spirit as workers. If the work is all of grace, and if God has a way of measuring that work, which is not at all according to the law, but of his own grace, then there are two things to be observed. First, do not be proud; secondly, do not be discouraged.

Do not be proud, for many that are first shall be last. Suppose, my dear friend, that you really are first, and are doing a great deal for God; will you be proud? Why, *you are only a greater debtor.* You owe all the more to that grace which has enabled you to be of some service in the kingdom of your Lord. Lie low at your Lord's feet, and be very humble.

Next, remember that though you may think that you are first, *you may, even now, be among the last.* Your assessment of your service may not be the divine assessment at all. You may think that you are *rich, and increased with goods, and have need of nothing;* and, in God's repute, you may be *wretched, and miserable, and poor, and blind, and naked* (Revelation 3:17). Your work may be like very big trusses of hay, and loads of straw, and stacks of stubble; and yet, when God comes to test it, it may be all burned down to a handful of ashes; whereas the friend of whom you think so little may only have built a small portion, but he has built it of gold, and silver, and precious stones.

Let us also recollect that even if it is true that we are among the first, we may, if we get proud of it, *find ourselves among the last.* O, how some of God's greatest servants have been shriveled up when they began to swell out with pride and vanity! God blessed them as long as they were feeble, and weak, and leaned upon his strength; but when they were strong, and relied on themselves, there came a dreadful failure.

There is one thing which is absolutely certain. *If you are among the first, you will reckon yourself to be among the last.* He that is best thinks himself worst. What a description Paul gives of himself in the seventh chapter of Romans! "Oh," says one, "I heard a person say that Paul was not a converted man when he wrote that!" Let me tell you that he had been in the third heaven when he wrote that bit of deep experience. He had so much likeness to his Lord that he excelled every other man then living, except, perhaps, John; and if it had not been for his extraordinary holiness, he would never have been able to pen those tremendous groanings wherein he says, *O wretched man that I am! who shall deliver me from the body of this death?* (Romans 7:24).

The man who thinks that he is holy has never seen the Holy God. If he had – if he had ever beheld him, he would say with Job, *I have heard of thee by the hearing of the ear: but now mine eye seeth thee. Wherefore I abhor myself, and repent in dust and ashes* (Proverbs 42:5-6). The superlative perfection of the Lord God, and the absolutely perfect example of our Lord Jesus Christ, are such that if a man has ever had communion with these, he shrinks into nothing in his own esteem. He that is really first is always the man who is willing to be counted last. Paul, though he is not one bit behind any of the apostles, still calls himself less than the least of all saints, and describes himself as having been the chief of sinners. Ah, beloved! a low idea of self is one of the labels with which God marks the best of his possessions; therefore, do not be proud.

In the next place, do not be discouraged. If you feel that you are last, *God's measure is not yours.* Though you may think that you are last, he may not think so at all. Though you say, "I am not worthy to be an apostle," yet he may think you worth putting into the apostleship. God's idea of your worthiness and your own idea of it may greatly differ; but his estimate is the true one.

Besides, suppose that you are last; *but he giveth more grace* (James 4:6). Christ has come, not only that we may have life, but also that we may have it *more abundantly* (John 10:10). Do not be content with what you have. *Covet earnestly the best gifts* (1 Corinthians 12:31). Covet still more the best graces. God is able to do for us *exceeding abundantly above all that we ask or think* (Ephesians 3:20). Go in for great things. Has not the Lord said, *Open thy mouth wide, and I will fill it* (Psalm 81:10)? I spoke to a man of God this morning, and I told him how God had graciously enabled me to draw near to him in prayer, and of the glorious way he had granted my requests. My friend said, "Yes, and he has made your mouth bigger than it used to be." Is it not so? The faculty of believing prayer grows by being used. The more you ask, the more you may ask; and the more you have asked, the more you will ask. The capacity to receive is increased by receiving. God grant that it may be so with us if we are last!

Remember, too, that if you really are among the least useful, yet *a right spirit may compensate* for your poverty, and make your little service very precious. If you cannot get a wide sphere, do not want it. A young minister said to an old one, "Ah, sir! I preach only to about one hundred people. I wish that I could get where I could gather a thousand." His friend answered, "Young man, a hundred people are quite enough for you to be accountable for; and if you faithfully discharge your duty to their souls, you have quite enough to do." Wish for a larger sphere if you are capable of filling it; but remember that the best preparation for greater usefulness is to be faithful in your present position.

My last word to God's children is this: What does it matter, after all, whether we are first or whether we are last? Do not let us dwell too much upon it, for *we all share the honor given to each.* When we are converted, we become members of Christ's living body; and as we grow in grace and get the true spirit that permeates that body, we shall say, when any member of it is honored, "This is honor for us." If any brother shall be greatly honored of God, I feel honored in his honor. If God shall bless your brother and make him ten times more useful than you are, then you see that God is blessing you – not only blessing your brother, but also you.

If my hand has something in it, my foot does not say, "Oh, I have not got it!" No, for if my hand has it, my foot has it; it belongs to the whole of my body. If my mouth alone eats, it does not eat for my mouth alone; but it also eats for my brain, my hand, my backbone, and for every part of me. So, when you get to feel your oneness with Christ, and your oneness with his people, your only thought will be, "Let God be glorified; let him be magnified. It does not matter whether I am first or last." You will stand up and say, "That brother, who was converted only a week or two ago, got his penny, and I am glad of it." Here is another, who has done very poor work, but you will thank God that he has got his penny.

He is one of the family. It all comes from the same hand, and it will all come home to the same house. We are something like men in a great shop, where there are different people serving. One young man has a counter where ladies come, and he serves them, and he takes a lot of money in the day; another counterman, at the back, sells goods that take a deal of trouble to dispose of, and upon which there is but a small profit. Does the master praise the men of the shop according to the quantity of money each one takes?

The one who is put in the back place, and sells poor goods, is just as diligent and just as worthy in his master's sight as the others. Suppose that they are all members of one family; when they meet at night, one will say, "I took so much." Another will say, "I took ten times as much as that"; but they are all glad, because it all goes into the firm; it is all a part of the same concern. Go then, dear brothers and sisters, and work away for Christ, and do not envy one another, but all be glad to be permitted, in this work of grace, to take any part or any portion for your Lord.

One thing more, and I will be done. I have only been talking to God's people all this while because you who are not saved cannot serve him. What a miserable position yours is! You are out of the pale of service. God will receive nothing from you until you come to Christ. The only way to bring a sacrifice is to bring it through the Great High Priest, the Lord Jesus Christ. *Except ye be converted, and become as little children, ye shall not enter into the kingdom of heaven* (Matthew 18:3); much less shall you be accepted as servants there. I beg you, by the thought of the grace of which I have been speaking, to rest not until you can say that Christ has saved you, made you a partaker of his grace, and sent you forth into his royal service. The Lord bless you! Amen.

Chapter 4

A Message to Nominal Followers of Religion

But what think ye? A man had two sons; and he came to the first, and said, Son, go work to day in my vineyard. And he answered and said, I will not: but afterward he repented himself, and went. And he came to the second, and said likewise. And he answered and said, I go, sir: and went not. Whether of the twain did the will of his father? They say, The first. Jesus saith unto them, Verily I say unto you, that the publicans and the harlots go into the kingdom of God before you. For John came unto you in the way of righteousness, and ye believed him not: but the publicans and the harlots believed him: and ye, when ye saw it, did not even repent yourselves afterward, that ye might believe him. (Matthew 21:28-32)

The sight of this vast arena, and of this crowded assembly, reminds me of other spectacles which, in days happily long past, were seen in the amphitheaters of the old Roman Empire. Around, tier upon tier, were the assembled multitudes, with their cruel eyes and iron hearts; and in the center stood a solitary, friendless man, waiting until the doors of the lion's den should be uplifted, that he might yield himself up as a witness for Christ and a sacrifice to the popular fury. There would have been no difficulty then to have divided the precious from the vile in that audience. The most thoughtless wayfarer who would enter into the amphitheater would know at once who was the disciple of Christ and who were the enemies of the Crucified One.

There stood the bravely calm disciple, about to die; but all around, in those mighty tiers of the Colosseum, or of the amphitheater of some provincial town, as the case might be, there sat matrons and nobles, princes and peasants, commoners and aristocrats, senators and soldiers, all gazing downward with the same fierce, unpitying look; all boisterous for their heathen gods, and all clamorous in the joy with which they gazed upon the agonies of the disciple of the hated Galilean, butchered to make a Roman holiday.

Another sight is before us today, with far more happy associations; but alas! it is a far more difficult task this day to separate the chaff from the wheat, the precious from the vile, than in the day when the apostle fought with beasts at Ephesus. Here, in this arena, I hope there are hundreds, if not thousands, who would be prepared to die for our Lord Jesus; and in yonder crowded seats, we may count by hundreds those who bear the name and accept the gospel of the Man of Nazareth; and yet I fear that both in these living hills on either side, and upon this vast floor, there are many enemies of the Son of God, who are forgetful of his righteous claims – who have cast from them those cords of love which should bind them to his throne, and have never submitted to the mighty love which showed itself in his cross and in his wounds.

I cannot attempt the separation. You must grow together until the harvest. To divide you would be a task which at this hour angels could not perform, but which one day they will easily accomplish, when at their Master's bidding, the harvest having come, they shall gather together first the tares in bundles to burn them, and afterwards the wheat into Jehovah's barn. I shall not attempt the division, but I shall ask each man to attempt it for himself in his own case. I say unto you, young men and maidens, old men and fathers, this day examine yourselves whether or not you are the faith. Let no man take it for granted that he is a Christian because he has helped to swell the numbers of a Christian assembly. Let no man judge his fellow, but let each man judge himself. To each one of you I say, with deepest earnestness, let a division be made by your conscience, and let your understandings separate between him that fears God and him that fears him not.

Though no man clothed in linen, with a writer's bottle of ink by his side, shall go through the midst of you to set a mark upon the foreheads of the men that sigh and cry for all the abominations of this city, let conscience take the bottle of ink and honestly make the mark, or leave the favored sign unmade, and let each man question himself this morning: "Am I on the Lord's side? Am I for Christ, or for his enemies? Do I gather with him, or do I scatter abroad?" "Divide! Divide!" they say in the House of Commons. Let us say the same in this great congregation this day. Political divisions are but trifles compared with the all-important distinction which I would have you consider. Divide as you will be divided to the right and to the left in the great day when Christ shall judge the world in righteousness. Divide as you will be divided when the bliss of heaven, or the woes of hell, shall be your everlasting portion.

If the whole of us were thus divided into two camps, and we could say these have made a covenant with God by sacrifice, and those on the other hand are still enemies to God by wicked works, looking at the last class we might still feel it necessary by way of personal application to make a division among them; for although all unbelievers are alike unpardoned and unsaved, yet they are not alike in the circumstances of their case and the outward forms of their sins. Alike in being without Christ, they are still very varied in their mental and moral condition. I trust I was guided by the Spirit of God to my text this morning, for it is of such a character that while it enables me to address the whole mass of the unconverted, it gives me a hopeful opportunity of getting at the conscience of each by dividing the great company of the unconverted into two distinct classes. O that for each tribe of unbelievers there may be a blessing in store this day.

We shall speak to those who are *avowedly disobedient to God,* and then to those who are *deceptively submissive to him.*

First, we have a word for those who are truly disobedient to God. There are many such here. God has said to you as he says to all who hear the gospel, *Son, go work to day in my vineyard;* and you have replied, perhaps honestly, but certainly very boldly, very unkindly, and very unjustly, *I will not.* You have made no bones about it, but have given a refusal point-blank to the claims of your Creator. You have spoken your mind right out, not only in words, but also in a more forcible and unmistakable manner, for actions speak far more loudly than words. You have said, over and over again, by your actions, "I will not serve God, or believe in his Son Jesus." My dear friend, I am glad to see you here this morning, and trust that matters will change with you before you leave this hall; but at present you have not yielded even an outward obedience to God, but in all ways have said, *I will not.*

Practically you have said, "I will not worship God; I will not attend a place of worship on Sunday – it is a weariness intolerable to me. I shall not sing the praise of my Maker – I will not pretend to bless the God for whom I have no love. In public prayer I shall not join – I have no heart for it. I shall not make a claim of repeating morning and nightly prayers in private – what is the good of it? I will not pray at all; I do not believe in its effectualness, and I will not be such a hypocrite as to follow a vain practice in which I have no belief whatever. As for what is called sin, I love it and will not give it up." You are proud of being called an honest man, for you acknowledge the claims of your fellow man upon you, but you scorn to be thought religious, for you do not admit the rights of your Maker.

To the righteous requests of others you yield a cheerful obedience, but to the just and tender requests of God you give a plain and evident denial. As clearly as actions can speak, you say by your neglect of the Sabbath, by your disregard of prayer, by your never reading the Bible, by your perseverance in known sin, and by the whole course of your life, *I will not.* Like Pharaoh, you have demanded, *Who is the Lord, that I should obey his voice?* (Exodus 5:2). You are of the same mind as those of old, who said, *It is vain to serve God: and what profit is it that we have kept his ordinance?* (Malachi 3:14).

Moreover, my friend, you have not as yet given an assent to the doctrines of God's Word; on the contrary, *intellectually* as well as practically, you go not at God's bidding. You have set up in your mind the idea that you must understand everything before you will believe it – an idea, let me tell you, which you will never be able to carry out, for you cannot understand your own existence; and there are ten thousand other things around you which you never can comprehend, but which you must believe or remain forever a gigantic fool. Still you quibble at this doctrine and that doctrine, railing at the gospel system in general; and if you were asked at a workingman's conference why you did not go to a place of worship, you would perhaps say that you stayed away from worship because you did not like this doctrine or that.

Let me say on my own account, that as far as I am personally concerned, it is a very small consideration to me whether you do like my doctrine or do not. For your own sake I am anxious above measure that you should believe the truth as it is in Jesus; but while you live in sin, your dislike of a doctrine will very probably only make me feel the more sure of its truth, and lead me to preach it with more confidence and vehemence. You think that we are to learn God's truth from the likings or dislikings of those who refuse to worship him and want an excuse for their sins.

O unconverted men and women, it will be a very long time before we shall come to you to learn what you would have us preach, and when we fall so low as to do that, you yourselves will despise us. What if the physician shall ask his patient what kind of medicine he would wish to have prescribed? Then the man needs no physician; he can prescribe for himself. Show the doctor out at the back door immediately. What is the use of such a physician? Of what service is a minister who will submit to depraved tastes and sinful appetites, and say, "How would you like me to preach to you? What smooth things shall I offer you?"

Ah souls! We have some higher end to be served than merely pleasing you. We would save you by distasteful truths, for honeyed lies will ruin you. That teaching which the carnal mind most delights in is the most deadly and deceitful. With many of you, your beliefs, and tastes, and likes must be changed, or else you will never enter heaven. I admit that in a measure I like your honesty in having said outright, "I will not serve God"; but it is an honesty which makes me shudder, for it betrays a heart as hard as the lower millstone.

Again, you have said, "I will not serve God," and up to this time it is very possible that you have never been in the temperament to repent of having said it, for the ways of sin are sweet to you, and your heart is fixed in its rebellion. You have never felt that conviction of sin which the Holy Spirit has effected in some of us; if you had felt it, you would soon have been shaken out of your *I will not.*

If God's power of grace, of which thousands of us bear witness that it is as real a power as that which guides the stars or dispatches the wind – if God's almighty grace should once get a hold of you, you would no longer say, "I do not believe this or that"; for, as tremblingly as any of those whom you now despise, you would cry out, *What must I do to be saved?* (Acts 16:30). Up until now you have never felt that power, and therefore I cannot wonder that you do not acknowledge it, although the testimony of honest witnesses ought to have some weight with you. You are practically, intellectually, and avowedly no Christian; you have never deceived yourself and others by making a profession which you do not honor, but you have gone on in your own chosen path, saying with more or less resolution, in answer to every call of the gospel, *I will not.*

We said just now that the answer of the son to his father as recorded in our text was very plain; it was not, however, very genuine, or such as his father might have expected. His father said, *Son, go work to day in my vineyard,* and the son rudely said, *I will not.* That is direct; and without another word of apology or reason he went his way. This is not quite as it should be, is it? Even so, my friend, you may have been too hasty and so have been unjust. Is it not very possible you have denied to God and to his gospel the respect which both really deserve? You have spoken very plainly, but at the same time very thoughtlessly, very harshly to the God who has deserved better things from you. Have you ever given the claims of the Lord Jesus a fair consideration? Have you not dismissed the gospel with a sneer quite unworthy of you? Have you not been afraid to look the matters between God and your soul fairly in the face?

I believe it to be the case of hundreds here; I know it to be the case of thousands and tens of thousands in London. They have put their foot down, and they have said, "None of your religion for me! I have made up my mind and I will never alter; I hate it and will not listen to it." Does no small voice within ever tell them that this is not fair to themselves or to God? Is the matter so easily to be decided? Suppose it should turn out that the religion of Jesus is true; what then? What will be the lot of those who despised him? My friend, the religion of Jesus is true, and I have proved its truth in my own case; so do, I pray you, consider it, and do not trifle away your immortal soul. *Thus saith the Lord of hosts: Consider your ways* (Haggai 1:7).

It is now time for me to tell the openly ungodly what is his real state. You have been more than a little proud of your honesty; and looking down upon certain professors of religion you have said, "Ah! I make no such claims as they do; I am honest, I am." Friend, you cannot have a greater abhorrence of hypocrites than I have; if you can find a fair chance of laughing at them, pray do so. If by any means you can stick pins into their windbags, and let the gas of their profession out, pray do so. I try to do a little of it in my way; you do the same!

You and I are agreed in this, I hope, in heartily hating anything like sham and falsehood; but if you begin to hold your head up, and think yourself so very superior because you make no profession, I must take you down a little by reminding you that it is no credit to a thief that he makes no profession of being honest, and it is not thought to be exceedingly honorable to a man that he makes no profession of speaking the truth. For the fact is, that a man who does not profess to be honest is a professed thief, and he who does not claim to speak the truth is an acknowledged liar; thus in escaping one horn you are thrown upon another; you miss the rock but run upon the quicksand.

You are a confessed and avowed neglecter of God, a professed despiser of the great salvation, an acknowledged disbeliever in the Christ of God. When our government at any time arrests persons suspected of Fenianism, they have no difficulty about those gentlemen who glory in wearing the green uniform and flaunting the big feather. "Come along," says the constable, "you are the man, for you wear the military clothing of a rebel." Even so, when the angel of justice arrests the enemies of the Lord, he will have no difficulty in accusing and arresting you, for, laying his hand upon your shoulder, he will say, "You wear the military clothing of an enemy of God; you plainly and unblushingly acknowledge that you do not fear God nor trust in his salvation."

No witnesses need be called concerning you at the last great day. You will stand up, not quite so bravely as you do today, for when the heavens are on a blaze, and the earth is rocking to and fro, and the great white cloud fills the field of vision, and the eyes of the great judge shall burn like lamps of fire, you will put on a different demeanor and a different posture from that which you maintain before a poor preacher of the gospel. Ah! my ungodly acquaintance, with such a case as yours there shall be no need to judge, for out of your own mouth shall you be condemned.

Yet I came not here to tell you of your sins only, but to also help you to escape from them. It is necessary that this much should be said, but we now turn to something far more pleasant. I am in hopes this day that some of you will listen to that little word in the text: *afterward*. *He answered and said, I will not: but* **afterward** *he repented, and went* (emphasis added). It is a long lane which has no turning; let us trust that we have come to the turning now. There is space left to you for repentance; though you may have been a drunkard, or a swearer, or impure, the die is not yet cast, and a change is still possible. May God grant that you may have reached the time when it shall be said of you, "Afterward he repented; he changed his mind; he believed upon Jesus, and obeyed the word of the Lord, and went."

Perhaps the son in the parable thought a little more calmly about it. He said to himself, "I will consider the matter; second thoughts are often best. I growled at my good father, and gave him a sharp answer, and I saw the tear standing in the good man's eye. I am sorry I grieved him. The thought of grieving him makes me change my mind. I said no to him, but I did not think about it. I forgot that if I go and work in my father's vineyard, I shall be working for myself, for I am his eldest son, and all that he has will belong to me, so that I am very foolish to refuse to work to my own advantage. Ah! now I see my father had my advantage at heart; I will even go as he instructed me." See, he shoulders his tools, and away he marches to labor with all his might. He said, *I will not,* but he repented and went, and it is admitted by all that he did the will of his father.

Oh, I hope that many a man and woman will this day cry, "I do retract what I have said. I will go to my Father, and will say to him, 'I will do your bidding. I will not grieve your love. I will not lose the opportunity of advancing my soul's best interest; I obey the gospel command.'" I will suppose that I see one such before me, and I will speak to him. Perhaps he said, *I will not,* because he really did not understand what religion was. How few after all know what the way of salvation is; though they go to church, and to chapel, they have not yet learned God's plan of pardoning sinners. Do you know the plan of salvation? Hear it and live by it. You have offended God; God must punish sin; it is a fixed law that sin must be punished. How then can God have mercy upon you?

Why, only in this way: Jesus Christ came from heaven and he suffered in the room, place, and stead of all who trust him; suffered what they ought to have suffered, so that God is just, and yet at the same time he is able to forgive the very chief of sinners through the merits of his dear Son. Your debts, if you be a believer in him, Christ has paid on your behalf. If you do but come and rest upon Jesus and upon Jesus only, God cannot punish you for your sins, for he punished Jesus for them, and it would not be just of him to punish Christ and then to punish you, to exact payment first from the guarantee and afterwards from the debtor.

My dear friend, whoever you may be, whatever your past life may have been, if you will trust Christ, you shall be saved from all your sin in a moment; the whole of your past life shall be blotted out. There shall not remain in God's book so much as a single charge against your soul, for Christ who died for you shall take your guilt away and leave you without a blot before the face of God. Read the last verse of my text, and you will see that it was by believing that men entered into the kingdom of God of old, and it is still by believing that men are saved. *Behold the Lamb of God,* said John the Baptist (John 1:36), and if you look to that bleeding Lamb, you shall live. Do you understand this? Is it not simple? Is it not suitable to you? Will you still refuse to obey it? Does not the Holy Spirit prompt you to yield? Do you not even now say, "Is it so simple? I will even trust in Jesus.

> Guilty, but with heart relenting,
> To the Savior's wounds I'll fly.

"I will come, by God's help, this morning, lest death should come before the sun sets. I will trust Christ to save me. Precious way of salvation! Why should I not be saved?"

It is possible too, that you may have said, *I will not,* because you really thought there was no hope for you. Ah! my friend, let me assure you – and oh! how glad I am to be able to do it – that there is hope for the vilest through the precious blood of Jesus. No man can have gone too far for the long arm of Christ to reach him. Christ delights to save the biggest sinners. He said to his apostles, *"Preach the gospel to every creature,* but begin" – where? *"beginning at Jerusalem* (Luke 24:47). There live the wretches who spit in my face. There live the cruel ones that drove the nails through my hands. Go and preach the gospel to them first. Tell them that I am able to save, not little sinners merely, but also the very chief of sinners. Tell them to trust in me and they shall live." Where are you, you despairing one? I know the devil will try to keep the sound of the gospel from your ears if he can, and therefore, I would *cry aloud, [and] spare not* (Isaiah 58:1). O you despairing sinners, there is no room for despair this side of the gates of hell. If you have gone through the foulest kennels of wickedness, no stain can stand out against the power of the cleansing blood.

> There is a fountain filled with blood,
>   Drawn from Immanuel's veins,
> And sinners plunged beneath that flood,
>   Lose all their guilty stains.

Oh, I trust, now that you know there is hope for you, you will say, "I will even come at once, and put my trust in Jesus."

While I would thus encourage you to repent of your neglect of God, let me invite you to come to Jesus, and press it upon you yet again. Ah! my dear friend, you will soon be dying, and though some wicked men, in their stupid insensibility, die very calmly, and as David said, *They are not in trouble as other men; neither are they plagued like other men. But their strength is firm* (Psalm 73:4-5); yet, whether they perceive it or not, it is a dreadful thing to die with unpardoned sin hanging around you. What will your guilty soul do when it leaves the body? Think of it for a minute. It is a matter worthy of your thought.

Some of you, in all probability, will die this week. It is not probable that so many thousands of us will march through a whole week and be found alive at the other end of it. Well then, as we *may* some of us go soon, and all of us *must go* before long, let us look before us and think a bit. Imagine your soul unclothed of the body. You have left the body behind you, and your disembodied spirit finds itself in a new world. Oh, it will be a glorious thing if that separated spirit shall see Jesus whom it has loved, and fly at once into his bosom, and drink forever of the crystal fountain of ever-flowing bliss. But it will be a horrible thing if instead of it, your naked, shivering spirit should wake up to find itself friendless, homeless, helpless, hopeless, tormented with remorse, and afflicted with despair.

What if it should have to cry out forever, "I knew my duty, but I did it not; I knew the way of salvation, but I would not run in it. I heard the gospel, but I shut my ears to it. I lived and at length left the world without Christ, and here I am, past hope, no repenting now, no believing now, no escaping now, for mercy and love no longer rule the hour." Have pity on yourself, my friend. I have pity on you. Oh, if my hand could pluck you from that flame, how cheerfully would I do it! Shall I pity you and will you not pity yourself?

Oh, if my pleadings should by God's grace persuade you to trust in Christ this morning, I would plead with you while voice, and lungs, and heart, and life held out! But oh, have pity on yourself! Pity that poor naked spirit which so soon will be quivering with utmost agony, a self-caused agony, an agony from which it would not escape, an agony of which it was warned, but which it chose to endure sooner than give up sin and yield to the scepter of sovereign grace.

I would rather hope that you are saying, "I do now repent, and by God's grace I will go." If so, let me tell you there are a great many in heaven who once, like you, said, *I will not,* but they afterwards repented and are now saved. I will give you one picture. Yonder, I see a company of men on horseback, and there is one, the proudest of them all, to whom they act as a guard; they are going to Damascus, so that he may take Christians to prison and compel them to blaspheme. Saul of Tarsus is the name of that cruel, murderous persecutor. When Stephen was put to death, God said to this man Saul, "Go, work in my vineyard," but Saul said plainly, "I will not," and to prove his hostility, he helped to put Stephen to death.

There he is riding in hot haste, upon his evil errand, none more set and determined against the Lord. Yet my Lord Jesus can tame the lion, and even make a lamb of him. As he rides along, a bright light is seen, brighter than the sun at noonday; he falls from his horse, he lies trembling on the ground, and he hears a voice out of heaven saying, *Saul, Saul, why persecutest thou me?* (Acts 9:4). Lifting up his eyes with astonishment, he sees that he had ignorantly been persecuting the Son of God. What a change that one discovery worked in him. That voice that said, *I am Jesus whom thou persecutes* (Acts 9:5), broke his hard heart, and won him to the cause.

You know how three days after that, that once proud and bigoted man was baptized upon profession of faith in Christ, whom he had just now persecuted! And if you want to see an earnest preacher, where can you find a better one than the apostle Paul, who, with heart on fire, writes again and again, *God forbid that I should glory, save in the cross of our Lord Jesus Christ* (Galatians 6:14)? I hope there is a Saul here, who is to be struck down this morning. Lord, strike him down! Eternal Spirit, strike him down *now!* You did not know, perhaps, that you had been fighting against God, but you thought the religion of Jesus to be a foolish dream. You did not know that you had insulted the dying Savior, but now you do know it; may your conscience be affected, and from this day forth may you serve the Lord.

I must leave this second point when I have just said this. If there be one here who, after a long refusal, at last yields, and is willing to become a servant of God by faith in Jesus Christ, let me tell him for his encouragement, that he shall not be one bit behind those who have been so long making a profession without being true to it, for the text says, *The publicans and the harlots go into the kingdom of God;* but what else? They *go into the kingdom **before*** (emphasis added) those who made a profession of serving God, but who were not true to it.

You great sinners shall have no back seats in heaven! There shall be no outer court for you. You great sinners shall have as much love as the best, as much joy as the brightest of saints. You shall be near to Christ; you shall sit with him upon his throne; you shall wear the crown; your fingers shall touch the golden harps; you shall rejoice with the joy which is unspeakable and full of glory. Will you not come? Christ forgets your past ill manners, and bids you to come today. *Come unto me,* says he, *all ye that labour and are heavy laden, and I will give you rest* (Matthew 11:28). Thirty years of sin shall be forgiven, and it shall not take thirty minutes to do it in. Fifty, sixty, seventy years of wickedness shall all disappear as the morning's hoarfrost disappears before the sun. Come and trust my Master, hiding in his bleeding wounds.

Raise thy downcast eyes and see
    What throngs His throne surround!
These, though sinners once like thee,
    Have full salvation found.
Yield not then to unbelief;
    He says, "There yet is room":
Though of sinners thou art chief,
    Since Jesus calls thee, come.

Bear with me a little time while I speak to the second character, the *deceptively submissive,* which are by far the most numerous everywhere in England, and probably the most numerous in this assembly. Oh you, my own regular acquaintances, you who have heard my voice these thirteen years, many of you are in this class. You have said to the Great Father, *I go, sir,* but you have not gone. Let me sorrowfully sketch your portraits: you have regularly frequented a place of worship, and you would shudder to waste a single Sunday in an excursion, or in any form of Sabbath breaking. Outwardly you have said, *I go, sir.*

When the hymn is given out, you stand up and sing, and yet you do not sing with the heart. When I say, "Let us pray!" you cover your faces, but you do not pray with real prayer. You utter a polite, respectful *I go, sir,* but you do not go. You give a theoretical assent to the gospel. If I were to mention any doctrine, you would say, "Yes, that is true; I believe that." But your heart does not believe. You do not believe the gospel in the core of your nature, for if you did, it would have an effect upon you.

A man may say, "I believe my house is on fire," but if he goes to bed and falls asleep, it does not look as if he believed it, for when a man's house is on fire he tries to escape. If some of you really believed that there is a hell, and that there is a heaven, as you believe other things, you would act very differently from how you do now. I must add that many of you say, *I go, sir* in a very solemn sense, for when we preach earnestly the tears run down your cheeks, and you go home to your bedrooms, and you pray a little, and everybody thinks that your concern of mind will end in conversion; but *your goodness is as a morning cloud, and as the early dew* (Hosea 6:4).

You are like dunghills with snow upon them: while the snow lasts,

65

you look white and fair, but when the snow melts, the dunghill remains a dunghill still. Oh, how many very impressible hearts are like that! You sin, and yet you come to a place of worship, and tremble under the Word; you transgress, and you weep and transgress again; you feel the power of the gospel to a certain extent, and yet you revolt against it more and more.

Ah! my friends, I can look some of you in the face and know that I am describing some of your situations to the letter. You have been telling lies to God all these years by saying, *I go, sir,* while you have not gone. You know that to be saved you must believe in Jesus, but you have not believed. You know that you must be born again, but you are still strangers to the new birth. You are as religious as the seats you sit on, but no more; and you are as likely to get to heaven as those seats are, but not one bit more, for you are dead in sin, and death cannot enter heaven.

O my dear friends, I lament that ever I should be called to say such a thing as this, and not be more affected by the fact; and, wonder of wonders, that you, some of you, know it to be true, and yet do not feel alarmed by it! It is the easiest thing in the world to impress some of you by a sermon, but I fear you never will get beyond mere transient impressions. Like the water when lashed, the wound soon heals. You know, and you know, and you know; and you feel, and feel, and feel again; and yet your sins, your self-righteousness, your carelessness, or your willful wickedness cause you, after having said, *I go, sir,* to forget the promise and lie unto God.

Now, I spoke very honestly to the other class, and must be equally plain with you. You, too, *incriminate yourselves.* There will be no need of witnesses against you. You have admitted that the gospel is true. You did not quarrel with the doctrine of future punishment or future glory. You attended a place of worship, and you said that God was good and worthy to be served. You confessed that you owed allegiance to him, and ought to render it. You have even knelt down and in prayer you have said, "Lord, I deserve your wrath." The great God has only to turn to some of your formal prayers to find quite enough evidence to secure your condemnation. Those morning prayers of yours, those evening prayers, hypocritical every one of them, will be more than sufficient to condemn you of your own mouth. Take heed! Take heed, I pray you, while you are yet in the land of hope.

All this while, as Matthew 11:32 reminds me, you have remained unsaved, you have seen publicans and harlots saved by the very gospel which has had no power upon you. Do you not know it, young man? You, I mean, the son of a godly mother? You know that you are not saved, and yet you had a drunken workman in your father's employment, and he has been these last few years a sober Christian man, he is saved, and you perhaps have taken to the habits which he has forsaken. You know that there have been picked off of the streets poor fallen women who have been brought to know Christ, who are among the sweetest and fairest flowers in Christ's garden now, though they were once castaways; and yet some of you respectable people who never committed any outward vice in your lives, are still unconverted, and still saying to Christ, *I go, sir*, but you have not gone.

You are still without God! Without Christ! Lost, lost, lost! Yet fairer outward characters could scarcely be found. I could rather weep for you! Oh! beware, beware of being like the apples of Sodom, which are green to look upon, but when crushed, crumble to ashes. Beware of being like John Bunyan's trees that were green outside, but inwardly rotten, and only fit to be tinder for the devil's tinderbox. Oh! beware of saying as some of you do, *I go, sir,* while you go not. I sometimes see sick people who quite alarm and distress me. I say to them, "My dear friend, you are dying; have you a hope?" There is no answer. "Do you know your lost state?" "Yes sir." "Christ died for sinners." "Yes sir." "Faith gives us of his grace." "Yes sir." They say, "Yes sir, yes sir, yes sir, yes sir, yes sir." I sometimes wish before God they would contradict me, for if they would but have honesty enough to say, "I do not believe a word of it," I would know how to deal with them. Stubborn oaks are leveled by the gale, but those who bend like the willow before every wind, what wind shall break them? O dear brethren, beware of being gospel hardened; or, what is the same thing, softened but only for a season. Beware of being a promising hearer of the Word, and nothing more!

I do not mean to close my discourse by speaking to you in this apparently harsh way, which, harsh as it seems, is full of love for your soul. I have a good word for you too. I trust that you will have a change worked in you by the Holy Spirit; for although these many years you have made false professions before God, there is yet room in his gospel feast for you. Did you notice the text? *The publicans and the harlots go into the kingdom of God **before you*** (emphasis added). Then it is clear you may come after them, because it could not be said they entered *before* you if you did not come after them.

If the Lord shall break your heart, you will be willing to take the Lord Jesus for your all in all in just the same way as a drunkard must, though you have not been a drunkard. You will be willing to rest in the merit of Jesus just as a harlot must, though you have never been such. There is room for you, young people, still, though you have broken your vows, and quenched your convictions. Alas, and you gray-headed people may be brought still, though you have lived so long in the outward means, but have never given up your hearts to Jesus. May the Lord bring you in this very place and lead you to say silently, "By the grace of God I will not be an open pretender any longer; I will give myself up to those dear hands that bled for me, and that dear heart that was pierced for me, and I will this day submit to Jesus' way."

The fact is, to close the subject, there is, my dear friends, the same gospel to be preached to one class of men as to every other class. I pray God the day may never come when we shall be found in our preaching talking about working classes, and middle classes, and upper classes. I know no difference between you; you are the same to me when I preach the gospel, whether you are kings and queens, or street sweepers; for satin and cotton, broadcloth and fustian are alike to the gospel. If you are peers of the realm, we trim not our gospel to suit you, and if you are the vilest of thieves, we do not exclude you from the voice of mercy. The gospel comes to men as sinners, all equally fallen in Adam, equally lost and ruined by sin.

I do not have one gospel for Her Majesty the Queen, and another gospel for the beggar woman. No; there is but one way of salvation, but one foundation, but one atoning sacrifice, but one gospel. Look to the cross of Christ and live. High was the brazen serpent lifted, and all that Moses said was, "Look." If a prince of the house of Judah was bitten, he was told to look; without looking, his lion standard of costly emblazonry could not help him; if some poor wretch in the camp was bitten, he must look, and the effectiveness was the same for him as for the greatest of the host. Look! Look! Look to Jesus. Believe in the Son of God and live. One brazen serpent for all the camp, one Christ for all ranks and conditions of men. What a blessing would it be if we were all enabled to trust Christ this morning! My brethren, why not? He is worthy of the confidence of all. The Spirit of God is able to work faith in all. O poor sinner, look to him!

Dear friends, I may never speak to some of you again, and I would therefore be pressing with you. By the hour of death, by the solemnities of eternity, I do implore and beg you to accept the only remedy for sin which even God himself will ever offer to the dying sons of men, the remedy of a bleeding Substitute, suffering in your room and stead, believed on and accepted in the heart. Cast yourself flat upon Christ. The way of salvation is just this – rest alone upon Christ! Depend wholly upon him.

A man was asked what he did, and he said, "I just fell down on the rock, and he that is down on the rock cannot fall no lower." Down on the rock, sinner! Down on the rock! The everlasting Rock of ages! You cannot fall lower than that. I will conclude with a well-known illustration. Your condition is like that of a child in a burning house, who, having escaped to the edge of the window, hung on by the windowsill. The flames were pouring out of the window underneath, and the poor lad would soon be burned, or if he fell, he would be dashed to pieces; he therefore held on with the clutch of death.

He did not dare to relax his grasp until a strong man stood underneath and said, "Boy! Drop! Drop! I'll catch you!" Now, it was no saving faith for the boy to believe that the man was strong – that was a good help towards faith – but he might have known that and yet have perished; it was faith when the boy let go and dropped down into his big friend's arms. There are you, sinner, clinging to your sins or to your good works.

The Savior cries, "Drop! Drop into my arms!" It is not doing, it is leaving off doing. It is not working, it is trusting in that work which Jesus has already done. Trust! That is the word – simple, solid, hearty, earnest trust. Trust and it will not take an hour to save you, for the moment you trust you are saved. You may have come in here as black as hell, but if you trust in Jesus you are wholly forgiven. In an instant, swifter than a flash of lightning the deed of grace is done. O may God the Spirit do it now, bringing you to trust, so that you may be saved.

Chapter 5

Work for Jesus

Son, go work to day in my vineyard. (Matthew 21:28)

I am not going to confine myself to the connection of these words, nor to using them strictly after the manner in which they were first spoken. I may, perhaps, explain the parable very briefly at the close; but I take leave to withdraw these words from their immediate context, and use them as a voice which, I believe, sounds often in the ears of God's people, and sometimes sounds in vain. *Son, go work to day in my vineyard.* It is certain that God still speaks to us. He has spoken to us in his Word. There are his precepts and promises, his statutes and testimonies. He that has ears to hear let him hear these sacred oracles. But beside this open revelation, there are counsels and rebukes more closely and personally addressed to the conscience; voices as soft sometimes as whispers, and at other times as loud as the thunders that pealed from Sinai.

The Lord has a way of speaking to men when *he openeth the ears of men, and sealeth their instruction,* as Elihu said (Job 33:16). Thus he speaks when he calls them effectively by his grace in conversion. So he once called *Samuel, Samuel,* until the child answered (1 Samuel 3:10). So he said, *Matthew, . . . Follow me* (Matthew 9:9). So he called out, *Zacchaeus, . . . come down* (Luke 19:5). So he cried out, *Saul, Saul, why persecutest thou me?* (Acts 9:4). So he bid some of us until the divine accents were clear and irresistible. In like manner we have, many of us, heard him say, *Son, give me thine heart* (Proverbs 23:26), and we have given him our hearts; we could do no otherwise. That voice exerted such a charming spell and swayed us with such a divine power that we were subdued by it, and we yielded our hearts to the God of love.

Since then, you who know the Lord must often have heard a voice speaking to you and bidding you to seek his face in prayer. Perhaps you have been busy with the world, but you found an impulse of a mysterious kind coming over you, and you have been willing to withdraw yourself for a few minutes to the closet, so that you might speak with God. You know how it has been when you have been meditating alone, and yet not alone. One whose presence you knew, whose face you could not see, was with you. You felt as if you must pray. It has not been any effort on your part. The exercise has been as easy as it is to breathe and as pleasant as it is to partake of your daily bread. You felt the Lord drawing you to the mercy seat and saying in your soul, "My son, *ask what ye will, and it shall be done unto you*" (John 15:7). You must have been conscious of such a voice as that.

And have you not at times, in the silence of your mind, heard the Lord call you to a closer communion with himself? Has not the sense, if not the words, of the spouse in the song been heard in your soul – *Come, my beloved, . . . let us see if the vine flourish* (Song of Solomon 7:11-12). *Come with me from Lebanon, my spouse, with me from Lebanon* (Song of Solomon 4:8)? You have been up and away. You have gone into the secret places where Christ has shown you his love, until you sat under his shadow with great delight, and his fruit has been sweet to your taste. Our experience makes us know that there are heavenly voices that invite prayer and that call to communion. And probably some of you have also been conscious of another voice which I earnestly desire we may all hear, namely, the more soldierly and stirring call to service for the Lord Jesus Christ.

Some of you have been obedient to the call these many years, and it calls louder and louder and louder still. You have been reaping, and bearing the heat and burden of the day, but you cannot throw down your sickle; your hand clings to it. Yes, rather do you take more gigantic strides and sweep down more of the precious wheat at every stroke you take. You feel that you can never cease from it until you do.

Your body with your charge lay down,
And cease at once to work and live.

A voice divine seems to be calling you and saying, *"Follow me, and I will make you [a fisher] of men. Behold, I have made you a chosen vessel unto me, to bear my name before the Gentiles"* (Matthew 4:19; Acts 9:15). You have heard that voice, and you are striving to obey it more and more.

Others either have never heard it or hearing it have forgotten it. There are none so deaf as those who will not hear, and there are some who have a very deaf ear to any admonitions of this kind. They are like Issachar – *a strong donkey couching down between two burdens* (Genesis 49:14), but yet lifting neither one. I fear lest upon them should come the curse of Meroz, *because [he] came not to the help of the Lord, to the help of the Lord against the mighty* (Judges 5:23). Now, perhaps this evening there are some Christian men or women here that shall feel as if the hand of the Crucified One were laid upon them, and they hear him say to them, *Know ye not that . . . ye are not your own? For ye are bought with a price: therefore glorify God in your body, and in your spirit, which are God's* (1 Corinthians 6:19-20). *Awake thou that sleepest, and arise from the dead, and Christ shall give thee light* (Ephesians 5:14).

The text, I hope, may be blessed of God to be such a voice as that. Listening to it, we notice four things. First, the character under which it calls us – *Son;* secondly, the service to which it calls us – *go work;* thirdly, the time for which it calls us – *go work to day;* and fourthly, the place to which it directs us – *in my vineyard.*

First, then, is the character under which it calls us.

It appears to me to be a very powerful selection of terms. *Son, go work to day in my vineyard.* It puts work on a very gracious footing, when we are bidden to work for the Lord, not as slaves, nor as mere servants, but as sons. The law of Moses speaks to us, and it says, "Servant, go and work for thy wages." But the Father in Christ speaks to us, and he says, *Son, go work to day in my vineyard.* No more as a servant, but as a son shall you serve the Lord. The returning prodigal said, *Make me as one of thy hired servants* (Luke 15:19). That was not an evangelical prayer and it was not answered.

The father said, *This my son was dead, and is alive again* (Luke 15:24), and so he received him, not as a hired servant at all, but as a son. Oh, dear people of God, I trust you always draw the distinction very clearly between the covenant of works and the covenant of grace. You do not try to serve Christ in order that you *may be* saved, but because you *are* saved. You do not obey his commands that you *may become* his children, but because you *are* his children, and therefore are imitators of God as dear children.

You say, *Abba, Father* because you feel the spirit of adoption within you, and you endeavor to obey the commands of your Father for the same reason. I do not, therefore, say to anyone here, "Go and work for God that you may be saved." I would not venture to put it on that footing. *Believe on the Lord Jesus Christ, and thou shalt be saved* (Acts 16:31). But turning to those who are saved, the gospel exhortation is put after a gospel sort – *Son, go work to day in my vineyard.*

And it has all the more strength on this account, because, in addressing us as sons, it reminds us of the great love which has made us what we are. We were by nature heirs of wrath even as others; but beloved, *Behold, what manner of love the Father hath bestowed upon us, that we should be called the sons of God* (1 John 3:1). Think of the love which chose us when we were still aliens and enemies; the love which adopted us, and put us into the family, itself wondering while it did it, for the Lord is represented as saying, *How shall I put thee among the children?* (Jeremiah 3:19), as if it were a strange thing that such as we are should ever be numbered among the children of God.

The love which adopted us did not stay there, but having given us the rights of children, it also gave us the nature of children, therefore we were born again – *Begotten . . . again unto a lively hope by the resurrection of Jesus Christ from the dead* (1 Peter 1:3); *being born again, not of corruptible seed, but of incorruptible, by the word of God, which liveth and abideth for ever* (1 Peter 1:23). Now, just think of election, adoption, conversion, and when the Lord addresses you by that term of *son;* think of all that and say, "I owe to God an immeasurable debt of gratitude for having enabled me to become his son: giving me power and privilege to become a child of God. Therefore do I feel the claims of obligation, and I would endeavor to work in the vineyard because I am his child, his son, his daughter, made so by his grace."

This, you see, dear friends, engages us to work in the vineyard all the more effectively, because we may reflect not only on the grace which has made us sons, but also on the privileges which that same grace bestowed upon us in making us sons; for, if children of God, the Lord will provide for us, will clothe us, will heal us, will protect us, will guide us, will educate us, and will make us suitable to be partakers of the inheritance of the saints in light. Remember, too, that precious passage: *If children, then heirs; heirs of God, and joint-heirs with Christ; if so be that we suffer with him, that we may be also glorified together* (Romans 8:17).

If heirs of God, how large is our inheritance; and if joint heirs with Christ, how sure that inheritance is. And we have been brought now, beloved, to such an estate as this that the angels themselves might envy us, for I venture to apply a passage of Scripture to this case – I hope without yanking it out – *Unto which of the angels said he at any time, Thou art my Son?* (Hebrews 1:5). But he speaks thus to us poor worms of the dust, and when he is bidding us to serve him, he comes to us under this character, and addresses us in this relationship, and he says, "Son, daughter, *go work to day in my vineyard.* I have given you bound-less privileges in making you my child. I have given you this world and worlds to come. Earth is your lodge, and heaven your home. And therefore, because I have done all this for you – and what could I have done more for you than have made you my child? – therefore I say, *Go work to day in my vineyard.*"

In appealing thus to us under the name of "son," it is supposed that we have some feelings within us correspondent to the condition to which our heavenly Father has called us. He says, *Son.* If any of you, being a son, has a father, and if that father wished you to do something for him, and he addressed you as "my son," you would feel at once that whatever you could do you were bound to do because you were a son. It would awaken in you the filial feeling which is swift at once to yield obedience and love. And when the Lord looks upon you, my brother, and says to you, *Son,* it is supposed that there is in your heart a child's nature given by his grace, and that this filial instinct prompts the quick response, "My Father, what do you say to me? Speak Lord, speak Father, for your son hears you. I long to do your will. I delight in it, for to me it is the greatest joy I know that you are my Father and my God.

Therefore, Lord, my heart stands ready now to listen to whatever you have to say, and my hand is ready to do it, as your grace shall enable me; only strengthen me in your ways." Son, daughter, *go work to day in my vineyard.*

By the use of that term "son," also, it is supposed that you have something of the qualification that will fit you to do what he bids you. A man who has a vineyard naturally supposes that his son knows something about vineyards. The boy will have learned something through his father, and you who know the Lord are the only people who can serve him in his vineyard – that is to say, in winning souls for Christ, none can do this but those who are won themselves. If there be a lost child to be reclaimed, he shall be brought in by one of the children who has himself been found. Unto the wicked God says, *What hast thou to do to declare my statutes?* (Psalm 50:16), but to you who are his sons and daughters he entrusts the gospel, putting you in trust with it so that you may bear it to others and bring others to know and love his name.

Oh, dear friends, it must be a dreadful thing to be trying to save the souls of others while you yourselves are lost; and what an unhappy mortal must he be who has to preach the gospel that he never knew – to tell of promises that he has never believed, and to preach a Christ in whom his soul has never trusted! But when the Lord speaks to you as his son and his daughter, the very fact that you stand in that relationship to him proves that you have some qualification for the service, and, therefore, dear brother or sister, you must not back out of it. You must not wrap your talent in a napkin, for you have got some talent in the very fact of being a child of God – a son or daughter of the Most High.

Thus have I tried to open up the character to whom the Lord speaks, but I cannot do it so as to interest those who are not his people. But I do say this to those of you who are a people near unto him, to whom he stands as a Father, that this fact has strong claims upon you. If I be a Father, where is my honor? If you be my children, where is your fear? If indeed the Lord has put you into his family, do you not owe to him the obedience and the love of children, and what can be more natural than that if there be a household work to do – vineyard work to do – your Father should look to you to do it, and turn to you whom he has loved so long and loved so well, and say, "Son, daughter, *go work to day in my vineyard*"?

Well now, secondly, let us turn to the next point, and that is, the service to which the Lord calls us – *Go work*.

I know some Christians who do not like the word *work,* and they look very black in the face if you say anything about duty. As for the matter of that, I do not mind how black they look, because there are some people who very much expose their own disposition by black looks and sullen moods; and when they turn sour, they only manifest what is in their own nature. He that quarrels with the precept quarrels with God. Let him mind that. And he that does not like the practical part of Christianity may do what he likes with the doctrinal part of it, for he has neither part nor lot in this matter.

The language of the true child of God is, *I will delight myself in thy statutes* (Psalm 119:16); and, as David put it, *Thy statutes have been my songs in the house of my pilgrimage* (Psalm 119:54). He would even sing about the precepts of the gospel. And now the text says, *Go work*. That is something practical, something real. *Go work*. He does not say, "My son, go and think and speculate, and make curious experiments, and fetch out some new doctrines and astonish all your fellow creatures with whims and oddities of your own." He says, *Son, go work*. And he does not say here, "My son, go and attend conferences one after another all the year-round, and live in a perpetual maze of hearing different opinions and going from one public meeting and one religious engagement to another, and so feed yourself on the fat things full of marrow."

All this is to be attended to in its proper proportion, but here it is, *Go work. Go work.* How many Christians there are that seem to read: "Go plan"; and they always figure in a way with some wonderful plan for the conversion of all the world, but they are never found laboring to convert a baby – never having a good word to say to the tiniest child in the Sunday school. They are always scheming, and yet never effecting anything. But the text says, *Son, go work.* Oh yes, but those who do not like to work themselves display the greatness of their talents in finding fault with those who do work, and a very clear perception they have of the mistakes and the quirks of the very best of workers, whose zeal and industry are equally inexhaustible.

Although the text does not say, "My son, go and criticize," what it distinctly says is, *Go work.* I remember that when Andrew Fuller had a very severe lecture from some Scotch Baptist brethren about the discipline of the church, he made the reply, "You say that your discipline is so much better than ours. Very well, but discipline is meant to make good soldiers. Now, my soldiers fight better than yours, and I think therefore that you ought not to say much about my discipline."

So the real thing is not to be forever calculating about modes of church government, and methods of management and plans to be adopted, and rules to be laid down, which it shall be counted a serious breach to violate. All are well in their place, for order is good in its way. But come now, let us go to work. Let us get something done. I believe the very best working for God is often done in a very irregular manner.

I feel more and more like the old soldier of Waterloo when he was examined about the best garment that could be worn by a soldier. The duke of Wellington said to him, "If you had to fight Waterloo over again, how would you like to be dressed?" The answer was: "Please, sir, I would like to be in my shirtsleeves." I think that is about the best. Get rid of everything superfluous and get at it and hack away. I would to God that some Christians could do that, just strip to it, get rid of the superfluities of orderliness and propriety, and everything else which hampers them in trying to get back poor souls. There they are, going down to hell, and we are contending about this mode and that, and considering the best way not to do it, and appointing committees to consider and debate, to adjourn and to postpone, and to leave the work in suspension. The best way is to arise and do it, and let the committee sit afterwards. *Son, go work to day.* Let it be something practical, something real, something actually done.

And by good work is meant something that will involve effort, toil, earnestness, self-denial, and perhaps something that will need perseverance. In good earnest you will need to stick to it. You will have to heartily yield yourself up to it and give up a good deal else that might hinder you in doing it. Oh, Christian men and women, you will not glorify God much unless you really put your strength into the ways of the Lord, and throw your body, soul, and spirit – your entire manhood and womanhood – into the work of the Lord Jesus Christ. To do this you need not leave your families, or your shops, or your secular engagements. You can serve God in these things. They will often be vantage grounds of opportunity for you, but you must throw yourself into it.

A man does not win souls to Christ while he is himself half asleep. The battle that is to be fought for the Lord Jesus must be fought by men who are wide-awake and invigorated by the Spirit of God. *Son, go work to day.* Do not go and play at teaching in Sunday schools. Do not go and play the preacher. Do not go and play at exhorting people on the corners of streets, or even play at giving away tracts. *Son, go work.* Throw your soul into it. If it is worth doing, it is worth doing well; and if it is worth doing well, it is worth doing better than you have ever yet done it; and even then it will be worth doing better still, for when you have done your best, you still have to reach forward to something far beyond; for the best of the best is all too little for such a God and for such a service. *Son, go work.*

Well now, such a claim as this may, perhaps, you think, sound rather hard; but I could tell you of many who would be very glad indeed if the Lord would say that to them. I might tell you of some who seldom leave their couches, some who can seldom sit upright through their weakness, some to whom the nights are often full of pain and the days are spent in weariness. They have learned, by God's teaching, to be content to suffer; but sometimes they cannot stifle an intense wish: they wish the Lord would let them serve him. They do not envy, but yet there sometimes crosses over their minds the shadow of something like envy when they recollect what opportunities some of you have, who are full of health and strength.

I have seen my brother minister laid aside, the voice perhaps gone, the lungs feeble, the heart prone to palpitate, and oh, how he has wished that he could preach. With what fervor has he said, "Oh, if I had but those opportunities over again, how I would try to use them better than when I was favored with them!" I tell you there are thousands of God's servants who would kiss the dust of his feet if he would only say to them, *Go work.* I remember reading of a minister who had been laboring in America until he had nearly broken down. He had to take a tour for his health.

He had not been away many days before he wrote in his diary, "There may be some ministers who count it a pleasure to be relieved from the duty of preaching, but I count it a misery. I would sooner preach as I have done in my own pulpit continually than see all the kingdoms of the world." And, indeed, there is no pleasure in the world like that of serving God. You will soon get tired if you have a vacation, but you will never get tired of a divine vocation, even if you may sometimes grow tired *in* it. Now, think that the Lord could have said to you, "Now, go and lie on that bed for ten years. Go and languish away in tuberculosis. I have nothing much for you to do. You have got to bear my will." Instead, at least for those of you who are able-bodied, are you not very glad that you are full of strength, or that you have some share of it, and that now your heavenly Father says, "*Son, go work. I have given you strength; go work*"? Lord, we thank you for so kind and gentle a command.

Besides, there is a great deal of honor in this work. You know how much your little boy wants to be a man. All boys do. When he first wears stand-up collars, he congratulates himself upon the sign of anything like being a man. How proud he is of it! And if you, being a father, were to say to your boy, "Son, you are now of such an age that I can trust you to do some work for me," see how the little man would begin to lift himself up: he is glad to do it. And I am sure that if we look at it rightly, we who are the children of God ought to feel honored by our heavenly Father saying to us, "You may do something for me."

We must be very humble, for, after all, we cannot do anything except as he works in us to will and to do. But it is really very gratifying and ennobling to a poor mortal spirit to be allowed to do anything for God, alas, and to do what perfect saints above and holy angels cannot do; for oh, dear brother, there is no glorified spirit that can go down that back street and up that blind alley, and up those staircases that seem as if they would tumble down under your feet. Go and talk to that dying woman about Christ. You have a privilege which honored Gabriel does not have, so be thankful that you have it. There is no angel that can take that little child in the Sunday school class and tell it of "Gentle Jesus, meek and mild," and carry the little lamb for the Good Shepherd. The Lord sends you to do it. And it should be a point of thankfulness with us all that he has counted us worthy and put us into the ministry – into any part or parcel of that ministry – to do something for his name's sake.

Well, we are always receiving – always receiving, and it is very blessed; but still in this, as in other things, it is more blessed to give than to receive; and when we can give back to God some little trifle of service, stained with our tears because it is no better than it is, oh, it is a happy and a blessed thing. How grateful you ought to be that the Lord does say to you, *Son, go work to day.*

And remember, once more, on this point, that the work to which the Lord calls us is very much varied; therefore, there is a great deal of change in it, and, besides that, it suits the different temperaments, constitutions, dispositions, and abilities of his people. He says, *Son, go work to day in my vineyard.* But he does not give you to do my work, and he does not give me to do your work.

Dear sister, you would like to do the work of such and such an excellent Christian woman, would you not? Yes, but that is naughty of you. Be satisfied to do your own work. Suppose your housemaid always wanted to do the cook's work; the house would soon be in bad order. Better keep to your own place, dear sister. Ah, there is a brother here who says, "I think I could preach if I only had such and such a congregation." Very likely, brother, but you had better preach to your own and do what good you can there. Very likely I would do better with my own congregation, and you will do better with yours than I would.

Every man had better keep to his own work in his own place. And how thankful we ought to be that if one can preach a sermon, still another can offer a prayer; that if one can go and speak to thousands, still another can speak to ones and twos. There is work in the school; there is work in the family; there is work in the street; there is work in the workshop; there is work everywhere for Jesus if you will but stretch out your hand to find it and follow Solomon's good advice: *Whatsoever thy hand findeth to do, do it with thy might* (Ecclesiastes 9:10).

Now, the time is the next thing. *Son, go work **to day*** (emphasis added). That means directly – now.

Brother, sister, I will not say a word about what it is your duty to do tomorrow. Let tomorrow take care of itself. I will have nothing to say about what it will be right for you to do in ten years' time. If you are alive, grace will be given to you for that. But what I have to say to you in God's name is, *Go work to day;* and as the sun has gone down, let it be, "Go work tonight in my vineyard," if there be opportunity, even tonight, before another day's sun has dawned upon the world. "And why today?" Because, brother, your Father wants you to be at it at once. *Why stand ye here all the day idle?*

If you have done nothing for Christ, you have wasted enough time. Do not rest today, but be at it now. He wants you to do it now, because the vines are in a certain condition that just now require work. There is somebody in the world who is in a tender state of mind, to whom you may speak successfully. There is a mourner here who wants comfort tonight. There is one struggling against his conscience, who wants urging-on tonight in the right way. If the case be neglected tonight, it will be like neglecting to trim the vines just at the proper time for taking away the superfluous wood. Now you can do it; you cannot do it on any other day. Therefore, *go work to day.*

To day, because there are certain dangers to which those whom you are about to bless are just now exposed. The devil is tempting them; it is needful that you go and help them against that temptation. They are just now in despair; it is needful that you step in with the word of comfort from your Master's mouth. They are, perhaps, this very night, before they go to their rest, about to commit a great sin. Perhaps the Lord means for you to intercede just now, before that sin is committed. *Son, go work to day;* you are needed.

There are very few laborers just now; many of them have gone. Son, go today, while the others have gone out for their recreation – while the others are asleep and have grown idle. There is a gap just now; it is at this moment. Many a brave deed of valor owed its success to being done at once. If Horatius had not kept the bridge just in that same moment when the enemy endeavored to pass over, we would never have heard of him, nor of the brave deeds of old. There is a time of lack – of need; there is an urgency. Son, God says to you, "Hasten you now, even now, and go work today in my vineyard." *Today* – mark that.

It means work all the day: work as long as ever you live. Son, if once you get into that vineyard, do not come home again until the day is done. I am always sorry when I hear of Christian people beginning to give up some of their work before the infirmities of old age come on; although I think that many a minister, when he gets old, had better give up a charge for which he is not equal and take one smaller for which his strength would avail. But I know that some give up this work and that work, and they say, "Let the young people come and take their turn." Yes, yes; but suppose the sun were to stop shining and say, "There is a star over there; let him have a turn and shine instead of me."

Suppose the moon were forever to give up shining in the night watches and say that she has had enough of being out at night; and suppose the earth were to say it has had enough of yielding harvests. "Why should I yield anymore? Let the sea take its turn and grow wheat." And so, dear Christian friends, keep on as long as you can. Who can blame dear old John Newton? When he got too feeble to get up the pulpit stairs of St. Mary Woolnoth, he was helped up, and then, leaning on his pulpit Bible he poured out his soul. A friend of his said to him, "Dear Mr. Newton, don't you think you ought to give up preaching?" "What!" said he, "shall the old African blasphemer ever give up praising the grace of God as long as there is breath in his body? Never." And so he went to his work again. Oh, for more of that spirit to persevere in the Master's service.

Only there is this thought: it is only a day. *Son, go work to day.* It will only be a day. The longest life is no more, and then the shadows of death will gather; but there will be no night, for instead, the day shall break and the shadows shall flee away, and then life's service here below will all be over. There will be no troublesome children to teach, no hard-hearted sinners to rebuke, no backsliding and lukewarm Christians to reprove, no deceivers to encounter, no skeptics to answer with the testimony that cannot be shaken, and no scoffers to put up with, patiently bearing their contempt. It will be all over then; and then shall those who have served their Master behold him girding himself and sitting down and serving them, and they shall feast at his table and enter into his joy. *Son, go work to day,* for you shall rest tomorrow. Work on, for there is rest enough in heaven; work on, for eternity shall well repay you for the toils of time.

Then, as to the place where the Lord calls us to the work, the text reads, *Son, go work to day in **my vineyard*** (emphasis added).

I like to think of this special sphere of labor, because it must be a pleasure to work in our Father's vineyard, for there everything that we do will be done for him. I trim this vine; it is my Father's vine. I dig this trench, but it is my Father's ground I turn. I gather up these stones; it is my Father's vineyard that I am engaged in clearing. I repair this fence; it is my Father's soil that I am thus hedging about. It is all done for him. Who would not do all that he could for the dear Redeemer, dying Lamb, and for the blessed Father of our spirits? *Go work to day in my vineyard.*

Then what interesting work it is, for it is our own vineyard because it is our Father's vineyard. All that belongs to him belongs to us. We are sons working in our Father's vineyard; so we can say, "This vine – why, I have an interest in it, for I am the heir of my Father's property. This ground that I endeavor to dig around and cultivate, it is my ground, it is my Father's. And this wall that I try to mend, it is mine, it is my Father's." It is always pleasant to work for ourselves, you know; and, in a blessed sense, when we are working for God, we are working for ourselves. You are laborers, you are God's husbandry, you are God's people; and when you are working for the Lord, you really are taking shares with him.

And what a work it is too! *Go work to day in my vineyard.* One likes working in a vineyard, because it pays. Working in a desert may be thankless toil; but working in a vineyard where there will be clusters is very different. One can think already of those juicy grapes that will be ready for the winepress, and for the festival, when the ruddy juice comes freely forth – when they make merry and joy in the wine. And you will have the new wine, and the wine on the dregs well refined. All sorts of pleasures await the man who serves the Lord.

"Go work in my vineyard." Does it not mean that the work is plentiful? There is always something to be done in a vineyard. If you ask those who keep vines, they will tell you that there is much labor required. From one part of the year right on, there is something still to be done, many dangers to be averted, and many enemies to be kept off from the vine; so there is plenty to do, brother. Go work in the vineyard, where there will be need of all your hands. It is close at hand; close by you; for the heavenly Father did not say, "Son, take a ship and go to Tarshish, or to Ophir." He said, "My son, go work in my vineyard"; and the vineyard was just out of the back door there.

Now, your heavenly Father's vineyard is close to you. Those streets where you live – the very house in which you dwell – perhaps the very chamber in which you sleep – is God's vineyard, where you are to work for him. It is your heavenly Father's own work, to be done by you in your heavenly Father's own strength. Oh, if I might set one young man on fire with love for Christ, I would be glad. If I could but be the humble means of inspiring some Christian woman with the high mission of being useful in her day and generation, how much would my soul rejoice!

There came into this tabernacle one evening a young gentleman who was well known as being a great hand with his cricket bat. He was a Christian and full of earnestness in laying hold upon the great truths of revelation, but he had never served his God. He thought it right to spend his leisure time in manly exercises, and in such pursuits he sought recreation. But while I spoke, a fire kindled within him, and he went home to begin to preach the gospel in the street of the city where he lived, and now he is the pastor of a large and influential church which he has gathered together.

Since then he has preached more than once in this place the gospel of Jesus Christ. Oh, that some other believer who may happen to be in that condition – some young man of ability who is spending all his strength on the world without going into anything grossly wrong but simply wasting his talent – might hear a voice saying to him tonight, as he goes down that aisle, "My son, *go work to day in my vineyard.*"

After dwelling so long upon the practical admonition, I have but little time left for that brief explanation of the parable, or more properly the parables of the vineyard with which at the outset I promised to close. The occasion on which they were spoken is memorable. Attacked *as he was teaching* (Matthew 21:23) – rudely interrupted by the legal Sanhedrin of the Jews with the high priest in the forefront, they confronted our Lord as it were with a warrant and propounded to him two questions: one as to the authority or title by which he acted, and the other as to the source from which his authority was derived. You all know how skillfully he evaded his unscrupulous antagonists. *I also will ask you one thing,* he said (Matthew 21:24). With that, he put to them a question that proved a puzzle, and left them to a ridiculous discussion, for *they reasoned with themselves* (Matthew 21:25), went aside to whisper, and then drew back in sheer timidity declining an answer, for they feared the people, or as you may read it, they were afraid of the mob.

The advantage our Lord thus gained he quickly followed up with a parable – in fact, with the parable we have been talking about. He opened it thus: *What think ye?* (Matthew 21:28), putting a query about two sons – the one bold in profession, yet utterly disobedient; and the other sullen in appearance, though afterwards repentant in spirit and diligent in labor. The thing was so obvious that they answer without hesitation with a reply that nailed the rebuke to their own breasts. *Whether of them twain did the will of his father? They say unto him, The first* (Matthew 21:31). Read it, read the parable for yourselves. Realize the force of it if you can.

The repentant harlot and the callous high priest are put in the scales. *In the way of righteousness* (Matthew 11:32) – according to the truthful caricature – the chief priests and elders themselves admit that *the first* of these two did the will of our heavenly Father. Digest this parable, I pray you. Almost without a break, the *vineyard* supplied him yet again with another parable which he insisted on their hearing – a parable that brought out the character of the dispensation and *the signs of the times* (Matthew 16:3) so distinctly, that they could not fail to read it in the light of their own prophets; and at the same time it so exposed the treachery of their counsel and conspiracy, that they recognized their own portrait at once and perceived that he spoke of them. The vineyard, you are all aware, was the constant symbol of the Jewish nation as a theocracy.

The men who sat in Moses' seat were the stewards in charge of that vineyard that was Jehovah's special property. They, like the perverse rulers of every age, sought to shelter their evil intentions under the cover of councils and conferences. But the words and warnings of Jesus, his proverbs and parables, were keen enough to probe all their subtleties, and leave them to stand uncomfortable without an excuse for the slyness of their hearts or the guilt of their conduct. Now remember that the kingdom of God was taken from them and given to a nation bringing forth the fruits thereof. To what nation is it given? Is it not to the church which is called *a chosen generation, a royal priesthood, an holy nation, a peculiar people; that ye should shew forth the praises of him who hath called you out of darkness into his marvellous light* (1 Peter 2:9)?

The vine is the express symbol of our Christian life, as all believers are incorporated with Christ. Well then, there is a vineyard of God's own planting; you believe that. He has let it out to husbandmen; you believe that. He will come seeking fruit of this vineyard; you believe that. You are, dear brethren, the children of the husbandmen; you believe that, or else you would not presume to sit at his table and drink of his cup. He says therefore to you, *Son, go work to day in my vineyard.* What answer do you give with your lips? What answer do you give with your life?

Thus far I have not been speaking to unconverted people. I have not said a word to them. To them, however, I have this word to say, and then I will be done. I shall not ask you to work for Christ. I cannot exhort you to do anything for him. You are not in a state of mind to do it. You must first believe in him. Oh, let it be a sorrow to you that you are incapable of serving Christ. Until you get a new heart and a right spirit, you have no capacity to serve him. You have first to trust Christ, and to prove in your own souls that this gospel is the power of God unto your salvation. Your eyes must be opened; you must be turned *from darkness to light, and from the power of Satan unto God, that [you] may receive forgiveness of sins, and inheritance among them which are sanctified by faith that is in [Jesus]* (Acts 26:18) before you can do anything for him.

Then, not until then, will you be fit to be made witnesses both of those things which you shall have seen, and of those things in the which he will hereafter appear unto you. You must be born again yourselves before you can toil in birth for others, until Christ be formed in them. You cannot testify, those of you by whom the testimony of Christ has not been received and in whom it is not confirmed. Your unskilled labor would be mischievous. Hands off such holy work until those hands have been washed clean by Jesus Christ. Come unto him, and trust him, and believe in him, and when he has saved you, then he will say to you, *Son, go work to day in my vineyard.*

Chapter 6

The Parable of the Wedding Feast

*The kingdom of heaven is like unto a certain king, which
made a marriage for his son, and sent forth his servants to
call them that were bidden to the wedding: and they would
not come. Again, he sent forth other servants, saying, Tell
them which are bidden, Behold, I have prepared my dinner: my oxen and my fatlings are killed, and all things are
ready: come unto the marriage. (Matthew 22:2-4)*

If God grants me strength, I hope to go through this parable; but at
this present time we shall confine our thoughts to the opening scene
of the royal festival. Before, however, we proceed further, it is most fitting that we give expression to our deep gratitude, that it has pleased
the infinite mind to stoop to our narrow capacities and instruct us by
parable. How tenderly condescending is God to devise similitudes, that
his children may learn the mysteries of the kingdom!

If it be sometimes marveled at among men that great minds are
ever ready to stoop, what a far greater marvel that God himself should
bow the heavens and come down to meet our ignorance and slowness
of comprehension! When the learned professor has been instructing
his class in the hall in profound matters of deep philosophy, and then
goes home and takes his child upon his knee, and tries to bring down
great truth to the grasp of his child's mind, then you see the great love

of the man's heart. And when the eternal God, before whom seraphim are but insects of an hour, stoops to instruct our childishness and make us wise unto salvation, we may well say, *Herein is love* (1 John 4:10).

Just as we give our children pictures so that we may win their attention, and may by pleasing means fix truth upon their memories, so the Lord with loving inventiveness has become the author of many a charming metaphor, type, and allegory by which he may gain our interest, and through his Holy Spirit enlighten our minds. If he who thunders until the mountains tremble, yet stoops to speak with us in *a still small voice,* let us gladly sit in Mary's place at his gracious feet, and willingly learn of him. O that God would give to each one a teachable spirit, for this is the greatest step towards understanding the mind of God.

He who is willing to learn, in a childlike spirit, is already in a considerable measure taught of God. May we all so study this instructive parable as to be invigorated by it to all that is well-pleasing in the sight of God, for after all, true learning in godliness may be judged by its result upon our lives. If we are holier, we are wiser; practical obedience to the will of the Lord Jesus is the surest evidence of an understanding heart.

In order to understand the parable before us we must first direct our attention to the plan of the *certain king* here spoken of. He had *a grand object* in view: he desired to do honor to his son upon the occasion of his marriage. We shall then notice the very *generous method* by which he proposed to accomplish his purpose: he made a dinner, and bade many to come. There were other ways of honoring his son, but the great king chose the way that would best display his bounty. We shall then observe, with sad interest, *the serious hindrance* which arose to the carrying out of his generous intention – those who were bidden would not come.

There was nothing to hinder the magnificence of the festival in the riches of the prince – he lavished out his stock for the feast; but here was a hindrance strange and difficult to remove – they would not come. Then our thoughts will linger admiringly over *the gracious response* that the king made to the opposers of his plan: he sent other servants to repeat the invitation, *Come unto the marriage.* If we shall drink deep into the meaning of these three verses, we shall have more than enough for one meditation.

A certain king of wide dominions and great power purposed to give a magnificent banquet, with a grand object in view. The crown prince, his well-beloved heir, was about to take to himself a fair bride, and therefore the royal father desired to celebrate the event with extraordinary honors. From earth, look up to heaven. The great object of God the Father is to glorify his Son. It is his will *that all men should honour the Son, even as they honour the Father* (John 5:23).

Jesus Christ, the Son of God, is glorious already *in his divine person*. He is unspeakably blessed, and infinitely beyond needing honor. All the angels of God worship him, and his glory fills all of heaven. He has appeared on the stage of action as *the Creator,* and as such, his glory is perfect, *for by him were all things created, that are in heaven, and that are in earth, visible and invisible, whether they be thrones, or dominions, or principalities, or powers: all things were created by him, and for him* (Colossians 1:16). He said, *Let there be light* (Genesis 1:3), and it flamed forth. He bade the mountains to lift their heads, and their summits pierced the clouds. He created the waterfloods, and he bade them to seek their channels, and he appointed their bounds.

Nothing is lacking to the glory of the Word of God, who was in the beginning with God, who spoke and it was done, who commanded and it stood forth. He is highly exalted also as *the preserver,* for *he is before all things, and by him all things consist* (Colossians 1:17). He is that nail fastened in a sure place, upon which all things hang. The keys of heaven, and death, and hell are fastened to his girdle, *and the government shall be upon his shoulder: and his name shall be called Wonderful* (Isaiah 9:6). He has *a name which is above every name* (Philippians 2:9), before which all things shall bow, in heaven, and earth, and under the earth. He is God over all. He is blessed forever. To him that is, and was, and is to come, the universal song goes up.

But there is another relation in which the Son of God has graciously been pleased to stand towards us. He has undertaken to be *a Savior,* in order that he might be *a Bridegroom.* He had enough glory before, but in the greatness of his heart, he would magnify his compassion even above his power, and he therefore stooped to take into union with himself the nature of man, in order that he might redeem the beloved objects of his choice from the penalty due to their sins, and might enter into the nearest conceivable union with them. It is as Savior that the Father seeks to honor the Son, and the gospel feast is not for the honor of his person merely, but also for the honor of his person in this new, yet anciently purposed, relationship. It is for the honor of Jesus as entering into spiritual union with his church that the gospel is prepared as a royal entertainment.

Brethren, when I said that here was a grand occasion, it certainly is so in God's esteem, and it should be so in ours; we should delight to glorify the Son of God. To all loyal subjects in any realm, the marriage of one of the royal family is a matter of great interest, and it is usual and fitting to give expression to congratulations and feelings by suitable rejoicings. In the instance before us, the occasion calls for special joy from all the subjects of the great King of Kings. For the occasion in itself is a subject for great delight and thankfulness to us *personally.* The marriage is with whom? With angels? He did not take up angels.

It is a marriage with our own nature: *He took on him the seed of Abraham* (Hebrews 2:16). Shall we not rejoice when heaven's great Lord is incarnate as a man, and stoops to redeem humanity from the ruin of the fall? Angels rejoice, but they have no such share in the joy as we have. It is the highest personal joy to manhood that Jesus Christ, who thought it not robbery to be equal with God, was made in the likeness of men, that he might be one flesh with his chosen. Arise you who slumber! If there was ever an occasion when you should stir up your spirits and cry, "Wake up my glory, awake psaltery and harp," it is now, when Jesus comes to be betrothed to his church, to make himself of one flesh with her, that he may redeem her, and afterwards exalt her to sit with him upon his throne. Here were abundant reasons why the invited guests should come with joyful steps, and count themselves three-times happy to be bidden to come to such a banquet. There is overwhelming reason why mankind should rejoice in the glorious gospel of Jesus and hasten to avail themselves of it.

Beside that, we must consider the *royal descent* of the Bridegroom. Remember that Jesus Christ our Savior is very God of very God. Are we asked to do him honor? It is right, for to whom else should honor be given? Surely, we should glorify our Creator and Preserver! Willful must be the disobedience which will not pay reverence to one so highly exalted and so worthy of all homage. It is heaven to serve such a Lord. His glory reaches unto the clouds; let him be adored forever and ever; O come let us worship and bow down, let us cheerfully obey those commands of God which aim at the honor of his Son.

Remember also the person of Immanuel, and you will desire his glory. This glorious Son, whose fame is to be spread abroad, is most certainly God – of that we have spoken, but he is also most assuredly man, our brother, bone of our bone, and flesh of our flesh. Do we not delight to believe that he, tempted in all points as we are, has never yet submitted to be stained by sin? Never has there been such a man as he, head of the race, the second Adam, the everlasting Father – who among us would not do him reverence? Will we not seek his honor, seeing that now he lifts our race to be next to the throne of God?

Remember, too, his *character*. Was there ever such a life as his? I will not so much speak of his divine character, though that furnishes abundant reason for worship and adoration, but will think of him even as a man. O beloved, what tenderness, what compassion, yet what holy boldness; what love for sinners, and yet what love for truth! Men who have not loved him have nevertheless admired him, and hearts in which we least expected to see such recognition of his excellencies have nevertheless been deeply affected as they have studied his life. We must praise him, for he is *chiefest among ten thousand,* and *altogether lovely.* It would be treason to be silent when the hour has come to speak of him who is incomparable among men and matchless among angels. Clap, clap your hands at the thought of the marriage of the King's Son, for whom his bride has made herself ready.

Think, too, of his *achievements*. We take into reckoning whenever we do honor to a prince all that he may have done for the nation over which he rules. What, then, has Jesus done for us? Rather let me say, what has he not done? Upon his shoulders were laid our sins; he carried them into the wilderness, and they are gone forever. Against him came forth our foes; he met them in the shock of battle, and where are they now? They are cast into the depths of the sea. As for death itself, that last of foes, he has virtually overcome it, and before long the weakest of us through him shall say, *O death, where is thy sting? O grave, where is thy victory?* (1 Corinthians 15:55).

He is the hero of heaven. He returned to his Father's throne amidst the acclamations of the universe. Do *we* not, for whom he fought, for whom he conquered, do *we* not desire to honor him? I feel I speak with bated breath upon a theme where all our powers of speech should be let loose. Bring forth the royal diadem and crown him! Is it not the universal verdict of all who know him? Ought it not to be the cry of all the sons of men? East and west, and north and south, ought they not to ring the joy bells and hang out streamers on his marriage day, for joy of him? Is the King's Son to be married? Is there a festival in his honor? O then let him be great, let him be glorious! Long live the King! Let the maidens go forth with their timbrels and the sons of music make sweet melody – yes, let all creatures that have breath break forth with his praises. "Hosanna! Hosanna! *Blessed is he that cometh in the name of the Lord*" (Matthew 21:9).

Secondly, here is a generous method of accomplishing the plan. A king's son is to be honored on the day of his marriage; in what way shall it be done? Barbaric nations have their great festivals, and alas, that men should have sunk so low that on such occasions rivers of human blood are made to flow. To this very day, on the borders of civilization, there is found a wretched tyrant whose hellish customs, for I dare not call them by a less severe term, command the murder of hundreds of his fellow creatures in cold blood, on certain high days and festivals. Thus would the monster honor his son by acting like a fiend.

No blood is poured forth to honor the Son of heaven's great King. I doubt not Jesus will have honor even in the destruction of men if they reject his mercy, but it is not so that God elects to glorify his Son. Jesus the Savior, on his wedding day with manhood, is glorified by mercy, not by wrath. If blood be mentioned on such a day, it is his own by which he is glorified. The slaughter of mankind would bring no joy to him; he is meek and lowly, a lover of the sons of men.

It has been the custom of most kings to distinguish a princely wedding by levying a fresh tax, or demanding an increased subsidy from their subjects. In the case of the anticipated wedding of our beloved queen's daughter, the dowry sought will be given with greater pleasure than upon any former occasion, and none of us would lift a whisper of complaint; but the parable shows that the King of Kings deals with us not after the manner of man. He asks no dowry for his Son; he makes the marriage memorable not by demands but by gifts. Nothing is sought for from the people, but much is prepared for them; gifts are lavishly bestowed, and all that is requested of the subjects is that they for a while merge the subject in the more honorable character of the guest, and willingly come to the palace, not to labor or serve at the table, but to feast and to rejoice.

Observe, then, that the generous method by which God honors Christ is set forth here under the form of a banquet. I noted Matthew Henry's way of describing the objects of a feast, and with the alliteration of the Puritans, he says, "A feast is for love and for laughter, for fullness and for fellowship." It is even so with the gospel. It is for *love;* in the gospel, sinner, you are invited to be reconciled to God; you are assured that God forgives your sins, ceases to be angry, and would have you reconciled to him through his Son. Thus love is established between God and the soul. Then it is for *laughter,* for happiness, for joy. Those who come to God in Christ Jesus, and believe in him, have their hearts filled with overflowing peace, which calm lake of peace often lifts itself up in waves of joy, which clap their hands in exultation.

It is not to sorrow but to joy that the great King invites his subjects, when he glorifies his Son Jesus. It is not that you may be distressed, but that you may be delighted that he bids you to believe in the crucified Savior and live. A feast, moreover, is for *fullness.* The hungry, famished soul of man is satisfied with the blessings of grace. The gospel fills the whole capacity of our manhood. There is not a faculty of our nature which is not made to feel its need supplied when the soul accepts the provisions of mercy; our whole manhood is satisfied with good things, and our *youth is renewed like the eagle's* (Psalm 103:5). *For I have satiated the weary soul, and I have replenished every sorrowful soul* (Jeremiah 31:25). To crown all, the gospel brings us into *fellowship* with the Father and his Son Jesus Christ.

God becomes our Father and reveals his paternal heart. Jesus manifests himself unto us as he does not unto the world, and the communion of the Holy Spirit abides with us. Our fellowship is like that of Jonathan with David, or Jesus with John. We feast on the bread of heaven, and drink wines on the dregs well refined. We are brought into the heavenly banqueting house where the secret of the Lord is revealed to us, and our heart pours itself out before the Lord. Very near is our communion with God; most intimate love and condescension does he show to us. What say you to this? Is there not here a rich meal worthy of him who prepares it? Here all your ample powers can wish, O sinner, shall be given to you; all you want for time and for eternity God prepares in the person of his dear Son, and bids you to receive it without money and without price.

I have already told you that all the expense lies with him. It was a very sumptuous festival: there were oxen, and there were fatlings, but none of these were taken from the pastures, or the stalls of the guests. The gospel is an expensive business; the very heart of Christ was drained to find the price for this great festival; but it costs the sinner nothing, nothing of money, nothing of merit, nothing of preparation. You may come as you are to the gospel feast, for the only wedding garment required is freely provided for you. Just as you are, you are bidden to believe in Jesus. You have nothing to do but to receive of his fullness, for to *as many as received him, to them gave he power to become the sons of God, even to them that believe on his name* (John 1:12). You are not asked to contribute to the provision, but to be a feaster at the divine banquet of infinite compassion.

How *honorable,* too, is the gospel to those who receive it. An invitation to a regal marriage was a high honor to those who were bidden. I do not suppose that many of us are likely to be invited to the princess's wedding, and, if we were, we would probably be greatly elated, for we would most of us feel it to be one of the great events of our lives. So was it with these people.

A king's son is not married every day, and it is not everybody that is bidden to the monarch's entertainment. All their lives long they would say, "I was at his wedding, and saw all the splendor of the marriage festival." Probably some of them had never before enjoyed such a feast as the luxurious potentate had prepared for that day, and had never before been in such good company. My brethren, nothing so honors a man as for him to accept the gospel. While his faith honors Christ, Christ honors him. It is no ordinary matter to be a king's son, but those who come to the marriage feast of God's own Son shall become the King's sons themselves – themselves participators in the glory of the great heir of all things.

While I am speaking of this generous method, my heart glows with sacred fervency, and my wonder rises that men do not come to the banquet of love which honors all its guests. When the banquet is so costly to the host, so free to the guests, and so honorable to all concerned, how is it that there should be found any so unwise as to refuse the favor? Surely here is an illustration of the folly of the unrenewed heart, and a proof of the deep depravity that sin has caused. If men turn their backs on Moses with his stony tablets, I do not marvel; but to despise the loaded tables of grace, heaped up with oxen and fatlings – this is strange.

To resist the justice of God is a crime, but to repel the generosity of heaven, what is this? We must invent a term of infamy with which to brand the wretched ingratitude. To resist God in majesty of terror is insanity, but to spurn him in the majesty of his mercy is something more than madness. Sin reaches its climax when it resolves to starve sooner than owe anything to divine goodness. I feel I must anticipate the period for delivering my message, and as I have described to you the way in which God honors his Son, I must at once proclaim the invitation, and cry to you, "Come to the wedding feast. Come you, and glorify Jesus by accepting the provisions of grace. Your works will not honor him if you set them up as a righteousness in competition with his righteousness. Not even your repentance can glorify him if you think to make it a rival to his precious blood. Come, guilty sinner, as you are, and take the mercy Jesus freely presents to you, and accept the pardon which his blood secures to those who believe in him."

It seems to me that when the messenger went out from the king and first of all marked signs of neglect among those who were bidden, and saw that they would not come, he must have been mute with astonishment. He had seen the oxen, and seen the fatlings, and all the goodly preparations. He knew the king, he knew his son, he knew what joy it was to be at such a feast; and when the bidden ones began to turn their backs on him, and go their way to their farms, the messenger repeated his message over and over again with eagerness, wondering all the while at the treason which dared insult so good a king.

I think I see him at first indignant for his master's sake, and afterwards melted to pity as he saw what would surely come of such an extravagance of ingratitude, such a superfluity of brashness. He mourned that his fellow citizens whom he loved should be such fools as to reject so good an offer, and spurn so blessed a proclamation. I, too, am tossed to and fro in soul, with mingled but vehement feelings. O, my God, you have provided the gospel; let none in this house reject it, and so insult your Son and dishonor you; but may all rejoice in your generous way of glorifying Jesus Christ, the Bridegroom of his church, and may they come, and willingly grace the festival of your love.

We now advance to our third point, and regretfully remember the serious hindrance which for a while interfered with the joyful event.

The king had thought in his mind, "I will make a great feast, I will invite a large number. They shall enjoy all my kingdom can afford, and I shall thus show how much I love my son, and moreover, all the guests will have sweet memories in connection with his marriage." When his messengers went out to announce to those who had received previously an express invitation that the time was come, it is written, *They would not come;* not they *could* not, but they *would* not come. Some for one reason, some for another; but without exception they would not come. Here was a very serious hindrance to the grand business.

Cannot the king drag his guests to the table? Yes, but then it would not accomplish his purpose. He does not want slaves to grace his throne. Persons compelled to sit at a marriage feast would not adorn it. What credit could it be to a king to force his subjects to feast at his table? None; for once, as I have said before, the subject must be merged in the guest. It was essential to the dignity of the festival that the guests should come with cheerfulness to the festival, but they would not come. Why? Why would they not come? The answer shall be such as to answer another question – Why do you not come and believe in Jesus?

With many of them it was an indifference to the whole affair. They did not see what concern they had in the king or his son. Royal marriages were high things and they concerned high people; they were plain-speaking men, farmers who went hedging and ditching, or tradesmen who made out bills and sold by the yard or pound. What did they care about the court, the palace, the king, the prince, his bride, or his dinner? They did not say quite that, but such was their feeling; it might be a fine thing, but it was altogether out of their line. How many run in the same groove at this hour?

We have heard it said, "What has a working man to do with religion?" and we have heard others of another grade in life affirm that persons who are in business cannot afford time for religion, but had better mind the main opportunity. The Lord have mercy upon your folly! Here is one great obstacle to the gospel, the empty indifference of the human mind concerning this grandest of all conceptions- – God's glorifying his dear Son by having mercy upon sinners.

At the bottom, the real reason for the refusal of those in the parable was that they were disloyal; they would not come to the supper because they saw an opportunity for the loyal to be glad, and not being loyal, they did not wish to hear the songs and acclamations of others who were. By staying away they insulted the king, and declared that they cared not whether he was a king or not, whether his son was a prince or not. They determined to disavow their allegiance by refusing the invitation. They said in effect, "Anyhow, if he be a king and his son a prince, we will do him no honor; we will not be numbered with those who surround his board and show forth his splendor. No doubt a feast is worth having, and such a feast as there will be provided it would be well for us to participate in, but for once we will deny our appetites that we may indulge our pride. We proclaim a revolt. We declare we will not go." Ah, you who believe not in Jesus, at the bottom of it your unbelief is hostility to your Maker, sedition against the great Ruler of the universe who deserves your homage. *The ox knoweth his owner, and the donkey his master's crib* (Isaiah 1:3), but you know not, neither do you consider; you are rebels against the majesty of heaven.

Moreover, the refusal was an insult to the prince as well as to his father, and in some cases the gospel is refused mainly with this intent, because the unbeliever rejects the deity of Christ, or despises his atonement. O sirs, beware of this. I know of no rock more fatal than to dishonor Christ by denying his sonship and his deity. Do not divide upon this, I beg you – *Kiss the Son, lest he be angry, and ye perish from the way, when his wrath is kindled but a little* (Psalm 2:12). Indifference covered the refusal in the text – *they made light of it* – but if you take off the film you will see that at the bottom there was treason against the majesty of the king, and distaste for the dignity of his son.

No doubt some of them despised the feast itself. They must have known that with such a king it could not be an inadequate meal, but they pretended to despise the feast. How many there are who despise the gospel that they do not understand; I say that they do not understand, for almost invariably if you hear a man depreciate the gospel, you will find that he has scarcely even read the New Testament and is an utter stranger to the doctrines of grace. Listen to a man who is fluent in condemnation of the gospel, and you may rest assured that he is loud because he is empty. If he understood the subject better, he would find, if he were indeed a man of honesty, that he would be led at least to be silent in admiration if he did not become loyal in acceptance.

Beloved friends, the feast is such as you greatly need; let me tell you what it is. It is pardon for the past, renewal of nature for the present, and glory for the future. Here is God to be our helper, his Son to be our Shepherd, and the Spirit to be our instructor. Here is the love of the Father to be our delight, the blood of the Son to be our cleansing, and the energy of the Holy Spirit to be life from the dead to us. You cannot want anything that you ought to want, but what is provided in the gospel, and Jesus Christ will be glorified if you accept it by faith. But here is the hindrance: men do not accept it; *they would not come.*

Some of us thought that if we put the gospel in a clear light, and if we were earnest in stating it, our hearers must be converted, and God forbid we should ever try to do otherwise than make it plain and be earnest. But for all that, the best ministry that ever was, or ever could be, will be unsuccessful in a measure; yes, and altogether so, unless the effective work of the Spirit be present. Still will the cry go up, *Who hath believed our report?* (Isaiah 53:1). Still will those who serve their Master best have reason to mourn that they sow on stony ground, and cast their bread on thankless waters. Even the prince of preachers had to say, *[Ye] search the scriptures; for in them ye think ye have eternal* life: . . . *And ye will not come to me, that ye might have life* (John 5:39-40). Alas, alas, that mercy should be rejected and heaven spurned.

So now we must close with the most practical matter of consideration: the gracious response of the king to the impertinence which interfered with his plans. What did he say? You will observe that they had been bidden, and then called. After the Oriental custom, the call suggested that the festival was now approaching, so that they were not taken unawares, but knew what they did.

The second invitation they rejected in cold blood, deliberately, and with intent. What did the monarch do? Set their city in a blaze, and at once root out the rebels? No, but in the first place, he winked at their former bold refusal. He said in himself, "Perhaps they mistook my servants; perhaps they did not understand that the hour had come. Perhaps the message that was delivered to them was too brief, and they missed its meaning. Or if, possibly, they have fallen into some temporary hostility against me, on reconsideration, they will wish that they had not been so rude and ungenerous to me. What have I done that they should refuse my dinner? What has my son done that they should not be willing to honor him by feasting at my table? Men love feasting; my son deserves their honor – why should they not come? I will pass over the past and begin again."

My friends, there are many of you who have rejected Christ after many invitations, and this morning my Lord forgets your former unkindnesses, and sends me again with the same message, again to bid you to come to the wedding. It is no small patience which overlooks the past and perseveres in kindness, honestly desiring your good.

The king sent another invitation – *all things are ready: come unto the marriage* (Matthew 22:4), but you will be pleased to observe that he changed the messenger. *Again, he sent forth other servants.* Yes, and I will say it, for my soul feels it: if a change of messengers will win you, much as I love the task of speaking in my Master's name, I would gladly die now, where I am, that some other preacher might occupy this platform, if thereby you might be saved. I know my speech to some of you must be monotonous. I seek out images fresh and many, and try to vary my voice and manner; but for all that, one man must grow stale to you when heard so often.

Perhaps my styles are not the sort to touch your peculiarities of temperament. Well, good Master, set your servant aside, and consider him not. Send other messengers if perhaps they may succeed. But to some of you I am another messenger – not a better one, but another one, since my brethren have failed with you. Oh, then, when my voice cries, "Come unto Jesus, trust in his atonement, believe in him, look to him and live," then let the new voice be successful, where former messengers have been disregarded.

You notice, too, that the message was a little changed. At first it was very short. Surely if men's hearts were right, short sermons would be enough. A very brief invitation might suffice if the heart were right, but since hearts are wrong, God bids his servants to enlarge, expand, and expound. "Come, for all things are ready. *I have prepared my dinner: my oxen and my fatlings are killed, and all things are ready: come unto the marriage.*" One of the best ways of bringing sinners to Christ is to explain the gospel to them. If we dwell upon its preparations, if we speak of its richness and freeness, some may be attracted whom the short message which merely tells the plan of salvation might not attract.

To some it is enough to say, *Believe on the Lord Jesus Christ, and thou shalt be saved,* for they are asking, *Sirs, what must I do to be saved?* (Acts 16:30-31). But others need to be attracted to the wedding feast by the description of the sumptuousness of the meal. We must try to preach the gospel more fully to you, but we shall never tell you of all the richness of the grace of God. As high as the heavens are above the earth, so high are his thoughts above your thoughts, and his ways above your ways. Forsake your sins and your thoughts and turn to the Lord, for he will abundantly pardon you. He will receive you to his heart of love and give you the kiss of his affection at this hour, if, like prodigal children, you come back and seek your Father's face.

The gospel is a river of love, it is a sea of love, it is a heaven of love, it is a universe of love, it is all love. There are no words to fully set forth the amazing love of God for sinners, no sin too big or too wicked, no crime too crimson or too closed for pardon. If you do but look to his dear crucified Son, all manner of sin and of blasphemy shall be forgiven you. There is forgiveness. Jesus gives repentance and remission. And then the happiness that will be brought to you here and hereafter are equally beyond description. You shall have heaven on earth and heaven in heaven; God shall be your God, Christ shall be your friend, and eternal bliss shall be your portion.

In this last message the guests were pressed very delicately, but still in a way which, if they had possessed any generosity of heart at all, must have touched them. You see how the Gospel writer puts it; he does not say, "Come, or else you will miss the feast; come, or else the king will be angry; come, come, or else you will be the losers." No, but he puts it, as I read it, in a very remarkable way. I venture to say – if I be wrong, the Master forgive me for saying so – the king makes himself the object of sympathy, as though he were an embarrassed host. See here: "My dinner is ready, but there is no one to eat it; my oxen and fatlings are all killed, but there are no guests. Come, come," he seems to say, "for I am a host without guests."

So sometimes in the gospel you will see God speaks as if he would represent himself as getting an advantage by our being saved. Now we know that herein he stoops in love to speak after the manner of men. What can he gain by us? If we perish, what is he – the loser? But he makes himself often in the gospel to be like a father who yearns over his child, longing for him to come home. He makes himself, the infinite God, turn as a beggar to his own creatures, and begs them to be reconciled. Wondrous stoop; for, like a merchant who sells his wares, he cries, *Ho, every one that thirsteth, come ye to the waters, and he that hath no money; come ye* (Isaiah 55:1).

Do you observe how Christ, as he wept over Jerusalem, seems to weep for himself as well as for them? *How often would I have gathered thy children together* (Matthew 23:37). And God, in the prophets, puts it as his own sorrow: *How shall I make thee as Admah? how shall I set thee as Zeboim?* (Hosea 11:8), as if it were not the child's loss alone, but the father's loss also, if the sinner died. Do you not feel, as it were, a sympathy with God when you see his gospel rejected? Shall the cross be lifted high, and none look to it? Shall Jesus die, and men not be saved by his death? O blessed Lord, we feel, if nothing else should draw us, then we must come when we see, as it were, yourself represented as a host under our embarrassment, for lack of guests. Great God, we come, we come gladly, we come to participate of the bounties which you have provided, and to glorify Jesus Christ by receiving as needy sinners that which your mercy has provided.

Brethren and sisters, since Christ finds many who detest honoring him, my exhortation is to you who love him: honor him the more since the world will not. You who have been constrained to come, remember to sing as you sit at his table, and rejoice and bless his name. Next, go home and intercede for those who will not come, that the Lord will enlighten their understandings, and change their wills, so that they may be yet constrained to believe in Jesus. And as for those of you who feel half inclined this morning by the soft touches of his grace to come and feast, let me bid you to come. It is a glorious gospel – the feast is good. He is a glorious King – the host is good. He is a blessed Savior, he who is married, he is good. It is all good, and you shall be made good too, if your souls accept the invitation of the gospel which is given to you this day. *He that believeth and is baptized shall be saved; but he that believeth not shall be damned* (Mark 16:16). *Believe on the Lord Jesus Christ, and thou shalt be saved.* The Lord send his Spirit to make the call effective, for his dear Son's sake. Amen.

Chapter 7

Making Light of Christ

But they made light of it, and went their ways, one to his farm, another to his merchandise. (Matthew 22:5)

Man has not much changed since the days of Adam. In his bodily frame he appears to be exactly similar, for skeletons many hundreds of years old are the exact counterparts of ours; and sure enough, that which was recorded in history as having been done by man centuries ago might be written again, for *there is no new thing under the sun* (Ecclesiastes 1:9). The same class of men is still to be discovered (although, perhaps, differently dressed) as that which existed ages long gone by. There are still men who answer the character given to others, in his day, by the Savior: *[They go] their ways, one to his farm, another to his merchandise,* making light of the glorious things of the gospel.

I am certain I have many such characters here tonight, and I pray the Lord that I may be enabled to discourse with them very solemnly and very pointedly. And I must ask all you who understand the heavenly art of prayer, to pray that God would be pleased to send home every thought into the breast where he intends it to lodge, that it may bring forth the comfortable fruit of righteousness in the salvation of many souls. *They made light of it;* so do too many in this day. I believe that to think lightly of Christ is a sin; and at all risks of being falsely called a legalist, or a free-willer, by those who are wise above what is written, I shall charge it upon you as such, for I hope I shall never belong to that class of Calvinists who do the devil's work by excusing sinners in their sins.

In the first place, we shall have a few words with you concerning *what it is that the sinner makes light of;* secondly, *how it is that he makes light of it;* and thirdly, *why it is that he makes light of it.* Then a general observation or two, and we shall not weary you.

In the first place, what is it that the sinner makes light of? According to the parable, the person alluded to made light of a marriage banquet which a king had provided, with all kinds of delicacies, to which they were freely invited, and from which they willfully kept themselves away. The spiritual meaning of this is easy to discover. Sinners who make light of Christ express their contempt for a glorious banquet which God has provided at the marriage of his Son. This is solemn ground to tread upon. Oh! for the teachings of the Holy Spirit.

Taking this parable as the basis of our remarks, we may observe, first, that the sinner makes light of *the messenger who brings him the news that the marriage supper is prepared.* These men refused to come; they went *one to his farm, another to his merchandise,* and so made light of the messenger; and every sinner who neglects the great salvation of Jesus Christ makes light of the gospel minister, which is no little insult in God's esteem. It is never reckoned a small offense by our great nation if our ambassador is treated with indifference; and take it for a truth, it is no light thing with God if you despise the ambassadors he sends to you. But this is comparatively little; the ambassadors are men like yourselves, who can well afford to be scorned, if that were all. In fact, we should be glad enough to forgive you if it were in our power to do so, and if this were all your guilt.

But these people *despised the feast.* Some of them imagined that the fatlings, and other provisions that would be upon the table, would be no better than what they had at home. They thought that the royal banquet would be no very great thing for which to give up their merchandise for a day, or to renounce their farming even for an hour. They scorned the banquet; at least it appears so, because they did not go to it. Oh sinner, when you neglect the great salvation, remember what you despise. When you make light of God's gospel, you make light of justification by faith; you make light of washing in the blood of Jesus; you make light of the

Holy Spirit; you make light of the road to heaven; and then you make light of faith, and hope, and love. You make light of all the promises of the eternal covenant, of all the glorious things that God has laid up for those who love him, and of everything which he has revealed in his Word as being the promised gift to those who come unto him.

It is a solemn thing to make light of the gospel, for in that word, *gospel* – "good tidings" or "good news" – is summed up all that human nature can require, and all that even the saints in bliss can receive. Oh! to despise the gospel of the blessed God, how mad! how worse than folly! Despise the stars, and you are a fool; despise God's earth, with its glorious mountains, with its flowing rivers, and its fair meadows, and you are a maniac; but despise God's gospel, and you are ten thousand maniacs in one. Make light of that, and you are far more foolish than he who sees no light in the sun, who beholds no fairness in the moon, and no brilliancy in the starry firmament. Trample, if you please, his lower works; but oh! remember, when you make light of the gospel, you are making light of the masterpiece of your great Creator – that which cost him more than to create a myriad of worlds – the bloody purchase of our Savior's agonies.

And, again, these people *made light of the king's son*. It was *his* marriage, and inasmuch as they kept themselves away, they did dishonor to that glorious one in whose honor the supper was prepared. They insulted him whom his father loved. Ah! sinner, when you make light of the gospel, you make light of Christ – of that Christ before whom glorious cherubs bow themselves – of that Christ at whose feet the high archangel thinks it happiness to cast his crown; you make light of him with whose praise the vault of heaven rings; you make light of him whom God makes much of, for he has called him *Christ . . . who is over all, God blessed for ever* (Romans 9:5).

Ah! it is a solemn thing to make light of Christ. Despise a prince, and you shall have little honor at the king's hand for it; but despise the Son of God, and the Father will have vengeance on you for his offended Son. Oh! my dear friends, it seems to me to be a sin, not unpardonable, I know, but still most heinous, that men should ever despise my blessed Lord Jesus Christ and treat him with cruel scorn. Make light of you, sweet Jesus? Oh! when I see you with your shirt of gore, wrestling in

Gethsemane, I bow myself over you, and I say, "O Redeemer, bleeding for sin, can any sinner make light of you?"

When I behold him with a river of blood rolling down his shoulder, beneath the cursed scourging of Pilate's whip, I ask, "Can a sinner make light of such a Savior as this?" And when I see him yonder, covered with his blood, nailed to a tree, expiring in torture, shrieking, *Eli, Eli, lama sabachthani?* (Matthew 27:46), I ask myself, "Can any make light of this?" Alas, if they do, then indeed, it would be sin enough to damn them, if they have no other sin – that they have lightly esteemed the Prince of Peace, who is glorious and altogether lovely.

Oh! my friend, if you make light of Christ, you have insulted the only one who can save you – the only one who can bear you across the Jordan – the only one who can unbolt the gates of heaven, and give you welcome. Let no preacher of smooth things persuade you that this is not a crime. O sinner, think of your sin, if you are making light of him, for then you are making light of the King's only Son.

And yet again, these people *made light also of the king* who had prepared the banquet. Ah! little do you know, O sinner, when you trifle with the gospel, that you are insulting God. I have heard some say, "Sir, I do not believe in Christ, but still I am sure I try to reverence God. I do not care about the gospel, I do not wish to be washed in Jesus' blood, nor to be saved in free-grace fashion; but I do not despise God; I am a natural religionist!" No sir, but you do insult the Almighty, inasmuch as you do deny his Son.

Despise a man's offspring, and you have insulted the man himself; reject the only begotten Son of God, and you have rejected the eternal one himself. There is no such thing as true natural religion apart from Christ; it is a lie and a falsehood; it is the refuge of a man who is not brave enough to say he hates God, but it is only a refuge of lies; for he who denies Christ in that act offends God, and shuts up heaven's gates against himself. There is no loving the Father except through the Son; and there is no acceptable worship of the Father except through the Great High Priest, the Mediator, Jesus Christ.

Oh! my friend, remember, you have not merely despised the gospel, but you have also despised the gospel's God. In laughing at the doctrines of revelation, you have laughed at God; in reviling the truth of the gospel, you have reviled God himself; you have bent your fist in the face of the Eternal; your oaths have not fallen upon the church, they have fallen upon God himself. Oh! remember, you that mock at the message of Christ! Oh! remember, you that turn away from the ministry of truth! God is a mighty one; how severely *can* he punish! God is a jealous God; oh! how severely *will* he punish! Make light of God, sinner? Why, this above all things is a damning sin, and in committing it, it may be that you will one day sign your own death warrant; for making light of God, of Christ, and of his holy gospel is destroying one's own soul, and rushing headlong into hell. Ah! unhappy souls, most unhappy must you be, if you live and die making light of Christ, and preferring your farms and your merchandise to the treasures of the gospel.

Again, remember, my poor, pitiful friend, in that you make light of all the things I have mentioned, *you are making light of the great solemnities of eternity.* The man who lightly esteems the gospel makes light of hell; he thinks its fires are not hot, and its flames not such as Christ has described them; he makes light of the burning tears that scald despairing cheeks forever; he makes light of the yells and shrieks that must be the sad songs and terrible music of perishing souls. Ah! it is no wise thing to make light of hell.

Consider again, you make light of heaven – that place to which the blessed ones long to go, where glory reigns without a cloud, and bliss without a sigh. You put the crown of everlasting life beneath your feet; you tread the palm branch beneath your unholy foot, and you think it little to be saved, and little to be glorified. Ah! poor soul, when you are once in hell, and when the iron key is turned forever in the lock of inevitable destiny, you will find hell to be something not so easy to despise; and when you have lost heaven and all its bliss, and can only hear the song of the blessed, sounding faintly in the distance, increasing your misery by contrast with their joy, then you will find it no little thing to have made light of heaven. Every man who makes light of religion makes light of these things. He misjudges the value of his own soul, and the importance of its eternal state.

This is what men make light of. "Oh! sir," says one, "I never indulge in any words hostile to God's truth, I never laugh at the minister, nor do I despise the Sabbath." Stop, my friend, I will acquit you of all of that; and yet I will solemnly lay to your charge this great sin of making light of the gospel. Hear me then!

How is it that men make light of it? In the first place, it is making light of the gospel and of the whole of God's glorious things, *when men go to hear and yet do not heed.* How many people frequent churches and chapels to indulge in a comfortable nap! Think what a fearful insult that is to the King of heaven. Would they enter into Her Majesty's palace, ask an audience, and then go to sleep before her face? And yet the sin of sleeping in Her Majesty's presence would not be so great, even against her laws, as the sin of willfully slumbering in God's sanctuary. How many go to our houses of worship who do not sleep, but who sit with a vacant stare, listening as they would to a man who could not play a lively tune upon a good instrument.

What goes in at one ear goes out at another. Whatever enters the brain goes out without ever affecting the heart. Ah, my friends, you are guilty of making light of God's gospel, when you sit under a sermon without paying attention to it! Oh! what would lost souls give to hear another sermon! What would yonder dying wretch, who is just now nearing the grave, give for another Sabbath! And what will you give, one of these days, when you shall be close by the river Jordan's brink, that you might have one more warning, and listen once more to the wooing voice of God's minister! We make light of the gospel when we hear it, without solemn and exceedingly great attention to it.

But some say they *do* pay attention. Well, it is possible to pay attention to the gospel and still make light of it. I have seen some men weep beneath a powerful sermon; I have observed the tears chasing each other – tears, blessed telltales of emotions within. I have sometimes said to myself, It is marvelous to see these people weep under some strong word from God, which is alarming them, as if Sinai itself were thundering in their ears. But there is something more marvelous than men's weeping under the Word. It is the fact that they soon, too soon, wipe all their tears away. But ah! my dear friend, recollect that if you hear of these things and shake off a solemn impression, you are, by doing that, insulting God and making light of his truth; and take heed how you do that, lest your own garments be red with the blood of your soul, and it be said, *O Israel, thou hast destroyed thyself* (Hosea 13:9).

But there are others who make light of it in a different fashion. They hear the Word and pay attention to it, but, alas! *they pay attention to something else with it.*

Oh! my friend, you make light of Christ if you put him anywhere except in the center of your heart. He who gives Christ a little of his affections, makes light of Christ, for Christ will have the whole heart or none at all. He who gives Christ a portion, and the world a portion, despises Christ, for he seems to think that Christ does not deserve to have the whole. And inasmuch as he says that, or thinks that, he has mean and unholy thoughts of Christ. Oh! carnal man, you who are half religious, and half profane; you who are sometimes serious, but as often frivolous; sometimes apparently faithful, but yet so often unholy, you make light of Christ.

And you who weep on Sunday, and then go back to your sins on Monday; you who set the world and its pleasures before Christ, you think less of him than he deserves; and what is that but to make light of him? Oh! I charge you, ask yourself, today, are not you the man? Do not you yourself make light of Christ? The self-righteous man who sets himself up as a partner with Christ in the matter of salvation, notwithstanding all his trivial good works, is such a ringleader among despisers, that I would expose him to public scorn in the very middle of them, and bid all like him to tremble, lest they also be found insulters of Jesus.

He makes light of Christ, again, *who makes a profession of religion and yet does not live up to it.* Ah! church members, you need a great deal of sifting; we have an immense quantity of chaff now mixed with the wheat, and sometimes I think we have something worse than that. We have some in our churches that are not so good as chaff, for they do not seem to have been near the wheat at all; they are nothing better than tares. They have come into our churches, just as they would into a trade association, because they think it will improve their business. It gives respectability to their name to take the sacrament; it makes them esteemed to have been baptized, or to be a member of a Christian church; and so they come in by crowds after the loaves and fishes, but not after Jesus Christ.

Ah! hypocrite, you make light of Christ if you think that he is a stalking horse to get you wealth. If you dream that you are to saddle and bridle Christ, and ride to wealth upon him, you make a grand mistake, for he was never meant to carry men anywhere except to heaven. If you suppose that religion was intended to gild your homes, to carpet your floors, and line your purses, you have greatly erred. It was intended to be profitable to the soul; and he who thinks to use religion to his own personal advantage thinks lightly of Christ, and at the last day this crime shall be laid to his charge – that he has *made light of it*; and the King shall send his armies to cut him in pieces, among those who have despised his Majesty and would not obey his laws.

And now, in the third place, I will tell you why they made light of it. They did so for different reasons.

Some of them made light of it *because they were ignorant;* they did not know how good the feast was; they did not know how gracious the king was; they did not know how fair the prince was, or else they might have thought differently. Now, there are many present tonight, I dare say, who think lightly of the gospel because they do not understand it. I have often heard people laugh at religion; but ask them what it is, and they know no more about religion than a horse, and worse than that, for they believe untruths about it, and a horse does not do that. They laugh at it, simply because they do not comprehend it; it is a thing beyond them.

We have heard of a foolish man who, whenever he heard a word of Latin mentioned, laughed at it, because he thought it was a joke; at any rate, it was a very outlandish way of talking, and so he laughed. So it is with many when they hear the gospel; they do not know what it is, and so they laugh at it. "Oh!" they say, "the man is mad." But why is he mad? Because you do not understand him. Are you so conceited as to suppose that all wisdom and all learning must rest with you? I would hint to you that the madness is on the other side. And though you may say of him, *Much learning doth make thee mad* (Acts 26:24), we would reply, "It is quite as easy to be made mad with none at all." And those who have none, and especially those who have no knowledge of Christ, are the most likely to despise him. Well did Watts say,

His worth, if all the nations knew,
Sure, the whole earth would love him too.

Oh! dear friends, if you once knew what a blessed master Christ is, if you once knew what a blessed thing the gospel is, if you could once be brought to believe what a blessed God our God is, if you could only have one hour's enjoyment such as the Christian experiences, if you could only have one promise applied to your heart, you would never make light of the gospel again. Oh! you say you do not like it! Why, you have never tried it. Should a man despise the wine of which he has never sipped? It may be sweeter than he dreams.

O taste and see that the Lord is good (Psalm 34:8); and as sure as ever you taste, you will see his goodness. I will venture to say, again, that there are many who make light of the gospel, simply through ignorance; and if that is so, I am somewhat in hopes that when they are a little enlightened by sitting under the Word, the Lord may be pleased graciously to bring them to himself; and then I know they will never make light of Christ again. Oh! do not be ignorant, for *that the soul be without knowledge, is not good* (Proverbs 19:2). Seek to know him, whom to know correctly is life eternal; and when you know him you will never make light of him.

Other people make light of it *because of pride.* "What is the good," said one, "of bringing me that invitation? Step into my house, my man, and I will show you a feast quite as good as any you can tell me of. Look here! there is good cheer for you; my table is as well spread as any man's. Begging his Majesty's pardon, the king cannot give a better feast than I; and I do not see why I should drag my bones around to get nothing better than I can get at home." So he would not go, out of pride.

And so it is with some of you. *You* need to be washed! No, you were never filthy, were you? *You* need to be forgiven! Oh no! you are rather too good for that. Why, you are so awfully pious in your own conceit, that if it were all true, you would make even the angel Gabriel blush to think of you. You do not think even an angel capable of holding a candle to you. What! You seek for mercy? It is an insult to you. "Go and tell the drunkard," you say, "go and fetch the harlot; but I am a respectable man; I always go to church or chapel; I am a very good sort of fellow. I may frolic now and then, but I make it up some other day. I am sometimes a little slack, but then I rein the horses in, and make up the distance afterwards; and I dare say I shall get to heaven as soon as anybody else. I am a very good sort."

Well, my friend, I do not wonder that you despise the gospel, for the gospel just tells you that you are entirely lost. It tells you that your very righteousness is full of sin. As for any hope of your being saved by it, you might as well try to sail across the Atlantic on a withered leaf as to try to get to heaven by your righteousness. And as for it being a garment fit to cover you, you might as well get a spider's web to go to court in and think it a dress fit to appear in before Her Majesty. Ah! my friend, I know why you despise Christ; it is because of your satanic pride. May the Lord pull the pride out of you; for if he does not, it will be the bundle of sticks that shall roast your soul forever. Take heed of pride; by pride the angels fell, so how can men, then, though they are the image of their Maker, hope to win by it? Shun it, flee from it; for as sure as you are proud, you will incur the guilt of making light of Christ.

Perhaps quite as many made light of the good news because *they did not believe the messenger.* "Oh!" said they, "stop a moment. What! A dinner to be given away? I do not believe it. What! The young prince going to be married? Tell that to fools; we do not believe any such thing. What! We all invited? We do not believe it; the story is incredible." The poor messenger went home and told his master that they would not believe him. That is just another reason why many men make light of the gospel, because they do not believe it.

"What!" they say, "Jesus Christ died to wash men from their sins? We do not believe it. What! A heaven? Who ever saw it? A hell? Who ever heard its groans? What! Eternity? Whoever returned from that last hope of every spirit? What! Blessedness in religion? We do not believe it – it is a moping, miserable thing. What! Sweetness in the promises? No, there is not; we believe there is sweetness in the world, but we do not believe there is any in the wells the Lord has dug." And so they despise the gospel, because they do not believe it. But I am sure that when a man once believes it, he never thinks lightly of it.

Let me once have the solemn conviction in my heart by the Holy Spirit that if unsaved, there is a gaping gulf that shall devour me; do you think I can go to rest until I have trembled from head to foot? Let me once heartily believe that there is a heaven provided for those who believe on Christ; do you think I could give sleep to my eyes, or slumber to my eyelids, until I have wept because it is not mine? I believe not.

But damnable unbelief thrusts his hand into the mouth of man, and plucks up his heart, and so destroys him; for it will not let him believe, and, therefore, he cannot feel because he does not believe.

Oh! my friends, it is unbelief that makes men think lightly of Christ; but unbelief will not do so by and-by. There are no infidels in hell: they are all believers there. There are many that were infidels here, but they are not so now; the flames are too hot to make them doubt their existence. It is hard for a man, tormented in the flame, to doubt the existence of the fire. It would be difficult for a man, standing before the burning eyes of a God, to doubt the existence of a God after that. Ah! unbelievers, turn you, or rather, may the Lord turn you from your unbelief, for this makes you think lightly of Christ, and this it is that is taking away your life and destroying your soul.

Another set of people thought lightly of this feast *because they were so worldly;* they had so much to do. I have heard of a rich merchant who was waited on one day by a godly man, and when he stopped him, he said to him, "Well, sir, what is the state of your soul?" "Soul!" he said, "bother you, I have no time to take care of my soul; I have enough to do to take care of my ships." About a week after, it so happened that he had to find time to die, for God took him away.

We fear that he said to him, *Thou fool, this night thy soul shall be required of thee: then whose shall those things be, which thou hast provided?* (Luke 12:20). You merchants of London, there are many of you who read your ledgers more than your Bibles. Perhaps you must, but you do not read your Bibles at all, while you read your ledgers every day. In America, it is said, they worship the almighty dollar. I believe that in London many men worship the almighty gold coin; they have the greatest possible respect for an almighty bank note; that is the god which many men are always adoring. The prayer book they carry so religiously in their hands is their cash book.

Even on Sunday, there is a gentleman over there who does not think his foreman knows it, but he was sitting indoors all this morning, because it was wet, adding up his accounts; and now he comes here in the evening, because he is a very pious man – extraordinarily so. He would shut the parks up on a Sunday, he would – he would not let a soul get a breath of fresh air, because he is so pious, but he himself may sit half a

Sunday with his ledgers and yet think it no sin. But many are too busy to think of these things. "Pray!" they say, "I have no time for that; I have to pay. What! Read the Bible? No, I cannot; I have to be looking over this thing and that thing, and seeing how the markets go. I find time to read the *Times,* but I could not think of reading the Bible." It will be marvelously unfortunate for some of you, that you will find the lease of your lives rather shorter than you expected. If you had taken a lease of your lives for eighty-eight years from this date, you would be foolish enough, perhaps, to spend forty-four years in sin. But considering that you are a tenant at will, and liable to be turned out any day, it is the height of folly, the very climax of absurdity, exceling all that the fool, with his cap and bells, ever did, to be living just to gather up the riches of this world, and not for things to come. Worldliness is a demon that has wrung the neck of many souls; God grant that we may not perish through our worldliness!

There is another class of people that I can only characterize in this way: *they are altogether thoughtless.* If you ask them concerning religion, they have no opinion at all about it. They do not positively detest it, and they do not mock at it; but they have not a thought about it. The fact of it is, they intend to think about it by and by. Theirs is a kind of butterfly existence: they are always moving about, never doing anything, either for others or themselves. And these are very amiable people, who are always ready to give a gold coin for a charity; they never refuse anybody, and they would give their gold coin all the same, whether it was for a cricket match or a church. Now, if I were forced to go back to the world and had to choose the character I would wish to be, the last position I would wish to occupy would be that of the thoughtless man.

I believe thoughtless persons are in the most danger of being lost of any class I know. I like sometimes to get under the Word a thoroughly obstinate, stiff hater of the gospel, for his heart is like a flint, and when it is struck with the hammer of the gospel, the flint goes to pieces in a moment. But these thoughtless people have India-rubber hearts – you hit them, and they give way; you strike them again, and they give way. If they are sick, and you visit them, they say yes. You talk to them about the importance of religion; they say yes. You talk to them about escaping from hell and entering heaven; they say yes.

You preach a sermon to them when they are better, and remind them of the vows they made in their sickness; "It is quite right, sir," they say. And they say the same whatever you may tell them. They are always very polite to you, but whatever you say to them is put aside. If you begin talking to them about drunkards, oh! they are not drunkards; they may have accidently gotten drunk once, but that was a little thing out of the usual way. And bring whatever sin you like to them; you may hit them and hit them, but it is no good, for they are not half so easily broken (speaking after the manner of men) as the real stubborn hater of the gospel is.

Why, there is a sailor who comes rolling home from sea, swearing, blaspheming, cursing. He comes into the house of God, and almost the first word is applied by the Spirit for the breaking of Jack's heart. Another young man says, "I know as much as any minister can tell me; for my own mother taught me, and my old father used to read the Bible for me until, I believe, I have gotten every bit of it in my head. I go to chapel out of respect to his memory, but I really don't care at all about it; it is very good for old people, it is quite right for old women, and those who are dying, and in time of cholera. It is a very good thing, but I don't care anything about it just now."

Now, I tell you, careless people, most solemnly, that you are the very devil's lifeguards; you are his reserve; he keeps you away from the battle; he does not send you out like he does a blasphemer, for he fears that a shot may by chance light upon you, and you may be saved. But he says, "Stand by here, and if you have to go out, I will give you an impenetrable coat of mail." The arrows go rattling against you; they all hit you, but alas! there is not one of them that penetrates your heart, for that is left elsewhere. You are only an empty chrysalis, and when you come to God's house, and his Word is preached, you make light of it, because it is your habit to be thoughtless about everything.

Very briefly I must touch on another case, and then I must dismiss you. You may make light of the gospel *out of sheer presumption*. Those who do this are like the foolish man who goes on, and is punished; not like the prudent man who *foreseeth the evil, and hideth himself* (Proverbs 22:3). They go on; that step is safe – they take it; the next step is safe – they take it; their foot hangs over a gulf of darkness; but they will try one step, and since that is safe, they think they will try the next; and as the last step has been safe, and as for many years they have been safe, they suppose they always shall be; and because they have not died yet, they think they will never die. And so out of sheer presumption, thinking "all men mortal but themselves," they go on making light of Christ. Tremble, you presumptuous ones, for you will not always be able to do that.

And, lastly, I fear there are a great many who make light of Christ *because of the commonness of the gospel.* It is preached everywhere and that is why you make light of it. You can hear it at the corner of every street; you can read it in this widely circulated Bible; and because the gospel is so common, therefore, you don't care for it. Ah! my dear friends, if there were only one gospel minister in London that could tell you the truth; if there were only one Bible in London, I believe you would be rushing to hear that Bible read; and the man who had the message would have no sinecure of it, for he would be obliged to work from morning to night, to tell it out to you.

But now, because you have so many Bibles you forget to read them; because you have so many tracts you pack up any article in them; because you have so many sermons you do not think anything at all of them. But why is that? Do you think less of the sun because it scatters its beams abroad? Do you think less of bread because it is the food which God gives to all his children? Do you think less of water, when you are thirsty, because every very small brook will give it to you? No. If you were thirsty for Christ, you would love him all the better, because he is preached everywhere; and you would not think lightly of him because of that.

They made light of it. How many today, I ask again, are making light of Christ? Many of you are, no doubt. I will give you, then, just one warning, and then a farewell. Make light of Christ, sinner! Let me say that again to you, and you will regret the day, when you come on your deathbed. It will go hard with you when the bony monster has got its grip on you, and when he is bringing you down the river to soak you in the lake of death. It will go hard with you when your eyestrings break, and when your death-sweat stands upon your brow.

Remember the last time you had a fever; ah! how you did shake. Remember last night, how you did quake in your bed when flash after flash of lightning came through your window, and how you did tremble when the deep-mouthed thunder spoke out the voice of God. Ah! sinner, you will tremble worse than when you shall see death for yourself, and when the bony rider on his white horse shall grasp his dart and plunge it into your bowels. It will go hard with you then, if you have no Christ to shelter you, no blood wherein to wash your soul! Remember, moreover, after death comes the judgment. It will go hard with you if you have despised Christ, and shall die a despiser. See that flying angel? His wings are made of flame, and in his hand he grasps a sharp two-edged sword. O angel, why do you wing your speedy flight? "Hark!" says he, "this trump shall tell you." And he puts a trumpet to his lips, and

> Blows a blast so loud and dread,
> Ne'er were prophetic sounds so full of woe.

Look! the sheeted dead have sprung up from their graves. Behold, the cloudy chariot is wheeled along by cherub's hand. Observe! there upon the throne there sits the King – the Prince. O angel, what in this terrible day must become of the man that has thought lightly of Christ? See there, he unsheathes his sword. This blade," says he, "shall find and pierce him through. This blade, like a sickle, shall reap each tare from the wheat, and this strong arm shall bind him up in his bundle to be burned; and this great arm of mine shall grasp him, and hurl him down, down, down, where flames forever burn, and hell forever howls." It will go hard with you then.

Mark this man's word; go away and laugh at it. But remember, I say to you again, it will be a solemn thing for you when Christ shall come to judgment if you have made light of him; and worse than all, if you should ever be locked up in the caverns of despair, if you should ever hear it said, *Depart from me, ye cursed* (Matthew 25:41), if you should ever mingle your awful shrieks with the sad howls of lost myriads, if you should see the pit that is bottomless, and the gulf that has walls of fire. It will be a fearful thing to find yourself in there, and to know that you can never get out again!

Sinner, this night I preach the gospel to you. Wherever you go, hear it, and believe it. May God grant you grace to receive it, so you shall be saved. *He that believeth and is baptized shall be saved; but he that believeth not,* so says the Scripture, *shall be damned.* To believe is to put your trust in Christ; to be baptized is to be plunged in water in the name of the Lord Jesus, as a profession that you are already saved, and that you love Christ. *He that believeth and is baptized shall be saved; but he that believeth not shall be damned.* O may you never know the meaning of that last word. Farewell!

Chapter 8

The Wedding Was Furnished with Guests

The wedding was furnished with guests. (Matthew 22:10)

Our discourse will follow the lines of the parable. A king desired to honor his son very royally. He loved his son well, for he merited richly from him; and therefore, as the most fitting time had come, he resolved to honor him. His son was about to take to himself a spouse; should not his marriage, which is a great event in life, be celebrated with honor? The father determined to honor his son on the joyful occasion by inviting a large number of guests to a sumptuous banquet. Not by the infliction of pain, or the pressure of taxation, but by liberality and festivity, would the king honor the crown prince.

It would be an extraordinary feast. Surely, it would be the simplest thing in the world to gather together a grateful company of guests. One would expect a competition for admission; everybody in the royal domain would eagerly ask for an invitation. But it turned out otherwise. There was a disloyal feeling abroad, and it now expressed itself; those who were bidden would not come, and means had to be used to secure the result spoken of in the text, so that *the wedding was furnished with guests.*

The parable is plain. The great Father delights to honor Jesus, his only begotten Son. The Father loves the Son, with whom he is one.

The Son has merited well at the Father's hands, for he has been *obedient unto death, even the death of the cross* (Philippians 2:8). It is the Father's aim in the work of grace to glorify his Son, who, as God and man in one nature, is the channel of grace to fallen men. He proposes to do this now that the Lord Jesus takes his church into marriage union with himself. The incarnate God calls a chosen company, the bride, the Lamb's wife, and celebrates thus early in the day this happy union by a wedding breakfast, to which he invites multitudes to come.

It is a feast of mercy, grace, and peace; a marriage feast of delight and joy. The feast is for the glorifying of the Lord Jesus Christ in a very special manner. Can any of us measure the glory which comes to our Lord Jesus by his union with the church? Angels, and principalities, and powers, intelligences now existing, and all intelligences yet to be created will wonderingly gaze upon the riches of his inheritance in the saints.

What a spectacle is this! The Word made flesh that he might dwell among us! Immanuel, God with us, taking unto himself a company of chosen men to be one with him forever. In the union of Christ and his church all wisdom centers, all grace shines forth. *The excellency of our God* (Isaiah 35:2) is to be seen in the salvation of the elect and the joining of them unto the Christ. Our glorious second Adam was like the first Adam in the garden, for whom no helpmeet was found. Neither cherubim nor seraphim, angels nor spirits, could be fit companions for him. He says, *My delights were with the sons of men* (Proverbs 8:31). He willed that his chosen church should stand to him in the same relation as Eve stood to Adam, to be the solace of his heart and the rest of his love. He chose men to be his companions, his friends, his joy, his crown.

One would have thought that every man hearing that manhood was thus to be honored by union with God would flock towards the marriage feast. It would have seemed certain that all would desire to know this heavenly mystery, and as soon as they knew it, they would press forward to be partakers in its bliss. Alas! this is not the case; and this morning my business is to tell you the story of how the purpose of divine love appeared in peril, but how, in the end, it is accomplished; and, according to the language of the text, *the wedding was furnished with guests.*

Our first point is, that it seemed as if none would come. The wedding feast was prepared: oxen and fatlings were killed, all things were ready; but where were the guests?

Those first invited, and naturally expected, would not come. Previous notice had been given to them of the festival, and afterwards a summons had been sent to say that the hour was come; but, instead of joyfully responding, they would not come.

These were, first of all, the Jews, to whom the gospel had been given by the Law and the Prophets long beforehand. *He came unto his own, and his own received him not* (John 1:11). Israel was not gathered: few out of the chosen nation recognized the Messiah. He came with a feast of mercy for them, but they would have none of it. He called, and they refused.

Today this same class will be found among the children of godly parents: dedicated from their birth, prayed for by loving devoutness, listening to the gospel from their childhood, and yet unsaved. We look for these to come to Jesus. We naturally hope that they will feast upon the provisions of grace, and like their parents will rejoice in Christ Jesus; but alas! how often it is the case that they will not come! Some such are here this morning. We greatly grieve over you. You do not choose your father's God, nor accept your mother's Savior. Ah me! if *you* will not come, who will? If you, who are taught concerning salvation by grace, yet refuse it, how can we wonder that the children of the godless and the profane reject our message? Who will come if you will not?

Dear friends, some of you are not privileged with godly parents, but you have been for many years willing listeners to the Word of Life, and yet you do not accept Christ Jesus as yours, nor accept the provisions of his grace. You do not rejoice with him in his union with his chosen, for you do not love him. How sad is this! Well may the dispirited preacher mourn and fear in his heart that the great festival of love will prove a failure! If such as you are will not come, how will the wedding be furnished with guests?

The outlook grew worse still when *they came not, though they were reasoned with.* When they would not come, the king sent other servants to bring them to a better mind; and this was the form of his reasoning: *Behold, I have prepared my dinner: my oxen and my fatlings are killed, and all things are ready: come unto the marriage.* No kinder argument could have been used. There was an appeal to all that was noble in them, and had they been worthy they would have come at once. I can well understand that the servants would repeat their lord's message with special eagerness as they thought of his waiting in the palace, and watching for the guests. They would cry to those who hesitated, "You have waited long enough, come at once.

The marriage cannot be delayed, so why should you delay? Delay no longer. *To day if ye will hear his voice, harden not your hearts* (Hebrews 3:15). Still they made light of it. When you have been invited to Jesus many a time; when tearful earnestness has pleaded with you, and yet men of God have had to return to their Master, saying, *Who hath believed our report?* it becomes a sorrowful business, and our anxious fears cannot see how the wedding will be furnished with guests. This would have been an overwhelming surprise to us if Jesus had not declared of men in his own day, *Ye will not come to me, that ye might have life.* If they refused his pleadings, we cannot wonder that they reject our sayings. Still it is a mournful fact that *many are called, but few are chosen* (Matthew 22:14).

The case looks darker still when we notice that, *though reasoned with by new messengers, they did not come.* It is said, *He sent forth other servants.* I tell you from my very soul, that if my Lord will only bring you to the banquet of his grace, I do not mind who shall be the successful messenger. If you will not believe in the Lord Jesus Christ unto eternal life through what I have to say, may the Lord remove me and send someone else to whom he will give power by his grace to reach your hearts. I shall be glad to remain in this pulpit for years to come, but not at the cost of a single soul. If somebody else can preach to you more efficiently, if someone else can get at your hearts better than I have done, may the Lord allow me to retire for your good! Do you wish it? *He sent forth other servants.*

A preacher may be too rhetorical: let a plain-speaking person be tried. He may be too weighty: let another come with parable and anecdote. Alas! with some of you the thing needed is not a new voice, but a new heart. You would listen no better to a new messenger than to the old one. After so many good and true men have spoken; after Paul, and Apollos, and Cephas have all failed, how shall the wedding be furnished with guests?

If you look at *the various characters who would not come,* you will see more and more cause for sorrow. Of some we simply read that *they would not come.* They made no excuses or apologies, but curtly said they would not come. There was an end of the matter. Many dismiss the gospel at once; they are not to be reasoned with: they do not want it, and will not have it. A large class of the community have heard of the way of salvation, but they care nothing for it. It is not with them a lack of information, but a lack of inclination. They have neither mind nor will for heavenly things.

A second class made light of it. They were indifferent to royal honors and duties. They were taken up with the care of what they had in possession, and went their way, each man to his farm, saying, "I have worked hard to get my farm, and I cannot afford to let it lay idle." Another was taken up with the care of getting an estate, and went to his merchandise, saying, "I have nobody to keep my shop. I must mind the main opportunity. If you do not look alive, everybody will run over you. I must attend to my buying and my selling." The worldly-wise make up a very numerous class. The rich man cannot be religious, his position in society prevents it; the poor man cannot mind the things of God, he is worn-out by earning his daily bread. Thus they all make excuses. Lord, when so many are unwilling, and so many more are occupied with other things, how shall the wedding be furnished with guests?

A third class were violently opposed. They would not be bothered, they had no patience with religious jargon. They *took his servants, and entreated them spitefully, and slew them* (Matthew 22:6). These are not so numerous as the others, but yet they are found among us. Skeptics, swearers, revilers of godliness, and "modern thought" men: these revile the cross, and are ferocious against the gospel. When we see these raging and raving, we are apt to ask very mournfully, How can the wedding be furnished with guests?

The most dreadful thought of all remains: *some of the invited had already perished.* The king in his wrath sent his troops and slew the murderers of his messengers and burned their city. During the years I have been preaching until now, many in my audience have died. Where are they now? If they died without Christ, they are now past hope. Ah me! they can never enter now, for the door is shut. If they died in their sins, they are in the outer darkness, where *there shall be weeping and gnashing of teeth* (Matthew 8:12). When you think of it, this is a dark prospect. Men are dying, dying without hope; and those who are still alive are resolved to perish in like manner, for they are earnestly invited to the feast of love, but they refuse to come. How can the wedding be furnished with guests?

The king tells us the real reason why they would not come: *they were not worthy.* Those who were invited specially, and about whom there was the greatest hope, had nothing in them to encourage that hope. They were not loyal, they were not kindhearted, they were not honest, they were not worthy, or else they would have come to do honor to the son of their king. Their not coming revealed the enmity of their hearts. It was a wretched way of showing their spite to the prince upon his wedding day. It is horrible that men refuse Christ and heaven out of enmity toward God. Rejectors of Christ are unworthy of pardoning grace, unworthy of a dying Savior, and unworthy of those marriage bonds into which Jesus enters with believing hearts. They are not worthy in the gospel sense of worthiness, and of course they were far less worthy in a legal sense.

The most mournful spectacle in the world is a heart that refuses the mercy of God. Objection is sometimes made to the doctrine of *total depravity.* I do not know what adjective can be too strong to describe human depravity when I perceive that it refuses God under his loveliest aspect: God in the greatness of his love, God sparing not his own Son. If men turn away from God in anger, I can understand it; if men turn aside from God in justice, I can understand it; but when they so hate God that they will not even have his salvation, when they refuse pardon through the precious blood of Christ, when they will sooner be damned than reconciled to God, this shows that their heart is desperately wicked. The cross rejected is the clearest proof of the heart depraved. There I leave this mournful subject and go a step further. Certainly, it did seem as if the wedding would not be furnished with guests.

Secondly, it was a mournful prospect. Imagine that there had been no guests at the wedding feast; what then?

First, *it would have been greatly to the king's dishonor.* The crown prince is married, and nobody comes to the wedding! The feast is free, costly, plentiful, but nobody will come to it. What an insult! The banqueting-hall is lighted, and the minstrels are in their place, but no eyes or ears are charmed. Oxen and fatlings make the tables groan, but none are there to make the hall resound with shout and song.

What a wretched spectacle! Empty halls, unfurnished benches, food untasted and carried out to the dogs! History does not record a more deliberate and unmistakable insult. Let me translate the parable. If no souls are saved, if the great plan of redemption does not save, what a farce the whole business will be! What a dishonor to the name of the great God! Look at the supposition, so that you may see the impossibility of it. Think for an instant of a defeated, disappointed, and dishonored King! Can it be? And yet, if the wedding had not been furnished with guests, the king would have been disappointed and insulted in the most tender point. If the chosen are not saved, if men are not brought to Christ, then the glorious name of the God of grace is dishonored. Do you think it can be so?

In the next place, suppose none had come to the wedding feast; then *the king's son would have been grieved.* His wedding, and nobody there! If it were your own, perhaps you could put up with it; for you do not stand in so public a position as the king's son, and you have not provided so vast a banquet. But the king's son! Only imagine that it is his wedding day, and the servants are mustered in the hall, but not a single guest arrives. He has no one to congratulate him upon the happy day, no one to wish him well, no one to welcome the bride.

Now, the same is true of our Lord Jesus Christ. If he dies, and men do not believe in him; if he rises again, and men do not accept him; if he enters heaven as a Prince and a Savior, and yet no one receives repentance and remission, where is his honor? where is his glory? Look at the dreadful supposition and think whether it can be. I am sure, as you gaze upon it, you will say, "Impossible! A bleeding Savior cannot die in vain. Our Christ could not in death have paid down the ransom price for nothing. He could not have stood as a substitute for men, and yet see men lost after all!"

If no guests had arrived, *how disappointed would the bride have been!* She, too, would have had to share in the failure of the day. Her wedding would not have been remembered with pleasure. She would have been happy in the bridegroom, but also unhappy because of the unkindness shown to him. In vain would have been her rich apparel, and her costly ornaments, for there are no eyes to gaze upon them. If souls are not saved, the church misses her greatest joy. When men believe in Jesus, how delighted we are! Our hearts leap for joy when men repent. But if sinners are not saved, if the preaching of the gospel is in vain, if they will not come to Christ, then are saints full of heaviness, and the church cries out in her anguish, "Have you forgotten to be gracious?"

Had none come to the marriage feast, *a store of provisions would have been wasted.* The king says, *My oxen and my fatlings are killed.* See the bullocks roasting whole! See yonder fatted calf killed for the feast! Observe how the sheep are led to the slaughter! All this will remain untasted. Yonder dainty dishes, and flowing bowls, and luscious fruits will have none to enjoy them. It will be a wretched business indeed! I want you to look at the dreadful picture until it vanishes out of sight. Can it be that Jesus has made himself the heavenly bread, and none will feed on him, or at best only a very few? Can it be that he has provided a robe of righteousness, and nobody will wear it? Is heaven prepared, and will it remain half occupied? I do but suppose it for the moment, to make you see what a melancholy fact a failure in the scheme of mercy would be.

Would it not have meant, also, *the enemy's triumph?* The king's foes would have heard of it and laughed him to scorn. At a royal wedding he could not command guests! How they would scoff at his wasted provision! "Ha, ha! Ha, ha!" The story would have been told on every bench in an alehouse. The sons of Belial would make rare merriment of it. The king, the prince, and the bride would all have been ridiculed because of a wedding in empty halls, and a feast with phantom guests! I do not believe that God intends to let Satan triumph in this way.

I cannot imagine that he will allow the powers of darkness thus to open their wicked mouths against him. If free will refuses the gift of God, free grace will come in and win the day. I have shown you already how free will threatens to empty the banqueting hall, and dishonor the King, the Son, and the bride; and if the business had been left to the free will of man, this is the result which would have come of it: a God dishonored, and men preferring to die rather than accept life through Jesus Christ. Then it could never have been said that *the wedding was furnished with guests.*

Let us go a step further and notice that in the parable this catastrophe was graciously prevented. *The wedding was furnished with guests.*

We are very much in the same case today as the servants were in when the invited ones would not come. We preach and teach the gospel, but we have to complain that so many will not come to the banquet of grace. God gives us many souls, but not as many as we desire. We are eager for many more, and we begin to be afraid lest, after all, God should not be glorified as we wish that he should be. In the parable, an unfurnished banquet was prevented, and so it will be in the reality. How was the calamity averted?

It was prevented, first, by *a fuller invitation.* At first the messengers only called those who had been previously bidden, a sort of aristocracy of hopeful persons. Since these would not come, we read: *Go ye therefore into the highways, and as many as ye shall find, bid to the marriage* (Matthew 22:9). They went out, not to a select band, but to all whom they might find. Brethren, it is a grand thing when we get a clearer idea of what the gospel really is. The more evangelical our notions become, so that we are prepared to preach the gospel to every creature under heaven, and to say, *He that believeth and is baptized shall be saved,* the more we may hope for great success.

If, by my preaching, I lead a man to look at himself, to see whether there is anything in him that entitles him to believe, I practically hide the gospel from him. If I preach up character unduly, so that the man mainly inquires whether he has that character, then I fix his eye upon himself, and this is not what I should aim at. If I go forth and gather together as many as I find, both good and bad, then their thoughts are on the banquet rather than on themselves. We want men to look to Jesus, and therefore we cry, *Whosoever will, let him take the water of life freely* (Revelation 22:17). When we get upon clear gospel lines, and stay there, we may expect to see the arm of the Lord revealed, and the wedding furnished with guests.

Again, *the invitation was now given more publicly.* They had simply gone to the houses of the invited guests and said, *All things are ready: come.* But now the servants go to the chief places of gathering, and they cry aloud, and spare nothing among the crowds of men. One has gone to the market center; another is preaching where four ways meet. Listen to the voice of one upon the village green, and to the songs of others as they travel the back slum! You cannot now go along a street without hearing the news of the great wedding feast. Many will be brought in when many are eager to bring them in. God is pleased to command the means which he has himself ordained.

The more constant and public the proclamation of the gospel becomes, the more numerously will men be saved through the Spirit of God. Then has the set time to favor Zion come. We are not to hide our lamp under a bushel. He that knows the gospel should speak it out as plainly as he can, and let his voice be as the silver trumpets of jubilee, so that every ear may hear. It came to pass that the king's message was more widely made known, and thus *the wedding was furnished with guests.*

Another matter assisted: *the servants were now thoroughly aroused.* I am sure I would have felt dreadfully agitated to see all those provisions and no one coming to eat them. Think of the halls decorated, the cooks working day and night, the big fires burning, bullocks roasting, the wines on the dregs set astir, and yet no guests. It would have worried me greatly and you too. You would have said, "It cannot be, it must not be, we cannot bear it. As for the king, how sadly he must feel! As for the good prince, how bitter it is for him! As for the dear bride, what must be her sadness when this great insult is put upon her! Here, I must fetch in some guests, or die in the attempt!"

I am sure we would have traveled six ways at once if we could; we would have invited with a thousand mouths if possible. Getting hold of one man's coat and of another man's sleeve, we would have compelled them to come in. This, also, is the Lord's way of blessing men. He arouses his own people, makes them sorrowful for the sins of the times, and then they grow earnest and troubled, and so they lay themselves out to snatch men as brands from the burning. *As soon as Zion travailed, she brought forth her children* (Isaiah 66:8). The lack of laboring causes the absence of conversion. When we begin to sigh, and cry, and mourn because the ways of God are forsaken, then our earnestness moves the heart, both of God and man, and the guests come to the wedding.

Again, the calamity of a wedding without guests was prevented by *a certain secret power that went with the messengers.* We read that they *gathered together all as many as they found, both bad and good*

(Matthew 22:10). They did not merely invite them, but they also gathered them in. Now people are not to be gathered in great numbers all of a sudden and led to a feast by mere words. Words are but air. There is nothing in our words to make men come to Jesus unless the Lord works by them. Yet the guests did come in crowds.

An influence went with the words of those servants that drew the people together; they could not wish to stay away; they came gladly. Their wills were sweetly inclined, and they thronged the palace. Beloved, all the hope of our ministry lies in the Spirit of God operating upon the spirits of men. I want all the members of this church to feel this more deeply and practically than ever. Do not put trust in the preacher; if he happens to be away, do not think that God is tied to him. Look for a blessing upon the gospel itself, no matter who preaches it. If the Holy Spirit be with us, we shall see thousands flocking to Jesus.

No sinner will ever come to Christ apart from the invigorating, enlightening, drawing, and converting power of the Holy Spirit supernaturally exercised upon the conscience and the heart. Let us believe this; and next, let us be assured that the Spirit of God is with us, and let us then go forth with all boldness. To the street corner, the cottage, the lodging house, and the wayside, let us go forth and publish abroad the invitation of the great King: *My oxen and my fatlings are killed, and all things are ready: come unto the marriage.*

Thus you have seen the outward means by which the Holy Spirit brings men to Jesus, and the wedding is furnished with guests.

I close by noticing, in the fourth place, that in the end the feast was a glorious success. *The wedding was furnished with guests.* Guests are a part of the furniture of a wedding feast. You may pile on your gold and silver plates, hang up your banners, load your tables, and sound your music; but if you have no guests, the feast is a failure. It is our solemn conviction that the Lord our God has never failed yet, and that he never will fail.

We believe that the Lord's eternal purpose will stand, and that he will do all his pleasure. We believe in no blind fate, but we trust in a predestination which is full of eyes, which accomplishes its purpose to the least jot and tittle. God's greatest work is redemption; will he fail in it? Salvation is the focus of his glory; shall this be frustrated? If God were to fail in connection with the cross, it would be a failure indeed; God would be dishonored, and his crown jewels cast into the mire. But it shall not be.

Turn to the parable, and we find *there were sufficient guests: the wedding was furnished with guests.* There were as many guests as were necessary to the honor of the king, and his son, and his bride. Oh yes, in the gathering up and consummation of all things, the wedding of the Lord Jesus will be amply furnished with guests: *He shall see of the travail of his soul, and shall be satisfied.* There will be no disappointment to Christ at the last great day. Satan may whisper disaster and disappointment to us at this hour, and for the moment it may seem as if the forces of darkness triumphed; but the end is not yet. The will of God, so full of grace and mercy, shall be accomplished; the preparations of grace shall be used, and the purpose of love fulfilled. As the wedding was furnished with guests, so shall heaven be filled with a number *which no man could number* (Revelation 7:9).

The feast was more of a success than it would have been had there been no opposition. *The persons who came to the wedding were more grateful* than the first persons invited might have been if they had come. The richer sort had a good dinner every day. Those farmers could always kill a fat sheep, and those merchants could always buy a calf. "Thank you for nothing," they would have said to the king if they had accepted his invitation. But these poor beggars picked off the streets, they had not tasted meat for months. Their half-starved bodies welcomed the fatlings.

How glad they were! One of them said to the other, "It's been a long time since you and I sat down to such a place as this," and the other answered, "I can hardly believe that I am really in a palace dining with a king. Why, yesterday I begged all the day and only had twopence at night. Long live the king, say I, and blessings on the prince and his bride!" I warrant they were thankful for such a feast. They said it was an ill wind that blew nobody any good: because their betters had refused to come, there was now room for them. When the Lord saves great sinners, such as you and me, he wins warm hearts for himself. When the Lord saves unlikely ones, he gets unusual thankfulness.

When he brings in the drunkard and the profane, the unclean and the hardened, and makes them pure, and holy, and puts them among the children, what gratitude he gets! The Pharisee may ask Christ to a cold dinner, but it is the woman that was a sinner who will wash his feet with tears and wipe them with the hairs of her head. If some of you moralists get saved – and God grant you may! – you will never prize the precious blood so much as those do who are washed by it from the foulest stains.

The joy that day was much more expressed than it would have been had others come. Those ladies and gentlemen who were first invited, if they had come to the wedding, would have seated themselves there in a very stiff and proper manner. Dear me, what a fine thing propriety is! And yet, what a dead thing it is! One said to me the other day, "I have gone to my place of worship for many years, and nobody ever did speak to me that I know of, and nobody ever will; for we are all too respectable to know one another." You know the dignified style of self-satisfied people. Among such there is no cordiality, no freshness, and no sweet naturalness.

Did you ever attend a breakfast or a dinner of beggars? Did you ever see a company of very hungry people feeding to their heart's content? They make a merry clatter; they are not muzzled by propriety; they are glad at the sight of every dish. They look at the waiters as angels; and when the hurrahing comes to be done, you admire the strength of their lungs. The dull monotony of respectability knows no joy like that which comes to poverty when it feasts to the full at the table of bounty. The crown prince was happier that day among his poor subjects than he would have been among the noblemen and the fashionables.

Those paupers, those laborers, those tramps, and those vagabonds, those were the fellows to make merry. To whom much is forgiven, the same loves much. Up in heaven they sing like the voice of many waters and like great thunder, because they have been cleansed from many sins and have partaken of great grace. Let the Pharisee and the moralist refuse the gospel; there are those around, who, in accepting it, will do it greater honor than their dull souls could ever render to it. Thus the wedding was furnished with guests, who expressed their joy enthusiastically.

How the provisions were relished! It does one good to see a hungry man eat his food. To him even every bitter thing is sweet. He does not turn over his food and cut off every little bit of gristle, as some of you do because of your delicate appetites. The true gospel hearer listens to the text – *Eat ye that which is good, and let your soul delight itself in fatness* (Isaiah 55:2). He does not act the critic and nitpick at this expression and that. He is too eager in appetite to be particular about the dishes and the carving. We marvel sometimes at the capacity of hungry men – there is no end to it; and it is the same with spiritual hunger as with natural hunger.

I think I can tell what happened at that wedding: the bride nudged the bridegroom and said, "See these poor people eat! Is it not a pleasure to give one's oxen and fatlings where they are so much needed?" The bridegroom was as happy as he could be, for he was of a sympathizing heart, and he greatly rejoiced in the joy of the poor people around him. The king himself that day was gladdened as he saw what a gallant company of hearty eaters they were, and how there was no niggling, nor finding fault, but only unbroken enjoyment and gratitude. The choicest kind of guests had been collected if the object was to give joy. Ah, dear friends! if you have a deep sense of sin, you will greatly appreciate free grace and Christ's dying love.

This is the lack of certain gentlemen who are always finding fault with the gospel: they never knew their own state by nature and by practice, and therefore they do not prize salvation. If they had felt a few lashes of the ten-thonged whip of the law upon their bare consciences, they would relish gospel forgiveness far more. He that has been in the prison of conviction prizes blood-bought freedom. He that has felt the chains of sin values the liberty by which Christ makes him free. So I say, that inasmuch as these poor creatures were brought in from the streets, and their splendid appetites enjoyed the feast, the wedding festival was no failure, but was all the greater success because of the king's enemies. The wedding was furnished with guests – guests who enjoyed the abundance provided by the king.

Certainly, *the occasion became more famous* than it would otherwise have been. If the feast had gone on as usual, it would have been only one among many such things; but now this royal banquet was the only one of its kind, unique, and unparalleled. To gather in poor men off the streets, laboring men and idle men, bad men and good men to the wedding of the crown prince – this was a new thing under the sun. Everybody talked of it. There were songs made about it, and these were sung in the king's honor where none honored kings before. In the kitchens, among the servants, this was a fine story to tell by the fireside, while Mary and Jane wished they had been there to see it.

In every lodging house for years to come this would be the favorite story – the tale of the poor man's prince, and the needy man's queen. On the exchange and in the market, men talked of the brave bride and bridegroom who had defied the customs of fashion, and had done a deed so daring in its goodness. Was ever such a thing heard of before? Here was a feast for men who never feasted before! Sensible men said, "And nothing could be better: they were feeding those that needed feeding; they were giving good cheer to those who have little enough of it." Among the poor themselves the prince's name was very famous, while the portrait of the princess was nailed up over the mantelpiece.

Children said to one another, "My father went to the wedding of the imperial prince." To many it seemed like a story out of *The Arabian Nights*. It did not read like a piece of common history at all, but like a fairy tale of the age of gold. Dear friends, when the Lord saved some of us by his grace, it was no common event. When he brought us great sinners to his feet, and washed us, and clothed us, and fed us, and made us his own, it was a wonder to be talked of forever and ever. We will never cease praising his name throughout eternity. That which looked as though it would defame the king turned out to his honor, *and the wedding was furnished with guests.*

One thing more: *the king's liberality was all the better seen.* If those who were first bidden had put in an appearance, they would have come arrayed in their own scarlet and fine linen. Some of the gentlemen would have bought a new suit on purpose. You may depend upon it, all the cunning women in the city would have been employed to get their ladyships ready for the banquet, that they might have honor in the court that day. Now these fine clothes would have been more for the glory of those who came in them, than for the honor of the king. There was nothing of this among those who were gathered from the highways. They were in sorry gear.

It was difficult, perhaps, in some cases, to tell which was the original stuff of their garments, so patched and mended were they. Anyhow, they were a ragged regiment; and what was the consequence? Why, then they must all be dressed in the prince's own garb, and all the glory of their apparel must be unto him. He said to his servants, "Go to my wardrobe. Bring forth changes of raiment." Everyone that came into the feast was invited to put on the king's wedding garments.

When he came in to see the guests, it was a grand sight, for everybody was royally arrayed. The king's wedding robes were much better than his subjects' best suits. It was a grand sight to see so many all in one royal garb, every guest wearing the uniform of mercy. So it is with us poor sinners, saved by grace. If we had possessed any true righteousness of our own, we should have worn it; but now we count our own righteousness but rubbish and dung so that we may win Christ and be found in him. His righteousness decorates all the saints: they could not be better arrayed. Thus is the feast made more glorious than it otherwise would have been, and the wedding is furnished with guests.

How I wish that I could gather in many this morning, both bad and good! I mean by *good,* those who are comparatively so, as to their moral conduct. You are bidden to come to the wedding feast of love. But even if you are bad, and obliged to acknowledge that you are so, I am equally anxious to gather you in to the feast. Do you ask me, What are we to do? What were these persons to do? To come just as they were, and freely receive what the king had freely provided.

Sometimes at our treats for Sunday school children, every child is told to bring his own mug and plate; but it is not so with our great King. His banquet is too royal for that. You are to bring nothing. Still, everybody must go home and wash, must he not? No, the washing and the clothing shall all be done for you at the King's palace. Come as you are. "But what do you mean by coming?" We mean trusting: trust your soul with Jesus Christ, and he will save it. Trust him, and you shall know that he died in your room, place, and stead, so that, believing in him, you shall not perish, but have everlasting life. May the Holy Spirit lead you to believe in Jesus, that is, trust him.

I have told you the gospel, and the whole of it. Trust the crucified Savior, and you shall live. Jesus says, *Look unto me, and be ye saved, all the ends of the earth* (Isaiah 45:22). Do not look within to see what is there, but look to Jesus hanging on the cross. A look at Christ crucified will save you. Look, dear boys and girls, young as you are, look to Jesus now! Look, you gray-headed men and women who have never looked before, look now! Strangers and foreigners, who have not heard this word before, there is life in a look at the Crucified One for you! You guiltiest of the guilty, and you most admirable of the admirable, turn away from anything there is in yourselves, bad or good, and look to Jesus only.

Receive from Jesus all he brings you – pardon, righteousness, sanctification, redemption, and himself. He that comes to a wedding feast has nothing to do but eat and drink. Give your mind up to this delightful exercise. Take the food that God provides for you. You shall do good works afterwards, for they will follow as a consequence of the strength that comes from receiving heavenly food through faith; but just now eat, drink, and be merry, as is suitable to a prince's marriage. May the Father be pleased, his Son be honored, and his church be comforted through you! Amen, and Amen.

Chapter 9

What Is the Wedding Garment?

And when the king came in to see the guests, he saw there a man which had not on a wedding garment: and he saith unto him, Friend, how camest thou in hither not having a wedding garment? And he was speechless. Then said the king to the servants, Bind him hand and foot, and take him away, and cast him into outer darkness, there shall be weeping and gnashing of teeth. (Matthew 22:11-13)

Two Sabbath mornings ago I preached from this parable, and I trust many were encouraged by it; but I noticed among inquirers who came to see me afterwards, a desire to know about the wedding garment, for they feared lest, in coming to join the church, they would come like the man of whom I shall now speak. Many true hearts are extremely sensitive to the impression of fear, and they seem to be on the watch for reasons for anxiety. I do not condemn them; on the contrary, I wish there were more of such holy tremblers. It is much better to be afraid of being wrong than to be indifferent as to what you are.

I perceive among the very best of the saints a considerable number who are deeply anxious as to their state before God. Those who will one day be cast out of the wedding feast are feeding themselves without fear, while those who have the most right to enjoy the banquet are full of gracious anxiety. Solomon says, *Happy is the man that feareth always* (Proverbs 28:14); he will cling closely to his God, and that will make him happy; he will not run risks like the presumptuous, and so he will be happy. Holy fear spreads few banquets, but it takes care that when there is a feast, we go to it in a wedding garment.

My chief object this morning will be to alleviate the fears of gracious ones. If they understand what the wedding garment really is, they will probably discover that they are wearing it; and, if not, they will know in whose wardrobe that garment of joy is to be found, and they will gladly ask to be arrayed therein. May the Holy Spirit, the Comforter, give a wedding joy this morning to each wedding guest, by causing him to see for certain that he is clothed in the wedding robe.

Immediately after our text, we find these solemn words: *Many are called, but few are chosen.* This is a conclusion drawn from the whole parable, in which we see processes at work, which separate the chosen few from the many who are called. A distinction was made by the summoning of the invited guests. The simple delivery of the invitation set a difference between the loyal and the rebellious – a distinction most marked and decisive. So it is in the preaching of the gospel: we preach it to every creature within our reach. Lovingly, tenderly, earnestly, not as well as we would, but still with all our heart we call men to the royal feast of grace, and immediately the very invitation begins to gather out the precious from the vile.

Pure gospel preaching is very discriminating. You can tell Cain from Abel as soon as the sacrifice is the subject. Preach salvation by grace, and you find that some will not have it at any price, others postpone all consideration of it, and a third party raises questions without end. Still do men make light of it and go their way to their farms and to their merchandise. Thus, dear friends, every Sabbath day, without our attempting to sit in judgment on men, the gospel is in itself a refining fire.

In the gospel, the son of David has a throne of judgment as well as of mercy. When men will not have Christ and his grace, the Word preached by his humble servant drives them away, and they go with the chaff. But the work of discrimination is not finished after the gospel has been heard and men have been brought into the church. Alas! even in the church, division has to be made; indeed, it is there that this is most fully carried out. *[His] fan is in his hand, and he will thoroughly purge his floor* (Matthew 3:12). If he uses a scourge nowhere else, he will be sure to use it in his own temple.

Among the sheep there are goats; among the virgins there are foolish ones; and among the guests at the wedding feast there are those who do not have on the wedding garment. Until we come to heaven itself, we shall always discover a necessity for the work of self-examination. Even in the apostolic college, Judas carried out his mischief, as if to warn us that no rank in service, no honor among brethren, no length of experience can screen us from the necessity of saying, *Lord, is it I?* (Matthew 26:22) when his warning voice says, *One of you shall betray me* (Matthew 26:21). In our text we see a man who has listened to the invitation and has come into the feast, and thus has passed the first test, and yet he is unable to withstand the second test; he has been received by the servants, but he cannot deceive their master. The king detects him as a spot in the feast, and he is cast out from the palace of mercy into the outer darkness, where there is weeping and wailing and gnashing of teeth. May none of us be of this sort.

I shall endeavor to answer four questions naturally arising out of the parable. First, *What is meant by the king's coming in? – when the king came in to see the guests;* secondly, *What is the wedding garment?* thirdly, *Who is he that does not have it;* and fourthly, *Why did he stand speechless* when he was asked, *How camest thou in hither not having a wedding garment?*

May the Holy Spirit help us while we consider, first, What is meant by the king's coming in?

The king came in to see the guests. They were all reclining at the tables, for *the wedding was furnished with guests.* They gathered while the sun was up, but darkness covered the world outside when *the king came in to see the guests.* They had feasted, and now the king came to honor the assembly.

It was the crown and the culmination of the feast. No matter how dainty the food, nor how bright the hall, the feast has not reached its height until his majesty appears in gracious condescension. It is so with us, beloved, in reference to our greater King. When we are gathered in this house, which has often proved to us to be a palace of delights, we never reach the height of our desire until the Lord manifests himself to us. You delight to hear the preacher, and to join in the song, and to say "Amen" to the prayer, but these are not all. Your heart and your flesh cry out for God, for the living God; you look to behold the King in his beauty.

When the glorious Father reveals himself in Christ Jesus, then the Sabbath is a high day, for our prayer is answered: *Make thy face to shine upon thy servant* (Psalm 31:16). Our glorious King is not always equally manifest in our solemn assemblies. Doubtless because of our sins he hides himself. In truth he is always with us, for the feast is his, and the hall is his, and every guest is brought in by his grace, and every dish on the table is placed there by his love; but yet there are times when he is specially seen among his people. Then our communion with the Father, and with his Son Jesus Christ is sweet indeed.

These are seasons of gracious visitation: times of refreshing from the presence of the Lord. When the King comes into the assembly, the preaching of the Word is in demonstration of the Spirit, and in power. Then the day of Pentecost has fully come, the Spirit is abundantly poured out, souls are saved, saints are edified, and Christ is glorified. The spiritual soon detect the divine presence, and the shout of a King is heard in the camp. When I think of it, my heart cries out with Isaiah, *Oh that thou wouldest rend the heavens, that thou wouldest come down, that the mountains might flow down at thy presence* (Isaiah 64:1). The presence of our God brings with it heavenly happiness, solemn content, and overflowing joy. Well does Dr. Watts sing,

> The King himself comes near,
> And feasts his saints today;
> Here we may sit and see him here,
> And love, and praise, and pray.

> One day amidst the place
> Where my dear God hath been
> Is sweeter than ten thousand days
> Of pleasurable sin.

Beloved friends, you know better than I can tell you when the King is near, and you know sorrowfully when he is not in the assembly. Alas, from how many congregations is he absent, and that absence is not mourned! When the Lord is gone, we spread our sails, but there is no wind; we bring the sacrifice, but there is no fire. The wedding would have been a failure without guests; but what would the feast have been if the host had refused to come in and see the guests? But the King came in due time. Alas, he came in among that crowd of wayfarers gathered from the highways at a moment's notice, and his presence crowned the festival with honor and rapture.

This coming in to see the guests indicates *a glorious revelation of himself.* When the king saw the guests, the guests saw *him;* but, inasmuch as his sight of them was the more important sight of the two, the chief thing is mentioned while the minor matter is implied. Do we know what it is to see God? This is the special privilege of the pure in heart. When the Lord's way is in the sanctuary, then his sanctified ones behold him. Spiritual eyes have looked to Jesus by faith, and he says, *He that hath seen me hath seen the Father* (John 14:9). Have you never been like John in Patmos, ready to swoon away because of the revelation of the Father in Christ? When Jesus has been set forth evidently crucified among us, we have in him beheld the face of the great King, and our hearts have leaped for joy, so that we have been ready to leap into heaven itself if the word had been given. When Augustine read those words, *Thou canst not see my face . . . and live* (Exodus 33:20), he was bold enough to answer, "Let me die to see thy face."

Blessed vision!

> Lord, let me see thy beauteous face!
> It yields a heaven below;
> And angels round the throne will say,
> 'Tis all the heaven they know.

The King delights to see his guests, and his guests delight to see him. Then is our worship full of bliss, and no place out of heaven is so like heaven as the place of our assemblies. We read in the Gospel of John: *Then were the disciples glad, when they saw the Lord* (John 20:20); and well they might be. Then are we glad also when we distinctly discern him as our Lord and our God. My own soul knows this joy unspeakable, but because it is unspeakable, I say no more.

For the king to come in and see the guests includes *a manifestation of special favor.* He comes in not to judge the guests, but to look upon them. You that were here last Thursday might will remember my text: *Look thou upon me, and be merciful unto me, as thou usest to do unto those that love thy name* (Psalm 119:132). The Lord is accustomed to looking with favor upon those who love his name, for he is pleased with them. O brothers and sisters, when the love of God is shed abroad in our hearts by the Holy Spirit, when the Father lifts upon us the light of his countenance, then our summer weather has come.

Can anything be compared with the favor of God? The smiles of kings, the friendships of emperors – do not mention them in the same day. Some of you know that the Lord loves you; yes, that he loved you from before the foundation of the world, and that he will love you when the world has ceased to be. Oh, that the King would come here this morning in that sense, and look into all your faces, and give you all the full assurance that you are in his heart, and shall be there to all eternity! Oh, that this whole church may be a living temple in which the Lord shall delight to dwell; may every stone of it be brilliant with the reflected light of his favor; may all our testimonies and labors be acceptable unto him; and may he be very gracious at the voice of our cry! O Lord, manifest yourself here as you did between the cherubim! For your sake we have borne reproach; Lord, be our glory! We have held fast your truth; we implore you, let the light of your countenance encourage us!

But here is the solemn point to which I call your attention: this visitation brings with it *a time of discovery and searching of heart.* When the king comes in to see the guests, the light grows stronger, and hidden things are revealed; for *all things are naked and opened unto the eyes of him with whom we have to do* (Hebrews 4:13). When the Lord visits his church, his fire is in Zion, and his furnace in Jerusalem; then the man without a wedding garment is winked at no longer. You can go on sleeping as a church when God is away, and no members will fall off; for those who know not the Lord will come in and go out among you as formerly.

The dead will remain quiet until the Lord sounds the trumpet of resurrection. Mere professing Christians will not know that they are making a false profession, but will remain at ease in our solemn feasts. But when the King comes in, all things are changed. *Who may abide the day of his coming? and who shall stand when he appeareth? for he is like a refiner's fire, and like fullers' soap* (Malachi 3:2). You cannot receive abundant spiritual life into the church without the discernment of the unworthy, and the expulsion of the spiritually dead.

One goes away because he is offended at the doctrine, another is grieved at the heart-searching experience, and a third feels himself too sternly rebuked as to his life. Thus the Lord's visitation of grace becomes a judicial inquest, and the finger of the Lord writes upon the wall, *Thou art weighed in the balances, and art found wanting* (Daniel 5:27). If the Lord our God were to come into his church today, there would be an awful shrinkage among the number of his guests; a panic would seize the assembly, and the door would be blocked with men hastening to escape his eye.

Look how the king's discernment is recorded in the text. Only one man had refused to put on a wedding garment, but the king at once fixed his eye upon him. The Savior, by a kind of heavenly charity, mentions only one intruder, but I fear we must regard the one as the type of many. If the King should come in at the time of our communion, I am afraid he would detect more than one. Still, if there were but one, he would concentrate his gaze upon that one, and speak to him by himself. If you are the only person who has dared to enter the church knowing that you are not converted, the King will spy you out. If you make a profession of religion out of bravado, and keep it up by sheer deceit, you may hide yourself away among your family connections, or think that your respectability will screen you; but you are mistaken.

You have to deal with one whose eyes are as a flame of fire, and he will so unmask you that you will not have a word to say in your own defense. This is a solemn matter. It will not make the truehearted wish the King to stay away, but those who are willful deceivers may well tremble. The King does come to this church. He is specially present in the midst of this people, and the consequence is that his judgment is strict with us. I have seen the rod of his discipline here in a very striking manner. I have seen the fair professing Christian wither in the heat of love, and the rootless Christian dried up in the noontide of grace. He might have gone on very well in any other church, but he has not been able to abide the brandished sword of the Spirit, and its *dividing asunder of soul and spirit, and of the joints and marrow* (Hebrews 4:12).

He has not been able to sit it out, but has been obliged to go away and find an easier rest. Just in proportion as we really have the King in the midst of us making glad the saints, we shall have the King in the midst of us discerning the false persons and casting them out, first into the outer darkness of the world, which lies in the wicked one, and at last into the outer darkness of weeping and wailing and gnashing of teeth. Still, be the result what it may, our prayer this morning is, *God be merciful unto us, and bless us; and cause his face to shine upon us* (Psalm 67:1).

Now I would answer the second question: What is the wedding garment? You are probably aware that this has been a point greatly disputed among theologians. Is the wedding garment justification, or sanctification, or what? I am not going to be theological and bring doctrinal matters to the text; but I shall read the parable as it stands, and interpret its details by its general run. It is called a *wedding garment* – a garment suitable for a marriage feast. Let us translate the figure of speech, rather than attempt to rivet a doctrine to it. What does a wedding garment mean? What is that which we must have in connection with our Lord's marriage or be cast out forever?

I think I may say plainly that it must signify *a distinguishing mark of grace*. Everybody does not wear a wedding garment: he who wears it has put it on because he is a wedding guest. You know the wedding guest at once by his attire. He dresses in a way that would be considered singular if he were so arrayed every day. Your steady citizen indulges in a white waistcoat on the nuptial occasion, but he never dreams of going down to his office in the city in such gear.

True members of the church of God wear a distinguishing mark. If you are not different from other people, you have no right to be in the church of God. If a servant can live with you for years and never discover your love for God, I would think there is none to discover. If you are just the same as those you lived with in your former days, if you have undergone no change, and are like the rest of men, then you have not the distinguishing mark that sets forth your right to be in the church of God. There ought to be a something about us which sets us apart – a something which can be seen and understood by common people, even as a wedding garment could be seen, and its meaning at once perceived. Your religion must not require a microscope to perceive it, nor should it be so indistinct that few can discover any meaning in it. It should be as visible as the white garment which was worn by Easterns at a marriage. Is it so?

I may boldly add here that the wedding garment was a distinguishing mark of grace; for as these people were fetched in from the highways, they could not have provided themselves with wedding garments. It the custom in the East for a king to provide robes for his guests; therefore, this wedding garment was a mark of grace, freely given and received. Is there, then, a something about you that the Lord in love has given you? Do you differ from others, not in natural accomplishments, but in spiritual grace? Does the difference mainly lie in what God himself has done for you? That is the question involved in the symbol of the wedding garment. Do you differ from what you used to be? Do you differ from what you were years ago? Do you differ from those with whom you used to associate, so that you seek other company and turn aside from those who once were charming fellows to you? If so, you have the wedding garment on.

It is a distinguishing mark. I do not mean to put this in a way that would grieve anybody here unless they ought to be grieved; but if they ought to be grieved, then we would have them cry to God for renewal by his grace. May the Lord make you to wear his garb! May he give you the spot of his children and cause you no longer to be of the world! A distinguishing mark is plainly the first meaning of the wedding garment.

In the next place, it was *a symbol of respect for the king.* To be fit for his company, the dress must be special. The absence of such a dress was, in the case before us, the badge of irreverence and disloyalty. This man said to himself, "I will feed at the feast without acknowledging its intent. Whoever stops me, I will push my way in, and I shall sit there in my everyday garments, to let the king know that I do not respect him in the least, and will not wear the robes he provides." It is as if you had lost a son, and some wretched man should say, "I will attend the funeral in a wedding suit. I shall thus wound the feelings of the mourners and show my contempt for the whole affair."

What an insult it would be! To turn the picture, suppose you were being married, and somebody forced his way into the wedding dressed in mourning, with crepe upon his hat, and black kid gloves upon his hands.

What a merciless insult! If such brashness were met with a horsewhip, who would be surprised? Now, this man acted in that fashion: he had no respect for the king; he showed his traitorous nature in the worst possible manner, spiting the king in his own halls on a tender occasion. Dear friends, I trust that you can truly say, "I have on the wedding garment of reverence for the King. I do not despise the Lord God; but I bow before him in true worship. I would come into his church, not to dishonor him, but to give glory to his name." The wedding garment was a token of respect for him who had provided the feast and presided over it. Judge you this day whether you have on the wedding garment, by inquiring whether you honor and reverence the Lord God, and labor to be obedient to him in all things.

The wedding garment was, moreover, *a token of honor for the prince.* Those who put on the wedding garment did as good as say, "We join in the joy of the prince, and come to this place today to show our attachment to him, and to wish him joy of his bride." My friends, do you feel a love for the Lord Jesus Christ? Many do not. I grieve to say we have a race of men sprung up nowadays who call themselves Christians, who pour contempt upon his precious blood, and ridicule the substitutionary sacrifice. Dreadful assertion! but it is a matter of fact. The name of Jesus, why, it is to our lives what the sun is to the skies, what the rivers are to the plains. Nothing makes us so glad as thoughts of Jesus. I am sure when I hear a sermon about Christ, my Master, that my very heart grows warm within me. Is it so with you? Well, then, you have on the wedding garment; that is to say, you do truly, though it be but in a simple way, pay homage to the Prince of Peace; you love the name and person of Jesus, and you come into his church because you do so.

The wedding garment also signified *a confession of sympathy with the great occasion.* Every man who ate of the fatlings, every man who drank of the wines, every man who gave his presence was a helper in the honors of that wedding feast, except this one intruder, who would not even pretend to join in the joy, for he refused the simple act of putting on a robe fit for the feast. Dear friend, do you feel sympathy with the Lord's purposes of grace? Do you rejoice that Jesus finds a bride among our race? Do you bless God for the covenant of grace, which includes incarnation, redemption, and sanctification? Do you bless the name of the incarnate God for taking into everlasting union with himself a people prepared of the Lord? Well, then, you are in sympathy with the marriage of the Lamb, and you have a right to be present at the feast. You evidently wear the wedding garment that denotes your joy in Christ, your interest in his church, and your part and lot in the joyous work of his salvation.

The wedding garment means, in a word, *conformity to the requirements of the occasion.* It was a wedding, and the guests must put on a suitable dress. This man refused to put it on. He was proud and would not wear the gift of grace; he was self-willed, and had to be unique and show his independence of mind. The regulation was by no means irksome, and to the rest of the guests the commandment was not grievous; but this man would have his own way in defiance of the Lord of the feast. What could come of such folly?

Now, beloved, one of the requirements of the feast is that you with your heart believe on the Lord Jesus, and that you take his righteousness to be your righteousness. Do you refuse this? If you will not accept the Lord Jesus as your substitute, bearing your sins in his own body on the tree, then you do not have the wedding garment. Another requirement is that you should repent of sin and forsake it, and that you should follow after holiness, and endeavor to copy the example of the Lord Jesus. You are to possess, as the work of divine grace, a godly and upright character. Have you such a character? Even though you are not perfect, yet, inasmuch as you follow after righteousness, you have the wedding garment. You say that you are a Christian; do you live like a Christian? Are you in a position and condition that agree with the gospel feast? If so, you have on the wedding garment.

Those who came unto the feast were, when they came, both bad and good, so that the wedding garment does not relate to their past character but relates to something with which they were invested when they came to the banquet. The putting on of a wedding robe cannot refer to an elaborate ceremony, or a feat of the intellect, or to a deep experience of the heart; and yet it involved joining in the wedding, or not joining in it. It involved reverence for the king, and homage to the prince, and sympathy with the whole matter. Look well to yourselves and see whether you truly yield yourselves to the Lord, and agree with him in the whole matter.

Thirdly, who is the man that that does not have on the wedding garment?

I should say, first, *he is the man who rejects God's revealed gospel so that he may follow his own thought and his own wisdom.* He says that he is loyal to Christ, and he expects all his fellow guests to be firm friends with him, for is he not in the banquet as much as they are? But he does not mean by *loyalty* what they mean by it. He is among believers, but he is not truly of them. He talks about atonement; he does not mean substitution. He talks about justification by faith; but he does not mean the old-fashioned doctrine. He speaks of conversion, but he means evolution. He girds himself with the garment of philosophy, but he refuses the robe of revelation, for the outside of it is too old-fashioned for him.

He is no more a wedding guest than he is one who fools around publicly, though perhaps, not so much so. He wears clothing in which the robe of righteousness and the garments of gladness are not to be seen. The looms of free grace and dying love have never woven him a wedding garment. His robe is not of God's provision, it is from his own wardrobe. He glories in his own culture, and not in the revelation of God, nor yet in the work of divine grace upon the heart. He is in the church, but he is not in Christ. He has a name to live, but he is dead.

The next person who does not have on the wedding garment is *the man who refuses the righteousness of God* because he has a righteousness of his own. He thinks his workday dress good enough for Christ's own wedding. What does he want with imputed righteousness? He scoffs at it as immoral – he who is himself immoral! What does he want with the precious blood of Jesus? He does not need to be washed from crimson stains. He writes a paper against the sensuousness of those persons who sing,

> There is a fountain filled with blood
> Drawn from Immanuel's veins.

His own righteousness, though it be of the law, and such as Paul rejected, he esteems so highly that he counts the blood of the covenant an unholy thing! Ah me, the brazenness of self-righteousness! Its pride is the very chief of sins, for it slights the righteousness of God. Practically, the self-righteous man does not see any wedding in the gospel system; he does not see anything in the gospel to make him glad, nothing for him to sing about, nothing to make him shout for joy of heart. He will not praise the Prince. Not he! He is under the law, and he is content to be a slave; he is trying to save himself by his own works, and law knows no holidays. He is not a wedding guest, but a mere laborer.

Another sort of person *has profession without feeling.* If he were outside of the church his conscience might trouble him; but he has come inside of it, and now he says to himself, "It is all right." He does not care to watch his feelings, for he never had any; he would rather not have any. To the power of the Word he is a stranger, though he knows the letter of it. As to repentance, and the burden of sin, he never knew them, and does not want to know them. He thinks Mr. Bunyan must have been superstitious or morbid when he wrote *Grace Abounding to the Chief of Sinners.*

Joy in the Lord is equally a thing unknown to him, for he hates all excitement. He has no solemn depressions and no raptures, for he has no spiritual life. As he has no holy feeling, so he has no holy action. He is a Christian, he says; but having put up the signboard, he carries on no trade. His religion operates far more upon his boots and his hat than it does upon his heart; that is to say, he comes out respectably dressed on a Sunday, but his religion never affects his conduct. Nobody can find much fault with him except that he is as dead as a doornail. He commits no gross sin; but he certainly performs no brilliant deeds of piety. Spiritually he is a very well-washed corpse – that is all.

We have others who are in the church who *think that what they have done themselves, or what nature has done for them, is quite enough.* They do not seek anything supernatural. They do not want any wedding garment more than their everyday coats. They are quite reputable in appearance even now, and with a little touching up they will be good enough without the new birth, and without the Holy Spirit. Alas, my friends! all that nature can ever do for you will leave you on the wrong side of heaven. You may cultivate nature to its utmost, but it will never bring forth the fruits of the Spirit. *Ye must be born again* (John 3:7). If you have not come into living contact with a living Savior by the work of the Holy Spirit, you may be in the church, but you are not in Christ, and do not have on the wedding garment.

Why, some dare to come into the church who *do not even have common morality.* It is shocking that we should have to say it, but nowadays we meet with those who call themselves Christians who can drink slyly, who can commit uncleanness with their bodies, who can be dishonest in their trading, who can be liars, who can hate their own flesh and blood and be at enmity with their brethren, and yet dare to come to the Communion table.

In the Highlands of Scotland it was at one time difficult to get Christian people to come to the Lord's Table, for they so trembled under a sense of their unworthiness. We do not want to push this too far, but that is a great deal better than that unholy daring, which is to be found in the minds of so many who serve Christ and Belial. God save his church from degradation! Unholy professing Christians do not have on a wedding garment; their outward robes by no means suit the King's feast, but rather they are a dishonor to him.

I do not see how that man can be said to have on a wedding garment *who takes no interest in the work of the church.* You see when a man put on the wedding garment, he did as good as to say, "I am interested in the wedding. I wish God's blessing on the bride and bridegroom." But many come in now to the King's feast who do not care a snap of the finger for the church of God, nor for Christ either. They come in because a sort of selfishness makes them anxious to be saved; but as to the bride, the Lamb's wife, they do not care whether she starves or flourishes.

Sad and wretched business this is! If members of the church only can distribute tracts or attend meetings for prayer – if they are doing this and show an interest thus in the wedding – they have on the wedding garment. But if all they do is simply hear, either to criticize or to enjoy, but never work for Christ, nor pray for the work of Christ, then they have no sympathy in the wedding feast, and therefore they do not have on a wedding garment.

To close, why was this man speechless? We do not often meet with people who have no excuse. Excuse-making is the easiest trade out there. A man can make an excuse out of nothing at all, or out of what is less than nothing, out of a direct lie. But here was a man who could not speak; why was that?

Well, I think, first, it was because *the affront was too barefaced. How camest thou in hither?* (Matthew 22:12). If he did not like the king, he could have stayed outside. There was no need for him to have come in at all and there display his malice. If any of you are resolved to be lost, you need not add to your eternal ruin by making a profession of religion, for hypocrisy is an excess of naughtiness. But this man willfully refused the wedding garment. Now those dear souls I mentioned at the beginning of the sermon do not willfully refuse the Lord's grace; I am sure they do not. Oh no, they are afraid they are not right, but they do not wish to be wrong. Such are not among those whom this parable condemns.

Next, *the affront was so audacious. How camest thou in hither?* said the king. He must have pushed past the deacons at the door. The fellow would come in. When the king said, *Bind him hand and foot* (Matthew 22:13), I think it was because he had used hand and foot to get in. He would get in. He said, "I will get in. I will defy the king to his face and sit in among his guests without a wedding garment." You, dear friend, do not wish to do that; I am sure it is the last thing you would do. Why, we have to persuade you to come in at all, for you are so tenderly jealous lest you should be mistaken. Do not let this parable condemn you.

But why was the man speechless? I answer once more, *because it was the king himself who spoke to him.* Ah! if I speak to you, what am I but flesh and blood? You do not mind me! But if the King himself were here today, and he said to any one of you, *Friend, how camest thou in hither not having a wedding garment?* the tone of his voice, the glory of his presence, would flash in upon your hearts; you would be obliged to feel it, and you could not invent an answer. If you do not love him, if you have no reverence for him, no sympathy with his Son, you will be speechless before his court.

Lastly, the reason why he was speechless was because, even if he could have spoken and been free from terror, *there was nothing to be said.* He could not cry, "Lord, I did not know it." He saw all the rest with wedding garments on. He could not say, "Lord, I could not get a wedding garment." Each one had received a garment *gratis,* and he might have received the same. He could not say, "Lord, I was pushed in here by somebody else." No, he had willingly chosen to come, and to defy the rule. The guests had all looked at him; some had edged a little ways off from him. Some had tenderly said, "Brother, will you not put on the wedding garment?"

He answered, "No." "Will you not go out before the king comes in?" "Why," he said, "I came on purpose to defy him. I mean to keep my place." I do not wonder that the king said, *Bind him hand and foot, and take him away, and cast him into outer darkness, there shall be weeping and gnashing of teeth* (Matthew 22:13). Our Lord Jesus Christ says very strong things about the future of the wicked.

I have been accused of representing the state of the lost in too horrible a manner. I have never gone beyond the dreadful descriptions given by our Lord himself. Do not risk your eternal future. Come to the church of God and join it, but do not join it unless you love the Lord. Do not come to the gospel feast unless you reverence the King, unless you love the Prince, and unless you are in sympathy with the great work of grace that is pictured as a wedding feast. If you have sympathy with the wedding, love for the Bridegroom, and delight in the bride, then come and welcome; for you have the wedding garment.

I am thinking just now of all those other hundreds of people at the wedding, all of them clothed with the wedding garment. What joy they felt! Many had been bad, and all had been poor; but they all had the wedding garment, and not one of them was cast out. If you will but put your trust in Jesus, and so honor the Son; and rest in the love of the Father, and so honor the King, then it is written, *Him that cometh to me I will in no wise cast out* (John 6:37). God bless you for Jesus' sake! Amen.

Chapter 10

The Wedding Garment

And when the king came in to see the guests, he saw there a man which had not on a wedding garment: and he saith unto him, Friend, how camest thou in hither not having a wedding garment? And he was speechless. Then said the king to the servants, Bind him hand and foot, and take him away, and cast him into outer darkness, there shall be weeping and gnashing of teeth. For many are called, but few are chosen. (Matthew 22:11-14)

Apparently, the parable of the marriage feast would have been complete without this addition, but there was infinite wisdom in appending this sequel. This is seen practically in the experience of the church of God. Those who are permitted to see large additions to the church will find this parable of the wedding garment to be uniquely appropriate and timely. Whenever there is a revival, and many are brought to Christ, it seems inevitable that at the same time a proportion of unworthy persons should enter the church. However diligent may be the oversight, there will be pretenders creeping in unawares who have no true part or lot in the matter, and therefore, when the preacher is most earnest for the ingathering of souls to Christ, he needs to couple that with a holy jealousy, lest those who come forward to make a profession of faith should be moved by carnal motives, and should not really have given their hearts to God.

We must use the net to draw in the many, but all are not good fishes that are taken therein. On the threshing floor of Zion the heap is not all pure wheat; the chaff is mingled with the grain, and therefore the winnowing fan is needed. God's furnace is in Zion, and there is good need for it, for the gold is yet in the ore, and needs to be separated from the dross. Wood, hay, and stubble building is quick work, but it is a waste of effort; we need continually to examine our materials, and see that we use only gold, silver, and precious stones. It is most needful in times of religious excitement to remind men that godliness does not consist in profession, but must be proved by inward vitality and outward holiness.

Everything will have to be tested by a heart-searching God, and if, when he comes to search us, we are found lacking, we shall be expelled even from the marriage feast itself, for there is a way to hell from the very gates of heaven. In a word, it is well for all men to be reminded that the enemies of the great King are not only outside the church, but they are also even in it; while a part of them refuses to come to the wedding of his Son, others press into the banquet and are still his foes. May God grant that this subject may have a heart-searching effect. May it be as the north wind when it blows through the marrow of the bones. May it lead us to desire to be searched and tested of God, whether we be truly in the faith, or are reprobates in his esteem.

The parable may be discussed under five topics. Here is *an enemy at the feast;* here is *the king at the feast;* that king becomes *the judge at the feast;* therefore, the enemy becomes *the criminal at the feast;* and he is swiftly removed by *the executioner at the feast.*

We see in the text an enemy at the feast.

He came into the banquet when he was bidden, but he came only in appearance, not in heart. The banquet was intended for the honor of the son, but this man meant not so; he was willing to eat the good things, but he intended to show no respect to the prince. He did not, like others, say, "I will not come, for I will not have this man to reign over me"; but he said, "I will come, but it shall be in such a way that the royal purpose shall not be served, but rather hindered. I shall be present as an onlooker, but take no share in the ceremony; I will, on the contrary, show that I have no care for the business in hand, except so far as it serves my purpose."

The man came in the full exercise of self-will and self-love. He resolved to yield no homage, but to assert his independent self-sovereignty. He would show the king even at his table, where his generosities were so largely dispensed, that he was not afraid to offend him. When he came to the door of the feast, he found the guests all putting on the garment suitable for the marriage banquet. As here, in our own country, at a funeral, each mourner is expected to put on the articles of mourning which are provided, so at the wedding feast each person was expected to wear the bridegroom's token of love, the garment which, as a badge, marked him as an attendant at the wedding, and as one who rejoiced in it.

While others cheerfully put on this wedding garment, the traitor would not; he resolved to defy the rules of the palace, and to insult the king by appearing in his own garments. He scorned to wear the garb of respectful joy; he preferred to make himself conspicuous by his daring brashness. The badge was intended to show that the wearer was a real participator in the joy of the feast, and for that very reason he would not put it on. He did not acknowledge the king nor the prince, nor care one atom about the cheerful event. He had no objection to being there, to eating the delicacies, or reclining upon the seats, and seeing the pomp and the show, but he was only in it, and not of it; he was there in body, but not in spirit.

Are there not crowds of people whose union to the church is nothing better than an insult to God? Custom sways them, and not sincere faith. They have no regard for the great head of the church or for the heart-searching God. They treat church membership as a trifle and have no tenderness of heart touching the matter. They, in effect, say, "*The table of the Lord is contemptible.* Spots are they in our feasts, *feeding themselves without fear*" (Malachi 1:7; Jude 1:12).

Many a time the question has been asked, "What was the wedding garment?" It is a question which need not be curiously pried into. So many answers have been given that I conclude that if our Savior had intended any one specific thing, he would have expressed himself more plainly, so that we should have been able, without so much theological disputing, to have understood what he meant. It seems to me that our Lord intended much more than any one thing. The guests were bidden to come to the wedding to show their respect to the king and prince;

some would not come at all, and so showed their revolt; this man came, and when he heard the regulation, that a certain garment should be put on, comely in appearance and suitable for the occasion, he determined that he would not wear it.

In this act of rebellion, he went as far in opposition as they did who would not come at all; and he went a little further, for in the very presence of the guests and of the king, he dared to declare his disloyalty and contempt. Alas, how many are willing enough to receive gospel blessings, but they are still at enmity with God, and have no delight in the only begotten Son. Such will dare to use the forms of godliness, and yet their hearts are full of rebellion against the Lord. The wedding garment represents anything which is indispensable to a Christian, but which the unrenewed heart is not willing to accept, anything which the Lord ordains to be a necessary accompaniment of salvation against which selfishness rebels.

Therefore it may be said to be Christ's righteousness imputed to us, for alas, many nominal Christians kick against the doctrine of justification by the righteousness of the Savior and set up their own self-righteousness in opposition to it. To be found in Christ, not having our own righteousness, which is of the law, but the righteousness which is of God by faith, is a very prominent badge of a real servant of God, and to refuse it is to manifest opposition to the glory of God, and to the name, person, and work of his exalted Son. But we might with equal truth say that the wedding garment is a holy character, the imparted righteousness that the Holy Spirit works in us, and which is equally necessary as a proof of grace. If you question such a statement, I would remind you of the dress which adorns the saints in heaven.

What is said of it? *They . . . have washed their robes, and made them white in the blood of the Lamb* (Revelation 7:14). Their robes, therefore, were such as once needed washing; and this could not be said in any sense of the righteousness of the Lord Jesus Christ – that was always perfect and spotless. It is clear, then, that the figure of speech is sometimes applied to saints in reference to their personal character. Holiness is always present in those who are loyal guests of the great King, for *without [holiness] . . . no man shall see the Lord* (Hebrews 12:14). Too many professing Christians pacify themselves with the idea that they possess imputed righteousness, while they are indifferent to the sanctifying work of the Spirit.

They refuse to put on the garment of obedience, and they reject the white linen which is the righteousness of saints. They thus reveal their self-will, their enmity toward God, and their non-submission to his Son. Such men may talk what they will about justification by faith, and salvation by grace, but they are rebels at heart; they do not have on the wedding garment anymore than the self-righteous do, whom they so eagerly condemn. The fact is, if we wish for the blessings of grace, we must in our hearts submit to the rules of grace without picking and choosing. It is vain to dispute whether the wedding garment is faith or love, as some have done; for all the graces of the Spirit and blessings of the covenant go together.

No man ever had the imputed righteousness of Christ without receiving at the same time a measure of the righteousness effected in us by the Holy Spirit. Justification by faith is not contrary to the production of good works; God forbid. The faith by which we are justified is the faith which produces holiness, and no man is justified by faith which does not also sanctify him and deliver him from the love of sin. All the essentials of the Christian character may be understood as making up the great wedding garment. In one word, we put on *Christ Jesus, who of God is made unto us wisdom, and righteousness, and sanctification, and redemption* (1 Corinthians 1:30).

The wedding garment is simply mentioned here as being a test of loyalty to those who came to the marriage feast, and as a mode by which rebellion was professed and loyalty made apparent. Here was a man, then, who came into the gospel feast and yet refused to comply with the command that related to that feast. He willfully preferred self to God, his heart was full of enmity and pride, he despised the gifts of grace, he scorned the rule of love, and he stood as a defiant rebel even at the banquet of mercy which his King had spread.

His sin lay, first of all, in coming in there at all without the wedding garment. If he did not mean to be of one heart with his fellow guests and his lord, why did he come? If a man does not intend to yield himself up to God's will, why does he profess to be a part of God's church? If a man is not saved by the righteousness of Christ, why does he profess to be a believer in Christ? If he will not be obedient to Christ's holy will, why does he pretend to be a follower of Christ? It is a grave mistake for any person to imagine that he can be in the church of God to his own advantage unless his heart is renewed, unless he means what he declares, and unless he sincerely loves the rule under which he professes to put himself.

The intruder's sin was aggravated by the fact that after he had unlawfully come into the feast, he still continued there without the wedding robe. He does not appear to have had any misgiving, or to have thought of amending his error. Only when the king came in and said, *Take him away,* had the bold rebel any idea of removing himself. Had he come in there, as I fear some of you have come into the church, under a mistake, thinking that there was no need of the wedding garment, when he looked around and saw all other persons wearing it, and observed that it was the peculiar mark of a guest, he would have felt uneasy and would have gone to those who kept the royal wardrobe to get such a robe for himself; and then his sin in the matter would not have been laid to his charge. But he persisted in remaining where he was and as he was.

O my dear friends, if you have already perpetrated the sin of union with the visible church of God without having the prerequisites, without being indeed submissive to God in heart and desirous to honor Christ, I entreat you, seek what is lacking, seek faith in God, seek a new heart, seek holiness of life, seek to become a loyal subject of the King, and be not content until you have these things, for the King will soon come in. He gives you time as yet, may he also give you grace to see to it that, being now where you ought never to have been, you may yet make your position a right one by obtaining that which will justify you in remaining where you are. The guest in his own clothes was a speckled bird among that company, and it was possible for him even then to have become one of them, but he would not; he continued to defy the King.

This persistence he retained though he probably knew the fate of those who had refused to come. He knew that the king had sent forth his armies and destroyed those wicked men who had molested his messengers, and yet he dared to recline at his ease in the very teeth, and defying the terrible power of the monarch. He made his brow as brass, and hardened his heart as adamant, and forced his way into a position where his seditious spirit would be able to display itself conspicuously. He said within his soul, "I care nothing for this marriage. I will make sport of it; I will intrude myself into that feast and show my contempt.

I will take the provisions, but the son shall have no honor from me, and the king shall not find me bending my will to his command." Thus he had the audacity to amuse himself as a willful rebel at the feast of mercy.

Are there any such among you here? The tendency will be for those who are not so to begin to condemn themselves. I know already one who has said, "I am that guest that did not have on a wedding garment." She is not that one, for she is not even a member of the church, and therefore it cannot concern her; but many like her write bitter things against themselves. Another will be saying, "I am that one," whereas if there be one that lives near to God and whose desire is to be like Christ, and to be in all things conformed to the divine will, he is the man. You who are most assuredly right will probably be suspicious that you are not, and you who are insincere and have never submitted yourselves to the will of God will probably say, "What does it matter? I am doing as well as others, I give as much, I heed the resources as much, so surely there can be no cause for concern in me." God grant that you may feel anxiety and fear before the Lord.

We pass on to the next point – the king at the feast.

The king came in to see the guests. What an honor and privilege this was to the poor creatures whom his royal lavishness had brought together! Was it not indeed the chief point of the entire festival? One of our greatest joys is to sing,

> The king himself comes near
> And feasts his saints today!

What would church fellowship be if it did not have the fellowship of God with it? To sit with my dear brethren and rejoice in their love is exceedingly delightful; but the best wine is fellowship with the Father and with his Son Jesus Christ. The king did not provide the banquet and leave his guests to eat by themselves, but he *came in;* and into every gospel church gathered according to his command the King will come. I am sure the most fervent desire of this church is that the King may personally visit us. We trust he is with us, but we want him yet more fully to reveal himself. Our cry is: "Come, great King, with all your glorious power, with your Spirit and with your glorious Son, and manifest yourself to us as you do not unto the world."

When the king came into the banqueting chamber, *he saw the guests* and they also saw him. It was a mutual revelation. Ever sweet is this to the saints, that their God looks upon them; his look brings no terror to our minds when we are loyal and loving. *Thou God seest me* (Genesis 16:13) is sweet music. We desire to abide forever beneath the divine inspection, for it is an inspection of unbounded love. He sees our faults, it is to remove them; he notes our imperfections, it is to cleanse them away. Behold me, O great King, and lift up your eyes upon me, accepting me in the beloved. What joy it is to us who are saved in Christ Jesus that we also can see him! *Through a glass, darkly* (1 Corinthians 13:12), I grant you we behold him, for as yet we are not fit to behold the full splendor of his diety! But yet how sweetly does he reveal himself to our souls and unveil his eternal love. Then it is that the feast is most fully a banquet of wine, when the banner of love waves over us, and the king's voice fills us with unspeakable delight.

The king came in to see the guests. This, I say, was the crowning point of the entire banquet. Observe that he came in after they were in their places. They did not see him before they had entered his halls. When an inferior entertains a superior, he always advances to the door to meet him and waits until he comes. If Her Majesty the Queen were entertained by one of her nobles, he would be in waiting, and at the threshold would meet her; but when a superior entertains an inferior, the inferior may take his seat at the table, and when all is ready the noble host will come in. It is so in the banquet of mercy. You and I see nothing of God, by way of communion with him, until first we have been brought in by the message of mercy to the marriage feast of the gospel; for, indeed, until then, a sight of God would strike us with terror:

> Till God in human flesh I see,
>   My thoughts no comfort find;
> The holy, just, and sacred Three
>   Are terrors to my mind.
>
> But when Immanuel's face appears,
>   My hope, my joy, begins;
> His name forbids my slavish fear,
>   His grace removes my sins.

When I get to the banquet of mercy, then it is that I can dare to look at the King of Kings, but not until then. What a joyous sight, a vision of the God and Father of our Lord Jesus Christ, the Father of glory as he appears in the gospel, feasting us upon his fatlings. An incarnate God makes God visible to us and makes us happy in the sight. "How can you see my face and live?" was the old question, but behold, it is answered this day. At the marriage union of Christ with his people we see the face of the King in his beauty and our souls not only live, but we also have life more abundantly.

Observe, dear brethren, that the King has special times for this. He is not always in the festal chamber; to our sorrow we sometimes miss the King's presence at his table. We have the ordinances always, but we do not always enjoy the God of ordinances. The means of grace are abiding, but the grace of the means will come and go according to the sovereign good pleasure of our God. The King has his times of coming in. These are glad times for his people, but they are trying times for the mass of professing Christians. When are these times? So far as unworthy guests are concerned, the times of God's visitation are those seasons when character is manifested. All times and periods do not reveal character.

A lion may lie all day asleep, and you may think it is tame; but when the night brings the time for it to go forth to its prey, then it howls and displays its ferocity. And so an ungodly man may lie down in the church of God with the lambs of the flock, and nothing may lead you to suspect his true character; but when the time comes for him to make profit by sin, or to get pleasure by sin, or to escape from persecution by sin, then you find out what he is. These providences are the King's coming in to scrutinize the guests. Changes in the conditions of the church, changes in the condition of the individual, all sorts of providential events go to make up the great sieve by which the wheat and the chaff are separated.

A great and most solemn coming in of the King to see the guests is, when having looked over the church, unknown to us, he decides that such and such a hypocrite has had space enough for repentance and time enough for mischief, and must now be summoned to the dread tribunal by death. The time when the King comes in to see his guests is not the last judgment, for that is the coming of the Son and not of the

Father; and if it were intended in the parable, we would read that *the prince* came in to see his guests. We are led to view the King himself as continually judging professing Christians and detecting the rebels who place themselves among the saints; by this judgment of God men are taken away from the church in their transgressions, bound hand and foot, and cast into the outer darkness, where there is weeping and gnashing of teeth.

I do not know, my dear brethren, when God may be visiting this church, and taking away the men that are rebels in our midst; but I do know that when professing Christians die it is not certain that all of them sleep in Jesus, but some of them are rooted up, like tares from among the wheat, and are bound up in bundles to burn. The division is going on constantly. The King's presence is known to believers in the joy which they feel, but it is made known to hypocrites by his cutting them off and appointing them their portion in eternal woe.

If, however, there is any one time when we may be quite sure that the King comes in to see the guests, it is after large ingatherings from the world; for notice here, when the servants had gathered in guests in large numbers, it was then that the king came in. Now it will be after the time of revival that we are feeling just now, when I hope a great many will be added to the church, that the Lord will search and sift us. If there has been no visitation of the church before for purposes of love or judgment – for they go together – we shall be quite sure to have such a visit from the great Lord himself at this time.

Solemnly think of the judge at the feast. To all the rest at the festival he was the king, the beloved monarch, the generous donor of a splendid banquet, and all eyes feasted as they looked at him. It was joy enough to behold the king in his beauty, and to see his son with all his royal jewels on, attired for the wedding feast; but he was a judge to the hypocritical intruder. The day of comfort to his saints is also the day of vengeance of our God. He who comes to comfort all who mourn, comes at the same time to strike the rebellious with a rod of iron.

The judge begins, as you perceive, by *seeing: He saw there a man.* What eyes are those of omniscience! The parable represents but one such man as present, yet the all-seeing king saw him at once, and he fixed his flaming eyes on that one. I suppose it was a greater crowd than this, but the king fixed his eyes on the solitary offender at once. Does the parable speak of only one because we may expect to find only one hypocrite in a church? Alas! there have been many such at the wedding feast, but one only is mentioned to show us that if there were but one, God would find him out; and, being many, the sinners in Zion may be the more sure that they will not escape.

It is possible that none of the guests may have noticed the man's garments; the parable makes no remark upon any expostulations made to him by others; perhaps they were all so taken up with the sight of the king, and so glad to be at the feast themselves, that they had no heart to make remarks upon others. But this is certain, that the king detected at once the absence of what was necessary to the marriage feast. It was not the presence of anything offensive, but the absence of something that was necessary. He did not say to the unworthy guest, "You have rags upon you," or "You are filthy," or "You have an unwashed lace"; he inquired solely into the absence of the peculiar badge which denoted a loving guest.

God will judge, and does continually judge, his church upon this question, the absence of what is absolutely necessary to being a Christian, the absence of honoring the Son and obeying the Father. O soul, if you are a professor of religion, and yet you do not love Jesus, and do not fear the great King of Kings, you lack the wedding robe, and what are you doing here? The king will see at once that you lack it. Your morality, your generosity, your high-sounding prayers, alas, and even your eloquent discussions – these cannot conceal from him the fact that your heart is not with him. The one thing needful is to accept loyally the Lord as King.

The king next began to deal with the rebel. Note how he spoke with him. He took him on his own ground. It was too high a day for the king to use rough speech; the man pretended to be a friend, and he addressed him as such, but though the word I doubt not was uttered softly, it must have stung him if he had any feeling left. Judas exemplified in his own person this character. When he gave to the Savior the traitor's kiss, our Lord addressed him as *friend*. He pretended himself to be a friend. A friend, indeed, to insult his king at his own table, and to select for the insult the delicate occasion of the prince's marriage to which he had been hospitably invited!

This was disgraceful! Friend indeed! Where will you find enemies if such shall be called friends? The king put it to him, *"How camest thou in hither?* What business have you here? What could have induced you so maliciously to defy me? To strike me in my most tender point, and mock my guests, and trample on my sin? Did you intend such daring brazenness? *How camest thou in hither? Into this place?* Was there nowhere else to pour forth your sabotage, no other spot in which to play the traitor? Do you need to come into my palace, and to my table, and before my son on his wedding day to reveal your animosity? Was there a need to do this?"

So may the Lord say to some of us. "Were there no other ways to sin, but that you must profess to be my servant when you were not so? Were there no other bowls that you could drink from, that you must profane the cups of my table? Was there no other bread that you could put into your wicked mouths but the bread that represents the body of my Son? Had you nowhere else to sin in that you needed to sin in the church? Could you do nothing else to show your spite but that you must make a lying profession of faith in my Son, who bled upon the cross to redeem the sons of men? Could you attack me nowhere else but through the wounds of my only begotten Son? Could you vex my Spirit by no other means than by pretending to be my friend, and thrusting yourself into this place, while defiantly rejecting that which was necessary to do me honor, and to do my Son honor, at the festival of my grace?" I dare not dwell upon the topic. I give you the text; I pray that your conscience may preach the sermon.

Notice, however, one thing, and that is, that the king, when he thus turned as a judge, dealt with this man only about himself. *How camest thou in hither?* (emphasis added). Did I hear a whisper in someone's mind: "Well, if I am unfit to be a church member, there are a great many others who are in the same condemnation." What is that to you? See to yourself! When the king came in to see the guests, he did not say to this man, "How came yonder persons here without the wedding garment?" His dealings were personal with him alone: *How camest* **thou** *in hither not having a wedding garment?*

Professing Christian, look to yourself, look to yourself. Let your charity begin at home. Cast out the beam from your own eye, and then may you see clearly to cast out the speck that is in your brother's eye. He fixed on the one man, made him his entire audience, and directed to him the solemn question: *Friend, how camest thou in hither?* Ah, my dear friends, as the pastor of this church, it has been a very great joy to me to see our numbers increased; many have been added to us, and many have gone forth from us to form other churches; my joy has been constant in God concerning this matter. Our beloved brethren associated with me in office have done their best to keep any of you back who have sought membership in whom we could see no fruits corresponding. We have not used our office deceitfully; as in the sight of God we have tried to be neither too severe nor too lax, but for all that, I cannot but know that there are some of you who are not Christians though you bear the name.

Like those of old, you say you are Jews and are not, but do lie. I am not now speaking of any who have fallen into sin and have suffered our rebuke, or have been separated from us by excommunication and yet remain in the congregation. I mean others of you whose lives are all that could be desired openly, and yet there is a worm at the heart of your profession; you are not vitally godly, you have a name to live, and you keep that name untarnished as yet, but you are dead. Search yourselves; do not from this tabernacle descend into hell. Let your prayer be, *Gather not my soul with sinners, nor my life with bloody men* (Psalm 26:9).

I am as concerned about myself as about you, that I should be found *accepted in the beloved* (Ephesians 1:6) lest after having *preached to others, I myself should be a castaway* (1 Corinthians 9:27). Do let it be a matter of solemn anxiety with each one. If you have never come to Jesus, come now; if you have never sought holiness of life, seek it now. If you have never had the wedding garment, it is yet procurable; go to him who freely gives it, and the Lord will not refuse you; go today and he will accept you.

He who was the unworthy guest is now the criminal at the feast. The king has now become a judge to him; the question has been personally put to him, and he is *speechless*. Why is he silent? Surely it was because he was convicted of open, undeniable disloyalty. No evidence was required; he had come there on set purpose with malice premeditated to display his disloyalty, and had done so in the presence of the king. I do not think he represents at all a person who enters the church through ignorance, with a sincere but ignorant intention; but he portrays one who makes a profession without care to make it true – willfully despising the Lord's commands.

He is a man willing to be saved by grace, and professing to be so, but refusing to acknowledge his duty to God and his obligations to the Son. He was speechless; he could not have chosen a worse place, nor a more brazen method of ventilating his disloyalty than that which he selected; there was nothing he could say in self-defense. At that moment, when the king looked him through and through, he saw the full horror of his position; his loins were loosed, like Belshazzar of old when he saw the handwriting on the wall; he saw now that his time to insult was over, and the day of retribution had come. He was taken in the very fact and could not escape.

He had been guilty of a superfluity of naughtiness, of an unnecessary extravagance of wickedness in coming into the feast to air his pride. He had committed a suicidal intrusion. He might have kept himself away at any rate, and not have thrust himself into the judge's presence. He saw now that the cause of sedition was hopeless; the king was there and he was in his power and none could rescue him. Why did he not burst into tears? Why did he not confess the wrong? Why did he not say, "My king, I have insulted you, have pity on me." His proud heart would not let him. Sin made him incapable of repentance. There is a verse in one of Hart's hymns which runs thus –

> Fixed is their everlasting state:
>   Could they repent, 'tis now too late.

That is true enough, but it supposes an impossibility, and I think it would have been far better to have said,

> Fixed is their everlasting state;
>   They can't repent, 'tis now too late.

Because the sinner goes on to sin, he continues still to suffer; he will not turn, he cannot turn. As the Ethiopian cannot change his skin, nor the leopard his spots, so when sin has reached its height the man cannot bend, or bow, or retrace his steps. Oh, if he could have repented even then! But he could not; and the tears that came after the king had pronounced the sentence were no tears of repentance, but only of despairing pride. He stood speechless. It was not only that he had no excuse, but also that he would not confess his wrong.

Have I anyone here in such a condition of heart, that while he has been sinning by making a false profession, and knows it, yet he sullenly refuses to confess his fault? Yield yourself, man! Yield at once. Fall at the King's feet at once. Even if you are not a hypocrite, if you have any suspicion that you are, fall down and say, "My King, make me sincere; I submit myself to your will, and am ready to put on the wedding badge. If there is any method by which I can honor your Son, I quibble not at it; let me wear his colors, and be known by all men to be truly a lover of the great Prince."

But now, lastly, while he stood speechless in the king's presence, the king gave place to the executioner, for he uttered these words: *Bind him hand and foot.* He was lawless, so make him feel the law. He said, "I am free, and I will do as I like," so let him never be free again; bind him, shackle him. Executioner, do your duty, prepare him for death, Alas, there are some who are bound and chained even before the breath is out of their bodies.

In their dying hours false professing Christians have often found that they could not pray, and could not repent. Like dying Spira, that arch-hypocrite and apostate, they have been conscious of misery, but not repentant, and no gospel promise has helped to comfort them. Their hearts were seared, they were twice dead before they were actually dead. Then came the sentence: *Take him away,* which is sometimes executed by the church in her excommunications – deceivers are taken away from the gospel feast by just discipline – but which is more fully carried out in the hour of death, when the man's hope fails him. Ah, sirs, what will you do if you have no true grace in your hearts when you are taken away from the Lord's Table, taken away from the baptism in which you gloried, taken away from the doctrines of the gospel which you understood so well in your head, but which you did not know in your heart?

John Bunyan's description of the man dragged by seven devils, bound with cords, comes up before my mind. *Bind him hand and foot, and take him away.* How thankful I am that the servants who brought them in are not the same ones who were commanded to take them away. The *douloi* (slaves) brought them in, the *diakonoi* (servants) took them away; the king has a special order of servants for the taking of deceivers away; his angels do that in the hour of death – they execute his vengeance. He gives us ministers a better office – he bids us to be his heralds of mercy.

Then the judge said, "*Cast him,* fling him like a useless, worthless thing. That wretch has dared pollute my marriage feast, so cast him away, as men fling weeds over the garden wall or shake off vipers into the fire." There is none in heaven or earth thought more despicable, more fit to be thrown away as rubbish and waste, than a man who had a Christian name, but had not the essentials of the Christian's nature. Cast him away. Where? *Into outer darkness,* far from the banquet hall where torches flame and lamps are bright; drive him out into the cold, chilly midnight air. He has once seen the light; it will be all the darker now for him when he is driven into the darkness.

There is no darkness so dark as the darkness of the man who once saw light. Cast him into the outer darkness. What will he do there? We are not told what would be done *to* him, it was not necessary. We learn elsewhere as much as could be revealed to us, but we are told *what he did,* for *there shall be weeping,* not the gush of tears which gives relief, but the everlasting dropping of scalding tears which creates fresh sorrow and enlarges their own source. The outcast shed no tears of regret, but of sullen disappointment, because he could not after all dishonor the king, and had even served to illustrate the royal justice and power, and so had brought glory to the king whom he hated in soul.

Then came the *gnashing of teeth,* caused by wrath and envy because he could do no more mischief. No sorrow is equal to that of a malicious spirit, that having attempted a daring deed of atrocious wickedness, has been defeated and has contributed to the triumph of the good and excellent. The misery of hell is not a misery that God arbitrarily creates; it is the necessary result of sin, it is sin itself come to ripeness. Here you see the picture of the man who was brash enough to come into the church without being a Christian, and now forever he gnashes with his teeth against that glorious majesty of heaven that it will never be in his power to injure, but that it will always be in his heart to hate. And this will be his hell – that he hates God; this his darkness – that he cannot see beauty in God; and this the outerness of the darkness – that he cannot enter into God's will.

Depart from me, ye cursed is only love repelling that which is not lovely; it is only justice giving to man what his fallen nature craved for. "Get away from me, for you did not honor me; when you did come to me, it was with your lips only. Go where your hearts were; *depart from me, ye cursed.*" Oh, may God grant that not one here may come under the lash of this terrible parable, but may we be found of the Lord in peace in the day of his appearing. You see, then, how the Lord sifts us. First, we are sifted by the preaching of the gospel, and many will not come – there is one heap of chaff; next, by the judgment of God in his church, and others are found lacking – there is another heap of chaff. Ah, when this is done, and the two great sieves are used, shall we be found among the wheat?

Do you say, "The sermon has nothing to do with me, I never made a profession, I shall go home easy enough." Come to this place, friend, I must not let you go. There is a vagabond brought before the magistrate accused of theft; he says he is perfectly innocent, but he is convicted, and has to suffer for it. After him comes a bragging fellow who says, "I do not make any profession of being honest; I rob anybody I can, and I mean to do so; I do not pretend to keep the law." Why, it seems to me that the magistrate would say, "I condemned the man who did at least pretend to be something decent, but to you I give double punishment; you are evidently incorrigible, and your case needs no consideration." You who do not say you are Christians, who confess you are not, and you declare yourselves the enemies of Christ, you will get no comfort therefore out of this parable; but I pray you, yield yourselves to the Savior, and believe in him, for *he that believeth and is baptized shall be saved.*

Chapter 11

Unprofitable Servants

And cast ye the unprofitable servant into outer darkness: there shall be weeping and gnashing of teeth.
(Matthew 25:30)

So likewise ye, when ye shall have done all those things which are commanded you, say, We are unprofitable servants: we have done that which was our duty to do.
(Luke 17:10)

His lord said unto him, Well done, thou good and faithful servant. (Matthew 25:21)

There is a narrow path between indifference and morbid sensibility. Some men seem to feel no holy anxiety: they place their Master's talent in the earth, leave it there, and take their pleasure and their ease without a moment's misgiving. Others profess to be so anxious to be right that they come to the conclusion that they can never be so, and fall under a horror of God, viewing his service as a drudgery, and himself as a hard master – though probably they never say so. Between these two lines there is a path, narrow as a razor's edge, which only the grace of God can enable us to trace; it is free equally from carelessness and from bondage, and consists in a sense of responsibility bravely borne by the help of the Holy Spirit.

The right way usually lies between two extremes: it is the narrow channel between the rock and the whirlpool. There is a sacred way which runs between self-congratulation and despondency, a very difficult track to find, and very hard to keep. There are great perils in the consciousness that you have done well, and that you are serving God with all your might; for you may come to think that you are a deserving person, worthy to rank among the princes of Israel. The danger of being puffed up can hardly be overestimated: a dizzy head soon brings a fall. But perhaps equally to be dreaded on the other side is that sense of unworthiness which paralyzes all exertion, making you feel that you are incapable of anything that is great or good. Under this impulse have men fled from the service of God into a life of solitude. They felt that they could not behave valiantly in the battle of life, and therefore they fled from the field before the fight began, to become hermits or monks, as if it were possible to do the Lord's perfect will by doing nothing at all, and to discharge the duties to which they were born by an unnatural mode of existence.

Blessed is that man who finds the straight and narrow way between high thoughts of self and hard thoughts of God, between self-esteem and a timid shrinking from all effort. My desire is that the Spirit of God may guide our minds into the golden midpoint where holy graces blend, and the contending vices, equally natural to our evil hearts, are all excluded. May the Spirit of God bless our three texts and the three subjects suggested by them, so that we may be put right, and then by infinite mercy may be kept right until the great day of account.

Let us read Matthew 25:30.

> *And cast ye the unprofitable servant into outer darkness:*
> *there shall be weeping and gnashing of teeth.*

In this our first text we have the verdict of justice upon the man who did not use his talent. The man is here called an *unprofitable servant* because he was slothful, useless, and worthless. He did not bring his master interest for his money nor render him any sincere service. He did not faithfully discharge the trust deposited to him as his fellow servants did.

Notice, first, that *this unprofitable person was a servant.* He never denied that he was a servant; in fact, it was by his position as a servant that he became possessed of his one talent, and to that possession he never objected. If he had been capable of receiving more, there is no reason why he should not have had two talents, or five; for the Scripture tells us that the master gave to every man according to his several abilities. He acknowledged the rule of his master even in the act of burying the talent, and in appearing before him to give an account. This makes the subject the more heart-searching for you and for me; for we, too, profess to be servants – servants of the Lord our God.

Judgment must begin at the house of God, that is, with those who are in the house of the Lord as children and servants. Let us, therefore, look well to our goings. If judgment first begins at us, *what shall the end be of them that obey not the gospel of God? And if the righteous scarcely be saved, where shall the ungodly and the sinner appear?* (1 Peter 4:17-18). If this in our text be judgment upon servants, what will be the judgment upon enemies? This man acknowledged that he was a servant even to the end; and though he was impertinent and brash enough to express a most wicked and slanderous opinion about his master, yet he neither denied his own position as a servant, nor the fact that his talent was his lord's, for he said, *Lo, there thou hast that is thine* (Matthew 25:25).

In thus speaking, he went rather further than some professing Christians do, for they live as if Christianity were all eating the fat and drinking the sweet and not serving at all; as if religion had many privileges but no precepts; and as if, when men were saved, they became licensed loiterers to whom it is a matter of honor to magnify free grace by standing all the day idle in the marketplace. Alas, I know some who never do a hand's turn for Christ, and yet call him Master and Lord. It will fare ill with them at his coming. Many of us acknowledge that we are servants, that everything we have belongs to our Master, and that we are bound to live for him. So far, so good; but we may get as far as that, and yet in the end we may be found as unprofitable servants, and so be cast into outer darkness, where there shall be weeping and gnashing of teeth. Let us take heed of this.

This man, though a servant, *thought ill of his master,* and disliked his service. He said, *I knew thee that thou art an hard man, reaping where thou hast not sown, and gathering where thou hast not strawed* (Matthew 25:24). Certain professing Christians who have stolen into the church are of the same mind: they dare not say that they regret their having joined the church, and yet they so act that all may conclude that if it could be undone, they would not do the same again. They do not find pleasure in the service of God but continue to pursue its routine as a matter of habit or a hard obligation. They get into the spirit of the elder brother, and they say, *Lo, these many years do I serve thee, neither transgressed I at any time thy commandment: and yet thou never gavest me a kid, that I might make merry with my friends* (Luke 15:29).

They sit down on the shady side of godliness, and never bask in the sun that shines full upon it. They forget that the father said to the elder son, *Son, thou art ever with me, and all that I have is thine* (Luke 15:31). He might have had as many feastings, as many lambs and kids as he desired; he would have been denied no good thing. The presence of his father ought to have been his joy and his delight, and better than all merrymakings with his friends; and it would have been so if he had been in a proper state of heart. The man who hid his talent had carried the evil and grumpy spirit much further than that elder brother did; but the germs are the same, and we must take care that we crush them at the beginning.

This unprofitable servant looked upon his master as one that reaped where he never sowed, and used the rake to gather together what he had never scattered. He meant that he was a hard, exacting, and unjust person, whom it was difficult to please. He judged his lord to be one who expected more of his servants than he had any right to look for, and he had such a hatred of his unjust conduct that he resolved to tell him to his face what he thought of him. This spirit may readily creep over the minds of professing Christians; I fear it is brooding over many even now, for they are not content with Christ. If they want pleasure, they go outside the church to get it; their joys are not within the circle of which Christ is the center. Their religion is their labor, not their delight; their God is their dread, not their joy. They do not delight themselves in the Lord, and therefore he does not give them the desire of their hearts, and so they grow more and more discontented.

They could not call him *God my exceeding joy* (Psalm 43:4), and so he is a terror to them. Devotion is a dreary engagement to them; they wish that they could escape from it with an easy conscience. They do not say as much to their secret selves, but you can read between the lines these words – *What a weariness is it!* (Malachi 1:13). It is no wonder when things come to this type of situation that a professing Christian becomes an unprofitable servant; for who can do a work well which he hates to do? Forced service is not desirable. God does not want slaves to grace his throne. A servant who is not pleased with his situation had better leave; if he is not content with his master, he had better find another, for their mutual relationship will be unpleasant and unprofitable. When it comes to this, that you and I are discontented with our God, and dissatisfied with his work, we had better look out for another lord, if any such will have us, for we shall certainly be unprofitable to the Lord Jesus from our lack of love for him.

Note next, that, albeit this man was doing nothing for his master, *he did not think himself an unprofitable servant.* He exhibited no self-depreciation, no humbling, no contrition. He was as bold as brass, and said unblushingly, *Lo, there thou hast that is thine.* He came before his master with no apologies or excuses. He did not join with those who have done all, and then say, *We are unprofitable servants;* for he felt that he had dealt with his lord as the justice of the case deserved; indeed, instead of acknowledging any fault, he turned to accusing his lord. It is even so with false professing Christians.

They have no idea that they are hypocrites; the thought does not cross their minds. They have no notion that they are unfaithful; hint at it and see how they will defend themselves. If they are not living as they ought to, they claim to be pitied rather than blamed; the blame lies with Providence; it is the fault of circumstances; it is the fault of anybody but themselves. They have done nothing, and yet they feel more at ease than those who have done everything. They have taken the trouble to dig in the earth and hide their talent, and they as good as ask, "What more do you want? Is God so exacting as to expect me to bring more to him than he gave me? I am as grateful and prayerful as God makes me – what more will he require?" There is, you see, no bowing in the dust with a sense of imperfection, but an arrogant casting upon God of all blame, and this, too, under the pretense of honoring his sovereign grace! Ah me! that men should be able to torture truth into such presumptuous falsehood.

Mark well, that the verdict of justice at last may turn out to be the very opposite of that which we pronounce upon ourselves. He who proudly thinks himself profitable shall be found unprofitable, and he who modestly judges himself to be unprofitable may in the end come to hear his Master say, *Well done, good and faithful servant* (Matthew 25:23). So little are we able, through the defects of our conscience, to form a right estimate of ourselves, that we frequently reckon ourselves to be rich and increased in goods, and having need of nothing, when, indeed, we are naked, and poor, and miserable. Such was the case with this unfaithful servant: he wrapped himself up in the conceit that he was even more just than his lord, and had an argument to plead which he thought would exonerate him from all blame.

It should give rise to much searching of heart when we notice *what this unprofitable servant did, or rather, what he did not do.* He carefully deposited his capital where no one was able to find it and steal it; and there was the end of his service. We ought to observe that he did not spend that talent upon himself or use it in business for his own benefit. He was not a thief, nor in any way one who misappropriated moneys placed under his charge. In this he excels many who profess to be the servants of God and yet live for themselves only. What little talent they have is used in their own business, and never upon their Lord's concerns.

They have the power of getting money, but their money is not made for Christ; such an idea never occurs to them. Their efforts are all for themselves, or – to use other words to express the same thing – *for* their families. Yonder is a man who has the gift of eloquent speech, and he uses it, not for Christ, but for himself, that he may win popularity, that he might arrive at a respectable position. The one end and object of his most earnest speech is to bring grist to his own mill and gain to his own estate. Everywhere this is to be seen among professing Christians, that they are living for themselves. They are not adulterers or drunkards, far from it; neither are they thieves or spendthrifts; they are decent, orderly, quiet sorts of people; but still, they begin and end with self.

What is this but to be an unprofitable servant? What is a servant to me if he works hard for himself and does nothing for me? A professing Christian may toil until he becomes a rich man, an alderman in the city, a Lord Mayor, a member of parliament, or a millionaire; but what does that prove? Why, that he could work and did work well for himself; and if all this while he has done little or nothing for Christ, he is all the more condemned by his own success. If he had worked for his Lord as he worked for himself, what might he not have accomplished? The unprofitable servant in the parable was not so bad as that, and yet he was cast into outer darkness. What then will become of some of you?

Furthermore, the wicked servant did not go and misspend his talent; he did not waste it in self-indulgence and wickedness as the Prodigal Son did, who spent his substance in riotous living. Oh no, he was a much better man than that. He would not waste a halfpenny; he was all for saving and running no risks. The talent was as he received it, only wrapped up in a napkin and hidden in the earth – put into a bank, in fact, but a bank that gave no interest. He never touched a penny of it for a feast or a romp, and therefore could not be accused of being a spendthrift with his lord's money; in all of which he was superior to those who yield their strength to sin, and use their abilities to gratify the guilty passions of themselves and others.

I grieve to add that some who call themselves servants of Christ lay out their strength to undermine the gospel they profess to teach; they speak against the holy name by which they are named, and thus they use their talent against their Master. This man did not do so; he was bad enough in heart for anything, but he had never openly become so wretched a traitor. He never employed learning in order to raise needless doubts, or to resist the plain doctrines of the Word of God; this has been reserved for religious leaders of these latter days – days which produce monsters unknown to less educated times.

This man's talent had not been wasted under his hand; it was as he had received it, and he therefore reckoned he had been faithful. Ah! but this is not what Christ calls faithfulness – just to stay where we are. If you think you have grace and only keep what you have, without obtaining more, it will be hiding your talent in the earth and keeping it a barren thing. It is not enough to retain; you must advance. The capital may be there, but where is the interest? To be living without aim or purpose beyond that of keeping up your position is to be a wicked and slothful servant, condemned already. While meditating upon this subject may we each say to ourselves, *Lord, is it I?*

His lord called this servant *wicked*. Is it, then, a wicked thing to be unprofitable? Surely wickedness must mean some positive action. No. Not to do right is to be wicked; not to live for Christ is to be wicked; not to be of use in the world is to be wicked; not to bring glory to the name of the Lord is to be wicked; to be slothful is to be wicked. It is clear that there are many wicked people in the world who would not like to be called so. *Wicked and slothful* – these are the two words which are riveted together by the Lord Jesus, whose speech is always wise. A schoolboy was asked by his master, "What are you doing, John?" He was called up, and thought he could get away by saying, "I was doing nothing, sir"; but his master answered, "That is the very thing for which I called you out, for you ought to have been doing the lesson which I set before you."

It will be no excuse at the last day for you to cry, "I was doing nothing, sir!" Were not those on the left hand made to depart with a curse upon them because they did nothing? Is it not written: *Curse ye Meroz, said the angel of the Lord, curse ye bitterly the inhabitants thereof; because they came not to the help of the Lord, to the help of the Lord against the mighty* (Judges 5:23)? He who does nothing is a *wicked and slothful servant* (Matthew 25:26).

This man was condemned to outer darkness. Notice this: he was condemned to be *as he was;* for hell, in one light, may be described as the great Captain's saying: "As you were." *He that is unjust, let him be unjust still: and he which is filthy, let him be filthy still* (Revelation 22:11). In another world there is permanence of character: enduring holiness is heaven, continual evil is hell. This man was outside of the family of his lord. He thought his lord to be a hard master, and so proved that he had no love for him, and that he was not really one of his household. He was outside in heart, and so his lord said to him, "Remain outside." Besides that, he was in the dark: he had wrong notions of his master; for his lord was not a harsh and hard man; he did not gather where he had not strawed, nor reap where he had not sown. Therefore his lord said, "You are willfully in the dark; abide there in the darkness which is outside."

This man was envious: he could not endure his master's prosperity; he gnashed his teeth at the thought of it. He was sentenced to continue in that mind, and so to gnash his teeth forever. This is a dreadful idea of eternal punishment, this permanence of character in an immortal spirit – *He that is unjust, let him be unjust still.* While the character of the ungodly will be permanent, it will also be more and more developed along its own lines: the bad points will become worse, and, with nothing to restrain it, evil will become viler still.

In the next world, where there are no hindrances from the existence of a church and a gospel, the man will ripen to a more hideous maturity of enmity against God, and a more horrible degree of consequent misery. Sorrow is bound up with sin: abiding in sinfulness, a man must necessarily abide in wretchedness; for the wicked is like the troubled sea that cannot rest, whose waters cast up mire and dirt. What must it be like to be forever outside the family of God! Never to be God's child! Forever in the dark! Never to see the light of holy knowledge, and purity, and hope! Forever to gnash one's teeth with painful contempt and abhorrence of God, whom to hate is hell! O for grace to be made to love him, whom to love is heaven. The unprofitable servant had a dreadful wage to take when his master reckoned with him, but who can say that he had not well earned it? He had the due reward of his deeds. O our God! grant that such may not be the lot of any one of us!

I must now call your attention to the second text:

> *So likewise ye, when ye shall have done all those things*
> *which are commanded you, say, We are unprofitable*
> *servants: we have done that which was our duty to do.*
> (Luke 17:10)

This is the verdict of self-abasement, given forth from the heart of servants who had laboriously discharged the full work of the day. This is a part of a parable intended to rebuke all notions of self-importance and human merit. When a servant has been plowing or feeding cattle, his master does not say to him, "Sit down, and I will wait upon you, for I am deeply in your debt." No, his master bids him to prepare the evening meal and wait upon him. His services are due, and therefore his master does not praise him as if he were a wonder and a hero. He is only doing his duty if he perseveres from morning light to setting of sun, and he by no means expects to have his work held up to admiration or rewarded with extra pay and humble thanks. Neither are we to boast of our services, but rather think little of them, confessing that we are unprofitable servants.

Whatever pain may have been caused by the first part of the discourse, I trust it will only prepare us the more deeply to enter into the spirit of our second text. Both these texts are graven on my heart as with an iron pen, by a merciless wound, inflicted when I was too feeble to bear it. When I was exceedingly ill in the South of France, and deeply depressed in spirit – so deeply depressed and so sick and ill that I scarcely knew how to live – one of those malicious persons who commonly haunt all public men, and especially ministers, sent me anonymously a letter, openly directed to "that unprofitable servant C. H. Spurgeon."

This letter contained tracts directed to the enemies of the Lord Jesus, with passages marked and underlined, with notes applying them to myself. How many Rabshakehs have in their day written to me! Ordinarily I read them with the patience which comes of use, and they go to light the fire. I do not look for exemption from this annoyance, nor do I usually feel it hard to bear, but in the hour when my spirits were depressed, and I was in terrible pain, this reviling letter cut me to the heart. I turned upon my bed and asked, Am I, then, an unprofitable servant? I grieved exceedingly, and could not lift up my head or find rest. I reviewed my life, and saw its infirmities and imperfections, but knew not how to put my case until this second text came to my relief and answered me as the verdict of my bruised heart.

I said to myself, "I hope I am not an unprofitable servant in the sense in which this person intends to call me so; but I am assuredly so in the other sense." I cast myself upon my Lord and Master once again with a deeper sense of the meaning of the text than I had felt before. His atoning sacrifice revived me, and in humble faith I found rest. By the way, I wonder that any human being should find pleasure in trying to inflict pain upon those who are sick and depressed; yet there are persons who delight to do so. Surely, if there are no evil spirits down below, there are some up above, and the servants of the Lord Jesus receive painful proofs of their activity. Let me, then, if you have felt any pain from the first text, lead you to the point at which I personally arrived when at last I could thank God for that letter and feel that it was beneficial medicine to my spirit.

This which is put into our mouths as a confession that we are unprofitable servants is meant to rebuke us when we think we are somebody and have done something worthy of praise. Our text is meant to rebuke us if we think that we have done enough, that we have borne the burden and heat of the day a long time, and have been kept at our post beyond our own watch. If we conclude that we have achieved a fine day's work of harvesting, and ought to be invited home to rest, the text rebukes us. If we feel an inordinate covetousness after comfort, and wish the Lord would give us some present and striking reward for what we have done, the text shames us. This is a proud, unchildlike, unservantlike spirit, and it must be put down with a firm hand.

In the first place, *in what way can we have profited God?* Eliphaz has well said, *Can a man be profitable unto God, as he that is wise may be profitable unto himself? Is it any pleasure to the Almighty, that thou art righteous? or is it gain to him, that thou makest thy ways perfect?* (Job 22:2-3). If we have given to God of our substance, is he our debtor? In what way have we enriched him to whom all the silver and gold belongs? If we have laid our lives out with the devotion of martyrs and missionaries for his sake, what is that to him, whose glory fills the heavens and the earth? How can we dream of putting the Eternal in debt to us? The right spirit is to say with David, *O my soul, thou hast said unto the Lord, Thou art my Lord: my goodness extendeth not to thee; but to the saints that are in the earth, and to the excellent, in whom is all my delight* (Psalm 16:2-3). How can a man place his Maker under an obligation to him? Let us not dote so blasphemously.

Dear brethren, we ought to recollect that *whatever service we have been able to render has been a matter of debt.* I hope our morality is not fallen so low that we take credit to ourselves for paying our debts. I do not find men in business priding themselves and saying, "I paid a thousand pounds this morning to such a one." "Well, did you give it to him?" "Oh no, it was all owing to him." Is that any great thing? Have we come to such a low state of spiritual morals that we think we have done a great deal when we give to God his due? *It is he that hath made us, and not we ourselves* (Psalm 100:3).

Jesus Christ has bought us: We are not our own, for we *are bought with a price.* We have also entered into covenant with him and given ourselves over to him voluntarily. Were we not baptized into his name and into his death? Whatever we may do is only what he has a right to claim at our hands from our creation, redemption, and professed surrender to him. When we have persevered in the hard work of plowing until no field is left untilled, when we have done the most pleasant work of feeding the sheep, and when we have finished by spreading the table of communion for our Lord, then we have done all we have done no more than was our duty to have done. Why should we boast, then, or cry for a discharge, or look for thanks?

Over and above this there is the sad reflection that, alas, *in all we have done we have been unprofitable through being imperfect.* In the plowing there have been obstacles, in the feeding of the cattle there has been harshness and forgetfulness, in the spreading of the table the provisions have been unworthy of such a Lord as we serve. How must our service appear to him of whom we read: *Behold, he put no trust in his servants; and his angels he charged with folly* (Job 4:18). Can any of you look back upon your service for your Lord with satisfaction? If you can, I cannot say I envy you, for I do not sympathize with you in the least degree, but tremble for your safety.

As for myself, I am compelled to say with solemn truthfulness that I am not content with anything I have ever done. I have half wished to live my life over again, but now I regret that my proud heart allowed me so to wish, since the probabilities are that I would do worse the second time. Whatever grace has done for me I acknowledge with deep gratitude; but so far as I have done anything myself, I beg pardon for it. I pray God to forgive my prayers, for they have been full of fault; I beg him to forgive even this confession, for it is not as humble as it ought to be; I implore him to wash my tears and purge my devotions, and to baptize me into a true burial with my Savior, that I may be quite forgotten in myself, and only remembered in him. Ah, Lord, you know how far we fall short of the humility we ought to feel. Pardon us in this thing. We are all of us unprofitable servants, and if you should judge us by the law, we must be cast away.

Once more, we cannot congratulate ourselves at all, even if we have had success in our Lord's work, since *for all that we have done we are indebted to our Lord's abundant grace.* If we had done all our duty, we should not have done anything if his grace had not enabled us to do it. If our zeal no respite knows, it is he that keeps the fire burning. If our tears of repentance flow, it is he that strikes the rock and fetches the waters from it. If there be any virtue, if there be any praise, if there be any faith, if there be any fervency, if there be any likeness to Christ, we are his workmanship, created by him, and therefore to ourselves we dare not take a particle of the praise. Of your own have we given unto you, great God! So far as anything has been worth your accepting, it was your own beforehand. Therefore the best are still unprofitable servants.

If we have special cause of regret because of some evident error, we shall be wise to go in a lowly spirit and confess the fault, and then go on doing the work of each day in a plodding, hopeful spirit. Whenever you get distressed because you cannot do what you would; whenever you see the faultiness of your own service, and condemn yourself for it, the best thing is to go and do something more in the strength of the Lord. If you have not served Jesus well up to now, go and do better. If you make a blunder, do not tell everybody and say that you will never try again, but do two good things to make up for the failure. Say, "My blessed Lord and Master shall not be more a loser by me than I can help. I will not so much fret over the past as amend the present and wake up for the future."

Brethren, try to be more profitable, and ask for more grace. The servant's business is not to hide himself in a corner of the field and cry, but to go on plowing; not to bleat with sheep, but to feed them, and so prove your love for Jesus. You are not to stand at the head of the table and say, "I have not spread the table for my Master as well as I could have desired." No, go and spread it better. Have courage; you are not serving a hard Master after all; and, though you very properly call yourself an unprofitable servant, be of good cheer, for a gentler verdict shall be pronounced upon you before long. You are not your own judge either for good or ill; another judge is at the door, and when he comes, he will think better of you than your self-abasement permits you to think of yourself. He will judge you by the rule of grace and not by law, and he will end all that dread which comes of a legal spirit and hovers over you with vampire wings.

Thus, I have brought you to the third text:

> *His lord said unto him, Well done, thou good and faithful servant.* (Matthew 25:21)

I shall not try to preach upon that cheering word, but shall only say a word or two upon it. It is much too grand a text to be expounded upon at the end of a sermon. We find the Lord saying to those who had used their talents industriously, *Well done, thou good and faithful servant.* This is the verdict of grace. Blessed is the man who shall acknowledge himself to be an unfaithful servant; and blessed is the man to whom his Lord shall say, *Thou good and faithful servant.*

Observe here that the "Well done" of the Master is *given in faithfulness.* It is not "Well done, thou good and brilliant servant"; for perhaps the man never shone at all in the eyes of those who appreciate glare and glitter. It is not "Well done, thou great and distinguished servant"; for it is possible that he was never known beyond his native village. He conscientiously did his best with his *few things,* and never wasted an opportunity for doing good, and thus he proved himself faithful.

The same praise was given to the man with two talents as to his fellow servant with five. Their positions were very different; but their reward was the same. *Well done, thou good and faithful servant* was won and enjoyed by each of them. Is it not very sweet to think that though I may have only one talent, I shall not thereby be debarred from my Lord's praise? It is my faithfulness on which he will fix his eye, and not on the number of my talents. I may have made many mistakes and have confessed my faults with great grief, but he will commend me as he did the woman of whom he said, *She hath done what she could* (Mark 14:8).

It is better to be faithful in the infant school than to be unfaithful in a noble class of young men. It is better to be faithful in a small village of forty or sixty people than to be unfaithful in a great city church, with thousands perishing in consequence. It is better to be faithful in a cottage meeting, speaking of Christ crucified to fifty villagers, than to be unfaithful in a great building where thousands congregate. I pray you be faithful in laying out all that you are and have for God. As long as you live, whatever faults you have, be not halfhearted or double-minded, but be faithful in intent and desire. This is the point of the judge's praise – the servant's faithfulness.

This verdict was *given by sovereign grace.* The reward was not according to the work, for the servant had been *faithful over a few things,* but he was made *ruler over many things* (Matthew 25:23). The verdict itself is not in accordance with the rule of works, but according to the law of grace. Our good works are evidences of grace within us; our faithfulness, therefore, as servants, will be the evidence of our having a loving spirit towards our Master – evidence, therefore, that our heart is changed, and that we have been made to love him for whom once we had no affection.

Our works are the proof of our love, and therefore they stand as evidence of the grace of God. God first gives us grace, and then rewards us for it. He works in us, and then counts the fruit as our work. We work out our own salvation, because he *worketh in [us] both to will and to do of his good pleasure.* If he shall ever say "Well done" to you and to me, it will be because of his own rich grace, and not because of our merits. And, indeed, this is where we must all come and where we must all stay; for the idea that we have any personal merit will soon make us find fault with our Master and his service, as being stern and hard.

I have sometimes admired how men who have denied the doctrine of salvation by grace, as a matter of theology, have, nevertheless, admitted it in their devotions. They have entered into controversy against it, and yet unconsciously they have believed it. An extreme case is that of Cardinal Bellarmine, who was one of the most hard-core enemies of the Reformation, and a renowned antagonist of the teaching of Martin Luther. I will quote from one of his works (Inst. *De Justificatione, Lib. V. c. 1*). He says, in summing up, "On account of the uncertain nature of our own works and the danger of vainglory, it is the safest course to place our whole trust in the mercy and loving-kindness of God."

You have well said, O Cardinal; and since the safest course is that which we would choose, we will place our whole trust in the mercy and loving-kindness of God. It is reported, and I believe on excellent authority, that this great man, who had all his life long been crying up salvation by works, when dying, breathed a prayer in Latin, the translation of which would be something like this: "I beg God, who weighs not our merits, but graciously pardons our offenses, that he would receive me among his saints and his elect." *Is Saul also among the prophets?* (1 Samuel 10:12). Does Bellarmine at the end pray like a Calvinist? Such a case makes one hope that many others may be saved in an apostate church.

Thank God, many are a great deal better than their creed, and in their hearts believe what, as controversial theologians, they deny. However this may be, I know that if I am saved or rewarded it must be of grace alone, for I can have no other hope. As for those who have done much for the church, we know that they will disclaim all praise, saying, *Lord, when saw we thee an hungred, and fed thee? or thirsty, and gave thee drink?* (Matthew 25:37). All the Lord's faithful servants will sing, "Non nobis Domine." Not unto us. Not unto us.

Lastly, brethren, with what infinite delight will Jesus fill our hearts if, through divine grace, we are happy enough to hear him say, *Well done, thou good and faithful servant.* Oh, if we shall hold on to the end despite the temptations of Satan, and the weakness of our nature, and all the entanglements of the world, and keep our garments unspotted from the world, preaching Christ according to our measure of ability, and winning souls for him, what an honor it will be! What bliss for him to say, *Well done.* The music of these two words will have heaven in them to us. How different it will be from the verdict of our fellow man, who are often finding fault with this and that, though we do our best. We never could please them, but we have pleased our Lord.

Men were always misinterpreting our words and misjudging our motives, but he sets all things right by saying, *Well done.* Little will it matter, then, what all the rest have said: neither the flattering words of friends nor the harsh condemnations of enemies will have any weight with us when he says, *Well done.* Not with pride shall we receive that commendation; for we shall reckon ourselves even then to have been unprofitable servants. But oh, how we shall love him for setting such an estimate upon the cups of cold water we gave to his disciples, and the poor broken service we tried to render to him. What condescension to call that "well done" which we feel was so ill done!

I pray God's servants here, who this morning first began with searching themselves, and then went on to confess their imperfections, now will close by rejoicing in the fact that, if we are believing in Christ Jesus, and are really consecrated to him, we shall conclude this life and begin the next with that blessed verdict of *Well done*. Remember, however, that you are those who are doing all and are faithful. I hear some people speak against self-righteousness, to whom I would say, "You need not say much about that matter, for it does not concern you, since you have no righteousness to be proud of."

I hear persons speak against salvation by good works who are in no danger of falling into that error, since good works and their lives have long parted company. What I do admire is seeing a man like Paul, who lived for Jesus, and was ready to die for him, yet saying at the close of his life, *But what things were gain to me, those I counted loss for Christ. Yea doubtless, and I count all things but loss for the excellency of the knowledge of Christ Jesus my Lord: for whom I have suffered the loss of all things, and do count them but dung, that I may win Christ, and be found in him, not having mine own righteousness, which is of the law, but that which is through the faith of Christ, the righteousness which is of God by faith* (Philippians 3:7-9).

Go on, brothers, and think not of resting until your day's work is done. Serve God with all your might. Do more than the Pharisees, who hoped to be saved by their zeal. Do more than your brethren expect of you, and then, when you have done all, lay it at your Redeemer's feet with this confession: "I am an unprofitable servant." It is to those who blend faithfulness with humility, and enthusiasm with self-abasement that Jesus will say, *Well done, thou good and faithful servant: . . . enter thou into the joy of thy Lord.*

Chapter 12

The Two Talents

He also that had received two talents came and said, Lord,
thou deliveredst unto me two talents: behold, I have gained
two other talents beside them. His lord said unto him, Well
done, good and faithful servant; thou hast been faithful
over a few things, I will make thee ruler over many things:
enter thou into the joy of thy Lord. (Matthew 25:22-23)

*E*very good gift and every perfect gift is from above, and cometh down
from the Father of lights (James 1:17). All that men have they must
trace back to the Great Fountain, the Giver of all good. Do you have
talents? They were given to you by the God of talents. Do you have
time? Do you have wealth, influence, and power? Do you have powers
of tongue? Do you have powers of thought? Are you a poet, a states-
man, or a philosopher? Whatever be your position and whatever be
your gifts, remember that they are not yours, but they are loaned to
you from on high. No man has anything of his own, except his sins.
We are but tenants at will. God has put us into his estates, and he has
said, *Occupy till I come* (Luke 19:13).

Though our vineyards bear never so much fruit, yet the vineyards
belong to the King, and though we are to take the hundred for our hire,
yet King Solomon must have his thousand. All the honor of our ability
and the use of it must be unto God, because he is the Giver. The parable

tells us this very pointedly, for it makes every person acknowledge that his talents come from the Lord. Even the man who dug in the earth and hid his Lord's money did not deny that his talent belonged to his master; for though his reply, *Lo, there thou hast that is thine,* was exceedingly impertinent, yet it was not a denial of this fact. So that even this man was ahead of those who deny their obligations to God, who arrogantly toss their heads at the very mention of obedience to their Creator, and spend their time and their powers rather in rebellion against him than in his service. Oh, that we were all wise to believe and to act upon this most evident of all truths, that everything we have, we have received from the Most High.

Now, there are some men in the world who have but few talents. Our parable says, *Unto one he gave five talents, to another two* (Matthew 25:15). To them I shall address myself this morning; and I pray that the few pointed things I say may be blessed of God to their edification or rebuke. First, I shall notice *the fact that there are many persons who have but few talents,* and I will try to account for God's dispensing only few to them. Secondly, I shall remind them that *even for these few talents they must be brought to account.* And thirdly, I shall conclude by making the comforting observation that *if our few talents be rightly used, neither our own conscience nor our Master's judgment shall condemn us for not having more.*

First, then, God has made some men with few talents. You very often hear men speak of one another as if God had made no mental differences at all. One man finds himself successful, and he supposes that if everyone else could have been as industrious and as persevering as himself, then everyone would necessarily have been as successful. You will often hear remarks against ministers who are godly and earnest men, but who do not happen to have much attracting power, and they are called loafers and lazy persons, because they cannot make much of a stir in the world, whereas the reason may be that they have but little talent, and are making the best use of what they have, and therefore ought not to be rebuked for the littleness of what they are able to accomplish. It is a fact, which every man must see, that even in our birth there is a difference.

All children are not equally precocious, and all men certainly are not equally capable of learning or of teaching. God has made notable and marvelous differences. We are not to suppose that all the difference between a John Milton and a man who lives and dies without being able to read, has been caused by education. There was doubtless a difference originally, and though education will do much, it cannot do everything. Fertile ground, when well tilled, will necessarily bring forth more than the best-tilled estate, the soil of which is hard and sterile. God has made great and decided differences, and we ought, in dealing with our fellow man, to recollect this, lest we should say harsh things of those very men to whom God will afterwards say, *Well done, thou good and faithful servant.*

But why is it that God has not given to all men similar talents? My first answer shall be, because God is a sovereign, and of all attributes, next to his love, God is the most fond of displaying his sovereignty. The Lord God will have men know that he has a right to do what he wills with his own. Therefore it is, that in salvation he gives it to some and not to others; and his only reply to any accusation of injustice is, *Nay but, O man, who art thou that repliest against God? Shall the thing formed say to him that formed it, Why hast thou made me thus?* (Romans 9:20). The worm is not to murmur because God did not make it an angel, and the fish that swims the sea must not complain because it has not wings to fly into the highest heavens.

God had a right to make his creatures just what he pleased, and though men may dispute his right, he will hold and keep it pure against all comers. That he may hedge his right around it and make vain man acknowledge it, in all his gifts he continually reminds us of his sovereignty. "I will give to this man," he says, "a mind so acute that he shall pry into all secrets; I will make another so dull that none but the plainest elements of knowledge shall ever be attainable by him. I will give to one man such a wealth of imagination that he shall pile mountain upon mountain of imagery, until his language seems to reach to celestial majesty. I will give to another man a soul so dull, that he shall never be able to originate a poetic thought."

Why this, O God? The answer comes back: *Is it not lawful for me to do what I will with mine own?* (Matthew 20:15). So then, *for the children being not yet born, neither having done any good or evil, that the purpose of God according to election might stand* (Romans 9:11), it was written, *the elder shall serve the younger* (Genesis 25:23). And so it is written concerning men, that one of them shall be greater than another; one shall bow his neck, and the other put his foot upon it, for the Lord has a right to dispose of places and of gifts, of talents and of wealth, just as seems good in his sight.

Now, most men quarrel with this. But observe, the thing that you complain of in God, is the very thing that you love in yourselves. Every man likes to feel that he has a right to do with his own as he pleases. We all like to be little sovereigns. You will give your money freely and liberally to the poor; but if any man should brazenly urge that he had a claim upon your charity, would you give unto him? Certainly not; and who shall impeach the greatness of your generosity in so doing?

It is even as that parable that we have in one of the Gospels, where, after the men had toiled, some of them twelve hours, some of them six, and some of them but one, the Lord gave every man a penny. Oh! I would meekly bow my head and say, "My Lord, have you given me one talent? Then I bless you for it, and I pray you bestow upon me grace to use it rightly. Have you given to my brother ten talents? I thank you for the greatness of your kindness towards him; but I neither envy him, nor complain to you." Oh! for a spirit that bows always before the sovereignty of God.

Again, God gives to one five, and to another two talents, because the Creator is a lover of variety. It was said that order is heaven's first law; surely variety is the second, for in all God's works, there is the most beautiful diversity. Look towards the heavens at night: all the stars shine not with the same brilliance, nor are they placed in straight lines like the lamps of our streets. Then turn your eyes below: see in the vegetable world how many great distinctions there are, ranging from the cedar of Lebanon to the hyssop on the wall, or the moss that is smaller still. See how from the huge mammoth tree, that seems as if beneath its branches it might shade an army, down to the tiny lichen, God has made everything beautiful, but everything full of variety.

Look on any one tree, if you please: see how every leaf differs from its fellow – how even the little tiny buds that are at this hour bursting at the scent of the approaching perfume of spring differ from each other – no two of them are alike. Look again, upon the animated world: God has not made every creature like another. How wide the range – from the colossal elephant, to the coney that burrows in the rock – from the whale that makes the deep foam with its lashings, to the tiny minnow that skims the brook; God has made all things different, and we see variety everywhere. I doubt not that it is the same even in heaven, for in heaven there are *thrones, [and] dominions, [and] principalities, [and] powers* (Colossians 1:16) – different ranks of angels, perhaps, rising tier upon tier.

One star differeth from another star in glory (1 Corinthians 15:41). And why should not the same rule stand firm in manhood? Does God cast us all in the same mold? It seems not so, for he has not made our faces alike; no two countenances can be said to be exactly the same, for if there be some likeness, yet there is a manifest diversity. Should minds, then, be alike? Should souls all be cast in the same fashion? Should God's creation dwindle down into a great factory in which everything is melted in the same fire and poured into the same mold? No, for variety's sake, he will have one man a renowned David, and another David's unknown armor-bearer; he will have one man a Jeremiah, who shall prophesy, and another a Baruch, who shall only read the prophecy; one shall be rich as the rich man in the parable, another poor as Lazarus; one shall speak with a voice as loud as thunder, another shall be dumb; one shall be mighty in word and doctrine, another shall be feeble of speech and slow in words. God will have variety, and the day will come when, looking down upon the world, we shall see the beauty of its history to be mightily indebted to the variety of the characters that entered into it.

But let us go a little further. God has a deeper reason than this. God gives to some men only a few talents because he has many small spheres, and he desires to have these filled. There is a great ocean, and it needs inhabitants. O Lord, you have made Leviathan to swim therein. There is a secret grotto, a hidden cavern, far away in the depths of the sea, and its entrance is small; if there were nothing but a Leviathan, it would remain unoccupied by a tenant forever; but a little fish is made, and that small place becomes an ocean unto it. There are a thousand sprays and twigs upon the trees of the forest; if all were eagles, how would the forests be made glad with song, and how could each twig bear its songster? But because God would have each twig have its own music, he has made the little songster to sit upon it.

Each sphere must have the creature to occupy it adapted to the size of the sphere. God always acts economically. Does he intend a man to be the pastor of some small church with four or five hundred inhabitants? Of what use is it in giving to that man the abilities of an apostle? Does he intend a woman to be a humble teacher of her own children at home, a quiet trainer of her own family? Would it not even disturb her and injure her if God should make her a poetess, and give her gifts that might electrify a nation? The littleness of her talents will to a degree fit her for the littleness of her sphere.

There is some youth who is quite capable of assisting in a ragged school (a free school for destitute children). Perhaps if he had a higher genius he might disdain the work, and so the ragged school would be without its excellent teacher. There are little spheres, and God will have little men to occupy them. There are posts of important duty, and men shall be found with nerve and muscle fitted for the labor. He has made a statue for every niche, and a picture for every portion of the gallery; none shall be left vacant. But since some niches are small, so shall be the statuettes that occupy them. To some he gives two talents, because two are enough, and five would be too many.

Once more, God gives to men two talents, because in them very often he displays the greatness of his grace in saving souls. You have heard of a minister who was deeply read in sacred lore; his wisdom was profound, and his speech graceful. Under his preaching many were converted. Have you never heard it not quite said, but almost hinted, that much of his success was traceable to his learning and to his graceful oratory? But, on the other hand, you have met with a man, rough in his dialect, uncouth in his manners, evidently without any great literary attainments. Nevertheless, God has given that man the one talent of an earnest heart; he speaks like a son of thunder; with rough, stern language he denounces sin and proclaims the gospel; and under him hundreds are converted.

The world sneers at him. "I can see no reason for all this," says the scholar. "It is all rubbish – jargon; the man knows nothing." The critic takes up his pen, dips it in the bitterest ink he can find, and writes a most delightful history of the man, in which he goes so far as to say, not that he sees horns on his head, but almost everything but that. He is everything that is bad, and nothing that is good. He utterly denounces him. He is foolish, he is vain, he is wretched, he is proud, he is illiterate, he is vulgar. There was no word in the English language that was bad enough for him, but one must be coined.

And now what says the church? What says the man himself? "Even so, O Lord, now must the glory be unto you forever, inasmuch as you have chosen the wretched things of this world, and the *things which are not, to bring to nought things that are*" (1 Corinthians 1:28). So it seems that out of the little, God sometimes wins more glory than he does out of the great; and I doubt not that he has made some of you with little power to do good, with little influence, and with a narrow sphere, so that he may, in the last great day, manifest to angels how much he can do in a little space. You know, dear friends, there are two things that always will attract our attention: one is skill embodied in a stupendous mass.

We see the huge ship, the *Leviathan,* and we wonder that man could have made it. At another time we see an elegant piece of workmanship that will stand upon less than a square inch, and we say, "Well, I can understand how men can make a great ship, but I cannot comprehend how an artist could have the patience and the skill to make so minute a thing as this." And ah! my friends, it seems to me that God is not a greater God to our understanding, when we see the boundless fields of the heavens and the unnumbered orbs swimming therein, than when we see a humble person living in a cottage, and behold God's perfect Word carried out in her soul, and God's highest glory effected from her little talent. Surely if in the little, man can honor himself as well as in the great, then the Infinite, and the Eternal, can most of all glorify himself when he stoops to the littlenesses of mankind.

Our second proposition was that even a few talents must be accounted for. We are very apt when we think of the day of judgment, to imagine that certain characters will undergo a more severe process than others. I know I have often involuntarily said, when reading the history of Napoleon, "Here is a man of tremendous ability, the world's master. A dozen centuries might be required to produce such another man; but here is a man who prostitutes all his ability to ambition, carries his armies like a destroying deluge across every country, makes widows of wives, and renders children fatherless, not by hundreds but by thousands, if not by millions. What must be his solemn account when he stands before the throne of God? Shall not the witnesses rise up from the fields of Spain, of Russia, of Italy, of Egypt, and of Palestine, and accuse the man who, to gratify his own bold ambition, led them to death?" But will you please remember that though Napoleon must be a prisoner at the bar, each of us must stand there also. And though our position is not very high, and we have not stood upon the pinnacle of fame, yet we have stood quite high enough to be borne under the observation of the Most High, and we have had just ability enough and power enough to have done mischief in the world, and to be accountable for it.

"Oh!" said one, "I thought that surely in the day of judgment he would pass me by. I have been no Tom Paine; I have not been a leader among low and vulgar infidels; I have been no murderer; I have not been a prince among sinners; I have not been a disturber of the public peace. What few sins I have committed have taken place quietly; nobody has heard of them; I don't think my bad example has gone far; perhaps my children have not been much blessed by my behavior, but, nevertheless, mine has been a very small amount of mischief, too small to have poisoned anyone besides myself. I have been, on the whole, so tolerably moral that though I cannot say I have served God, yet my failures in veering from the path of duty have been slight indeed!"

Ah! truly friends! you may think yourselves never so little, but your making yourselves insignificant will not excuse you. You have had but little entrusted to you! Then the less trouble it is for you to make use of your talents. The man who has many talents requires much hard labor to use them all. He might make the excuse that he found five talents too many to put out in the market at once; you have only one; anybody can lend out his one talent to interest – it will cost you but little trouble to apply that. And inasmuch as you live, and inasmuch as you die, without having improved the one talent, your guilt will be exceedingly increased by the very fact that your talent was only little, and, consequently, the trouble of using it would have been only little too.

If you had only little, God required only little of you; why, then, did you not render that? If any man holds a house at a rental price of a pound a year, let it be never so small a house for the money; for if he brings not his rent, then there is not one-half the excuse for him that there would be if his rent had been a hundred pounds, and he had failed to bring it. You shall be the more inexcusable on account of the little that was required of you. Let me, then, address you, and remind you that you must be brought to account.

Remember, my friend, that in the day of judgment your account must be personal; God will not ask you what your church did – he will ask you what you did yourself. Now there is a Sunday school. If God should try all members of the church in a body, they would each of them say, "O Lord, as a body we had an excellent Sunday school, and had many teachers," and so they would excuse themselves. But no; one by one, all professing Christians must come before him. "What did you do for the Sunday school? I gave you a gift for teaching children – what did you do?" "O Lord, there was a Sunday school." That has nothing to do with it. What did *you* do? You are not to account now for the company with which you were united, but for yourself as an individual.

"O," says one, "there were a number of poor ministers; I was at the Surrey Hall, and so much was done for them." No, what did *you* do? You must be held personally responsible for your own wealth, for your own ability. "Well," says one, "I am happy to say there is a great deal more preaching now than there used to be; the churches seem to be roused." Yes sir, and you seem to take part of the credit to yourself. Do *you* preach more than you used to? You are a minister; do *you* make any greater efforts? Remember, it is not what your brethren are doing, but it is what *you* do that you will be called to account for at the bar of God; and each one of you will be asked this question: "What have you done with *your* talent?" All your connection with churches will profit you nothing; it is your personal doings – your personal service towards God that is demanded of you as an evidence of saving grace. And if others are idle – if others pay not God his due – so much the more reason why you should have been more exceedingly diligent in doing so yourself.

Recollect, again, that your account will have to be particular. God will go into all the items of it. At the day of judgment you will not have to cast up a hurried account in the sum, but every item shall be read. Can you prove that? Yes. *That every idle word that men shall speak, they shall give account thereof in the day of judgment* (Matthew 12:36). Now, it is in the items that men go astray. "Well," says one, "if I look at my life in the bulk, I am not very much ashamed; but it is those items, those little items – they are the troublesome part of the account that one does not care to meddle with." Do you know that all of yesterday was made up of littles? And the things of today are all little, and what you do tomorrow will all be little things?

Just as the tiny shells make up the gray limestone hills, and the gray limestone hills together make up the range, so the trifling actions make up the whole account, and each of these must be pulled asunder separately. You had an hour to spare the other day – what did you do? You had a voice – how did you use it? You had a pen – you could use that – how did you employ it? Each particular shall be brought out, and there shall be demanded an account for each one. Oh, that you were wise, that you did not insult this matter, but would take every note in the music of your behavior, and seek to make each note in harmony with its fellow, lest, after all, the psalm of your life may prove to be a hideous discord. Oh, that you who are without God would remember that your life is assuredly such that the trial of the last great day must end in your condemnation.

Again, that account will be very exact, and there will be no getting off without those little things. "Oh! they were a few slight offenses and very small matters indeed; I never took stock of them at all." But they will all be taken stock of then. When God comes to look into our hearts at last, he will not only look at the great but also at the little; everything will be seen into, the pence sins as well as the pound iniquities – all must be brought against us, and an exact account given.

Again, remember, in the last place, upon this point, that the account will be very impartial at the day of judgment, when all will be tried without any reference to their position. The prince will be summoned to give an account of his talents, and side by side must stand his member of the royal court and his slave. The mightiest emperor must stand at God's bar, as well as the lowliest one who inhabits a cottage. All must appear and be tried according to the deeds they have done in the body. As to our professions, they will profit us nothing. We may have been the proudest hypocrites that ever made the world sick with our pride, but we must be searched and examined as much as if we had been the vilest sinners.

We must take our own trial before God's eternal tribunal, and nothing can bias our judge, or make him give an opinion for or against us, apart from the evidence. Oh, how solemn this will make the trial, especially if we have no blood of Christ to plead! The great Advocate will get his people an acquittal, through his credited merits, even though their sin in itself would condemn them. But remember that without him we shall never be able to stand the fiery ordeal of that last dread judicial inquest. "Well," said an old preacher, "when the law was given, Sinai was all in smoke, and it melted like wax; but when the punishment of the law is given, the whole earth will quake and cower. For who shall be able to endure the day of the Lord, the day of God's fierce anger?"

The last point is this: if by divine grace – and it is only by divine grace that this can ever be accomplished – our two talents be rightly used, the fact that we had not five will be no injury to us.

You say, when such a man dies, who stood in the midst of the church, a triumphant warrior for the truth, that the angels will crowd to heaven's gates to see him, for he has been a mighty hero, and has done much for his Master. A Calvin or a Luther, with what acclamations shall they be received! – men with talents, who have been faithful to their trust. Yes, but do you not know that there is many a humble village pastor whose flock scarcely numbers fifty, who toils for them as for his life, who spends hours in praying for their welfare, who uses all the little ability he has in his endeavor to win them to Christ; and do you imagine that his entry into heaven shall be less triumphant than the entry of such a man as Luther? If so, you do not know how God deals with his people.

He gives them rewards, not according to the greatness of the goods with which they were entrusted, but according to their fidelity thereto; and he that has been faithful to the least, shall be as much rewarded as he that has been faithful in much. I want you briefly to turn to the chapter to see this. You will note, first, that the man with two talents came to his lord with as great a confidence as the man who had five. He said, *Lord, thou deliveredst unto me two talents: behold, I have gained two other talents beside them.* I will be bound to say, that while that poor man with the two talents was trading with them, he frequently looked upon his neighbor with the five talents and said, "Oh, I wish I could do as much as he is doing! See now, he has five talents to put out, and how much interest he has coming every year. Oh, that I could do as much!"

And as he went on, he often prayed, "O my Lord, give me greater ability, and greater grace to serve you, for I long to do more." And when he sat down to read his diary, he thought, "Ah, this diary does not tell much. There is no account of my journey through fifty counties; I cannot tell how I have traveled from land to land, as Paul did, to preach the truth. No, I have just had to continue in this church, and been pretty well starved to death, toiling for this people, and if I have added some ten or a dozen to the church, that has meant a very great deal to me. Why, I hear that Mr. So-and-so was privileged to add two or three hundred in a year; oh, that I could do that! Surely when I go to heaven, I shall creep in at the door somehow, while he by grace will be enabled to go boldly in, bringing his sheaves with him."

Now stop, poor Little-faith, stop; your Master will not deal so with you. When you shall come to die, you will through his grace feel as much confidence in dying with your two well-used talents as your brother with his ten, for you will, when you come there, have your Lord's sweet presence, and you will say, "I am complete in Christ. Christ's righteousness covers me from head to foot, and now in looking back upon my past life, I can say, Blessed be his holy name. It is little that I could do, but I have done as much as I could for him. I know that he will pardon my defects, and forgive my incompetent management, and I shall never look back upon my humble village charge without much joy that the Lord allowed me to labor there." And oh, it seems to me that that man will have even a richer commendation in his own conscience than the man who has been more publicly applauded, for he can say to himself, after putting all his trust in Christ, "Well, I am sure I did not do this for fame, for I blushed unseen – I have lost my sweetness on the desert air. No one has ever read my deeds; what I did was between myself and my God, and I can render up my account to him and say, 'Lord, I did it for you, and not to honor myself.'"

Yes, friends, I might tell you now of many a score of earnest evangelists in this our land who are working harder than any one of us, and yet win far less honor. Yes, and I could bring up to you many a score of city missionaries whose toil for Christ is beyond all measure of praise, who never get much reward here; no, instead they meet with insults and disrespect. You see the poor man start as soon as he goes from his place of worship today. He has got three hours this afternoon to go and spend among the sick, and then you will see him on Monday morning. He has to go from house to house, often with the door slammed in his face, often exposed to mobs and drunken men, sometimes jeered and scoffed at, meeting with persons of all religious persuasions and of no persuasion.

He toils on. He has his little evening meeting, and there he gets a little flock together and tries to pray with them, and he gets now and then a man or a woman converted; but he has no honor. He just takes him off to the minister, and he says, "Sir, here is a good man; I think he is convicted. Will you baptize him and receive him into your church?" The minister gets all the credit for that, but as for the poor city missionary, there is little or nothing said of him.

There is, perhaps, just his name, Mr. Brown, or Mr. Smith, mentioned sometimes in the report, but people do not think much of him, except, perhaps, as an object of charity they have to keep; whereas he is the man that gives them the charity, giving all the sap and blood and marrow of his life for some poor sixty pounds a year, hardly enough to keep his family above need. But he, when he dies, my friend, shall have no less the approval of his conscience than the man who was permitted to stand before the multitudes and raised the nation into excitement on account of religion. He shall come before the master clothed in the righteousness of Christ, and with unblushing face shall say, "I have received two talents; I have gained beside them two talents more."

Furthermore, and to conclude, you will notice there was no difference in his master's commendation – none in the reward. In both cases, it was, *Well done, good and faithful servant; thou hast been faithful over a few things, I will make thee ruler over many things: enter thou into the joy of thy Lord.* Here comes Whitfield, the man that stood before twenty thousand at a time to preach the gospel, who in England, Scotland, Ireland, and America has testified the truth of God, and who could count his converts by thousands, even under one sermon!

Here he comes, the man that endured persecution and scorn, and yet was not moved – the man of whom the world was not worthy, who lived for his fellow man, and died at last for their cause. Stand by angels and admire, while the Master takes him by the hand and says, "Well done, well done, good and faithful servant; enter thou into the joy of thy Lord!"

See how free grace honors the man whom it enabled to do valiantly. Hark! Who is this that comes there? A poor thin-looking creature that on earth had tuberculosis; there was a hectic flush now and then upon her cheek, and she lay three long years upon her bed of sickness. Was she a prince's daughter, for it seems heaven is making much stir about her? No, she was a poor girl that earned her living by her needle, and she worked herself to death! Stitch, stitch, stitch, from morning to night! And here she comes.

She went prematurely to her grave, but she is coming, like a shock of wheat fully ripe, into heaven; and her Master says, *Well done, thou good and faithful servant: thou hast been faithful over a few things, I will make thee ruler over many things: enter thou into the joy of thy Lord.* She takes her place by the side of Whitfield. Ask what she ever did, and you find out that she used to live in some back attic down some dark alley in London; and there used to be another poor girl who would come to work with her, and that poor girl, when she first came to work with her, was an animated and lively creature, and this tuberculosis-ridden child told her about Christ; and when she was well enough, they used to creep out on an evening to go to chapel or to church together.

It was hard at first to get the other one to go, but she used to press her lovingly; and when the girl went wild a little, she never gave her up. She used to say, "O Jane, I wish you loved the Savior"; and when Jane was not there, she used to pray for her, and when she was there, she prayed with her; and now and then when she was stitching away, she read a page out of the Bible to her, for poor Jane could not read. And with many tears she tried to tell her about the Savior who loved her and gave himself for her. At last, after many a day of hard persuasion, and many an hour of sad disappointment, and many a night of sleepless, tearful prayer, at last she lived to see the girl profess her love for Christ; and she left her and got sick, and there she lay until she was taken to the hospital, where she died.

When she was in the hospital, she used to have a few tracts, and she used to give them to those who came to see her; she would try, if she could, to get the women to come around, and she would give them a tract. When she first went into the hospital, if she could creep out of bed, she used to get by the side of one who was dying, and the nurse used to let her do it, until at last she got too ill. Then she used to ask a poor woman on the other side of the ward, who was getting better, and was going out, if she would come and read a chapter to her; not that she wanted her to read to her on her own account, but for her sake, for she thought it might strike her heart while she was reading it. At last this poor girl died and fell asleep in Jesus; and the poor tuberculosis-ridden needle woman had said to her, *Well done* – and what more could an archangel have said to her? – *she hath done what she could.*

See, then, the Master's commendation, and the last reward will be equal to all men who have used their talents well. Ah! if there be degrees in glory, they will not be distributed according to our talents, but according to our faithfulness in using them. As to whether there are degrees or not, I know not; but this I know, he that does his Lord's will shall have it said to him, *Well done, good and faithful servant.*

And now, friends, this one word only. I have told you that there are many in our denomination who are preaching the gospel continually. I could bring a few of the letters, written by the poor ministers, to us to read, but sometimes I think this a violation of delicacy, and I do not like to do it. But when I did that one year, the collection was almost twice as good; so I think I might almost commit a breach of etiquette in order to help them. However, I can solemnly assure you, that if there is poverty anywhere, it is to be found among the ministers in the Baptist churches, and I am sorry to say that one cause of it is the fault of the people themselves; they are so little in the habit of giving, that their ministers are starved.

Now, if Christ will say "Well done" in the hereafter to many a humble preacher, do you think he intends the church to starve them while they are here on thirty or forty pounds a year? Now, brethren, if Christ will say "Well done" at the last day, we may anticipate his verdict, and say, "Well done today." And can we better say "Well done" than by unmuzzling the ox that treads out the wheat, and give these poor ministers something out of our own wealth, as God may help us, that their necessities may be supplied? There will be pretty well a score of persons who will be dependent during the next year upon what you give this year; perhaps you will remember that and assist them. One kind gentleman, who usually comes here, says, "I could not come today, so I forward my pound to be put into the box by the minister." And I trust, if there are any not here today who will be here next Sunday, that they will not forget this collection. It is always very dear to the heart of my church.

Chapter 13

The Reward of the Righteous

When the Son of man shall come in his glory, and all the holy angels with him, then shall he sit upon the throne of his glory: and before him shall be gathered all nations: and he shall separate them one from another, as a shepherd divideth his sheep from the goats: and he shall set the sheep on his right hand, but the goats on the left. Then shall the King say unto them on his right hand, Come, ye blessed of my Father, inherit the kingdom prepared for you from the foundation of the world: for I was an hungred, and ye gave me meat: I was thirsty, and ye gave me drink: I was a stranger, and ye took me in: naked, and ye clothed me: I was sick, and ye visited me: I was in prison, and ye came unto me. (Matthew 25:31-36)

It is exceedingly beneficial to our souls to mount above this present evil world to something nobler and better. The cares of this world and the deceitfulness of riches are apt to choke everything good within us, and we grow fretful, despondent, perhaps proud, and carnal. It is well for us to cut down these thorns and briars, for heavenly seed sown among them is not likely to yield a harvest, and I do not know a better sickle with which to cut them down than thoughts of the kingdom to come.

In the valleys in Switzerland many of the inhabitants are deformed and dwarfish, and the whole of them wear a sickly appearance, for the atmosphere is charged with miasma, and is close and stagnant; you cross the valleys as rapidly as you can, and are glad to escape from them. Up yonder on the mountain you will find a hardy race who breathes the clear, fresh air as it blows from the virgin snows of the Alpine summits. It would be well for their frames if the dwellers in the valley could frequently leave their abodes among the marshes and the fever mists and get themselves up into the clear atmosphere above. It is to such an exploit of climbing that I invite you this morning.

May the Spirit of God bear us as upon eagles' wings, that we may leave the mists of fear and the fevers of anxiety, and all the ills which gather in this valley of earth, and get ourselves up to the mountains of future joy and blessedness where it is to be our delight to dwell world without end! Oh, may God disentangle us now for a little while, cut the cords that keep us here below, and permit us to mount! We sit, some of us, like chained eagles fastened to the rock, except that unlike the eagle, we begin to love our chain, and would, perhaps, if it came really to the test, hate to have it snapped. May God now grant us grace if we cannot at once escape from the chain of mortal life as to our bodies, yet to do so as to our spirits; and leaving the body like a servant at the foot of the hill, may our soul, like Abraham, go to the top of the mountain, and there may we have communion with the Most High.

While expounding my text, I shall ask for your attention this morning, first, *to the circumstances which surround the rewarding of the righteous;* secondly, *to their portion;* and thirdly, *to the persons themselves.*

There is much teaching in the surrounding circumstances.

We read: *When the Son of man shall come in his glory.* It appears, then, that we must not expect to receive our reward until by-and-by. Like the hireling we must fulfill our day, and then at evening we shall have our penny. Too many Christians look for a present reward for their labors, and if they meet with success, they begin doting upon it as though they had received their recompense. Like the disciples who returned saying, *Lord, even the devils are subject unto us* (Luke 10:17), they rejoice too exclusively in present prosperity; whereas the Master bade them not to look upon miraculous success as being their reward, since that might not always be the case. "Nevertheless," said he, "rejoice not in this, *but rather rejoice, because your names are written in heaven*" (Luke 10:20).

Success in the ministry is not the Christian minister's true reward: it is a pledge, but the wages still wait. The praise of your fellow man you must not look upon as being the reward of excellence, for often you will meet with the reverse; you will find your best actions misconstrued, and your motives ill interpreted. If you are looking for your reward *here,* I may warn you of the apostle's words: *If in this life only we have hope . . . we are of all men most miserable* (1 Corinthians 15:19), because other men get their reward; even the Pharisee gets his: *Verily, I say unto you, they have their reward* (Matthew 6:2); but we have none here. To be despised and rejected of men is the Christian's lot. Among his fellow Christians he will not always stand in good repute.

It is not unmitigated kindness nor unmingled love that we receive even from the saints. I tell you that if you look for your reward to Christ's bride herself, you will miss it; if you expect to receive your crown from the hand even of your brethren in the ministry who know your labors, and who ought to sympathize with your trials, you will be mistaken. *When the Son of man shall come in his glory,* then is your time of recompense; but not today, nor tomorrow, nor at any other time in this world. Reckon nothing which you acquire, no honor which you gain, to be the reward of your service to your Master; that is reserved for the time *when the Son of man shall come in his glory.*

Observe with delight the dignified person by whose hand the reward is given. It is written, *When the **Son of man** shall come* (emphasis added). Brethren, we love the King's courtiers; we delight to be numbered with them ourselves. It is no ordinary thing to do service to him whose head "though once 'twas crowned with thorns, is crowned with glory now." But it is a delightful thought that the service of rewarding us will not be left to the courtiers. The angels will be there, and the brethren of the King will be there; but heaven was not prepared by them, nor can it be given by them. Their hands shall not yield us a coronation; we shall join their songs, but their songs would be no reward for us. We shall bow with them and they with us, but it will not be possible for them to give us the recompense of the reward – that starry crown is all too weighty for an angel's hand to bring, and the benediction all too sweet to be pronounced even by angelic lips.

The King himself must say, *Well done, good and faithful servant.*

What say you to this, my dear brother? You have felt a temptation to look to God's servants, to the approval of the minister, to the kindly look of parents, to the word of commendation from your fellow worker; all these you value, and I do not blame you; but these may fail you, and therefore never consider them as being *the* reward. You must wait until the time when the King comes, and then it will neither be your brethren, your pastors, your parents, nor your helpers, but the King himself who shall say to you, *Come, ye blessed.* How this sweetens heaven! It will be Christ's own gift. How this makes the benediction doubly blessed! It shall come from his lips, which drop like myrrh and flow with honey. Beloved, it is Christ who became a curse for us, who shall give the blessing to us. Roll this as a sweet morsel under your tongues.

The character in which our Lord Jesus shall appear is significant. Jesus will then be revealed as truly "the King." *When the [King] shall come.* It was to him as King that the service was rendered, and it is from him as King that the reward must therefore come; and so upon the very threshold a question of self-examination arises: "The King will not reward the servants of another prince – am I therefore his servant? Is it my joy to wait at the threshold of his gates, and sit like Mordecai at the courts of Ahasuerus – at the entrance of his door? Say, soul, do you serve *the* King?"

I mean not the kings and queens of earth; let them have loyal servants for their subjects; but saints are servants of the Lord Jesus Christ, the King of Kings – are you so? If you be not so, then when the King comes in his glory, there can be no reward for you. I long in my own heart to recognize Christ's kingly office more than I have ever done. It has been my delight to preach to you Christ dying on the cross, and *God forbid that I should glory, save in the cross;* but I want for my own self to realize him on his throne, reigning in my heart, having a right to do as he wills with me, so that I may get to the condition of Abraham, who, when God spoke, though it was to tell him to offer up his own Isaac, never asked a question, but simply said, *Here am I* (Genesis 22:11). Beloved, seek to know and feel the controlling power of the King, or else when he comes, since you have not known him as King, he cannot know you as servant; and it is only to the servant that the King can give the reward which is spoken of in the text – *When the [King] shall come.*

Now I move on. *When the [King] shall come in his **glory*** (emphasis added). The fullness of that it is impossible to conceive.

> Imagination's utmost stretch,
>   In wonder dies away.

But this we know – and it is the sweetest thing we can know – that if we have been partakers with Jesus in his shame, we also shall be sharers with him in the luster which shall surround him. Are you, beloved, one with Christ Jesus? Are you of his flesh and of his bones? Does a vital union knit you to him? Then you are today with him in his shame; you have taken up his cross, and gone with him outside the camp bearing his reproach; you shall doubtless be with him when the cross is exchanged for the crown. But judge yourself this morning; if you are not with him in the regeneration, neither shall you be with him when he shall come in his glory.

If you start back from the black side of Communion, you shall not understand its bright, its happy period, when the King shall come in his glory and all his holy angels with him. What, are angels with him? And yet he did not take up angels, he took up the seed of Abraham. Are the holy angels with him? Come, my soul, then you cannot be far from him. If his friends and his neighbors are called together to see his glory, what do you think if you are married to him? Shall you be distant? Though it be a day of judgment, yet you cannot be far from that heart, which having admitted angels into intimacy, has admitted you into union.

Has he not said to you, O my soul, "I have betrothed you unto me in faithfulness, and in judgment, and in righteousness"? Have not his own lips said it: "I am married unto you, and my delight is in you"? Then if the angels, who are but the friends and the neighbors, shall be with him, it is abundantly certain that his own beloved Hephzibah, in whom is all his delight, shall be near to him and shall be a partaker of his splendor.

It is when he comes in his glory, and when his communion with angels shall be distinctly recognized, that his unity with his church shall become apparent. *Then shall he sit upon the throne of his glory.* Here is a repetition of the same reason why it should be your time and my time to receive the reward from Christ if we be found among his faithful servants. When *he* sits upon his throne, it would not be fitting that his own beloved ones should be in the mire. When he was in the place of shame, they were with him, and now that he is on the throne of gold, they must be with him too. There would be no oneness – union with Christ would be a mere matter of talk – if it were not certain that when he is on the throne, they shall be upon the throne too.

But I want you to notice one particular circumstance with regard to the time of the reward. It is *when he shall have divided the sheep from the goats.* My reward, if I be a child of God, cannot come to me while I am in union with the wicked. Even on earth you will have the most enjoyment of Christ when you are most separated from this world. Rest assured, although the separated path does not seem an easy one, and it will certainly impose upon you persecution and the loss of many friends, yet it is the happiest walking in the world.

You conforming Christians who can enter into the world's mirth to a certain degree, you cannot, you never can, know as you now are, the inward joys of those who live in lonely but lovely fellowship with Jesus. The nearer you get to the world, the further you must be from Christ; and I believe the more thoroughly a bill of divorce is given by your spirit to every earthly object upon which your soul can set itself, the more close will be your communion with your Lord. *Forget also thine own people, and thy father's house; so shall the king greatly desire thy beauty: for he is thy Lord; and worship thou him* (Psalm 45:10-11).

It is significant that not until the King has separated the sheep from the goats does he say, *Come, ye blessed;* and though the righteous will have enjoyed a gladness as disembodied spirits, yet as risen from the grave in their bodies, their gladness is not fully accomplished until the Great Shepherd shall have appeared to separate them once and for all by a great gulf which cannot be passed, from all association with the nations that forget God. Now then, beloved, these circumstances all put together come to this, that the reward of following Christ is not today, is not among the sons of men, is not from men, is not even from the excellent ones of the earth, is not even bestowed by Jesus while we are here; but the glorious crown of life which the Lord's grace shall give to his people is reserved for the second advent, *when the [King] shall come in his glory, and all his holy angels with him.* Wait with patience, wait with joyful expectation, for he shall come, and blessed be the day of his appearing.

We have now to turn to the second point – the portion itself. Every word is suggestive. I shall not attempt to exhaust, but merely to glance at all. The reward of the righteous is set forth by the loving benediction pronounced to them by the Master, but *their very position* gives some foreshadowing of it. He put the sheep on his right hand. Heaven is a position of the most elevated dignity authoritatively conferred, and of divine complacency manifestly enjoyed. God's saints are always at his right hand according to the judgment of faith, but hereafter it shall be more clearly manifested. God is pleased to be close to his people, and to place them near to himself in a place of protection.

Sometimes it seems as if they were at the left hand; they certainly have, some of them, less comfort than the worldlings. *I have seen the wicked in great power, and spreading himself like a green bay tree* (Psalm 37:35); their eyes stand out with fatness, and they have more than a heart could wish; whereas his people are often made to drink waters of a full cup, and their meat and their drink are bittered with wormwood and gall. The world is upside down now; the gospel has begun to turn it the right way uppermost, but when the day of grace is over, and the day of glory comes, then shall it be righted indeed; then those that wandered about in sheepskins and goatskins shall be clothed in glittering apparel, being transfigured like the Savior upon Tabor. Then those of whom the world was not worthy shall come to a world that shall be worthy of them. Then those who were hurried to the stake and to the flames shall triumph with chariots of fire and horses of fire, and swell the splendor of the Master's pompous appearing.

Yes, beloved, you shall eternally be the object of divine complacency, not in secret and unmanifested communion, but your state and glory shall be revealed before the sons of men. Your persecutors shall gnash their teeth when they see you occupying places of honor at his right hand, and themselves, though greater far than you on earth, will be condemned to take the lowest room. How shall the rich man bite his fire-tormented tongue in vain as he sees Lazarus, the beggar on the dunghill, made to sit at the right hand of the King eternal and immortal!

Heaven is a place of dignity. "There we shall be as the angels," says one, but I know we shall be even superior than they. Is it not written of him who in all things is our representative, *Thou hast put all things under his feet* (Psalm 8:6)? Even the very seraphs themselves so richly blessed, what are they but *ministering spirits, sent forth to minister for them who shall be heirs of salvation?* (Hebrews 1:14).

But now turning to the welcome uttered by the judge, the first word is *Come.* It is the gospel symbol. The law said "Go"; the gospel says "Come." The Spirit says it in invitation; the bride says it in intercession; *let him that heareth* say it by constantly, laboriously endeavoring to spread abroad the good news. Since Jesus says *Come,* we learn that the very essence of heaven is communion. "Come!" You came near enough to say, "Lord, we believe, help our unbelief!" On the cross you looked to me and were lightened. You had fellowship with me in bearing my cross. You filled up that which was behind of the sufferings of Christ for his body's sake, which is the church.

Still come! Ever come! Forever come! Come up from your graves, you risen ones! Come up from among the ungodly, you consecrated ones! Come up from where you cast yourselves down in your humiliation before the great white throne! Come up to wear my crown and sit with me upon my throne! Oh, that word has heaven lurking within it. It shall be to you your joy forever to hear the Savior say to you, *Come.* I protest before you that my soul has sometimes been so full of joy that I could hold no more when my beloved Lord has said "Come" to my soul; for he has taken me into his banqueting house, and his love banner has waved over my head, and he has taken me away from the world, and its cares and its fears, and its trials and its joys, up to *the top of Amana, from the top of Shenir and Hermon* (Song of Solomon 4:8), where he manifested himself to me.

When this "Come" shall come into your ear from the Master's lips, there shall not be the flesh to drag you back; there shall be no sluggishness of spirit, no heaviness of heart. You shall come eternally then; you shall not mount to descend again, but mount on and on in one blessed Excelsior forever and forever. The first word indicates that heaven is a state of communion – *Come.*

Then it is *Come, ye blessed,* which is a clear declaration that this is a state of happiness. They cannot be more blessed than they are. They have their hearts' desire, and though their hearts have been enlarged and their desires have been expanded by entering into the Infinite, and getting rid of the cramping influences of corruption and of time, yet even when their desire shall know no bounds, they shall have all the happiness that the utmost stretch of their souls can by any possibility conceive.

This much, and this is all we know – they are supremely blessed. Their blessedness you perceive does not come from any secondary joy, but from the great primary Source of all good. *Come, ye blessed of my Father.* They drink the unadulterated wine at the winepress itself, where it joyously leaps from the bursting clusters; they pluck celestial fruits from the unwithering boughs of the immortal tree; they shall sit at the wellhead and drink the waters as they spring with unrivaled freshness from the depths of the heart of the Deity. They shall not be basking in the beams of the sun, but they shall be like Uriel, the angel in the sun; they shall dwell in God, and so their souls shall be satisfied with favor, and full and more than full with his presence and benediction.

Notice, once again, that according to the words used, it is a state where they shall recognize their right to be there; a state therefore of perfect freedom, and ease, and fearlessness. It is – *inherit the kingdom.* A man does not fear to lose that which he wins by lineage from his parent. If heaven had been the subject of earning, we might have feared that our merits had not really deserved it, and therefore suspected that one day a Writ of Error would be issued and that we would be ejected. But we do know whose sons we are; we know whose love it is that makes glad our spirits, and when we "inherit" the kingdom, we shall enter it not as strangers or as foreigners, but as sons coming to their birthright.

Looking over all its streets of gold and surveying all its walls of pearl, we shall feel that we are at home in our own house, and have an actual right, not through merit but through grace, to everything that is there. It will be a state of heavenly bliss; the Christian shall feel that law and justice are on his side, and that those stern attributes have brought him there as well as mercy and loving-kindness. But the word *inherit* here implies full possession and enjoyment. They have inherited in a certain sense before; but now as an heir when he has arrived at full maturity begins to spend his own money, and to farm his own acres, so do they enter into their heritage.

We are not full-grown as yet, and therefore are not admitted to full possession. But wait a while; those gray hairs indicate, my brethren, that you are getting ripe. These, these, these my still youthful locks show me, alas, that I may have to wait for a little longer, and yet I know not, for the Lord may soon permit me to sleep with my fathers; but later or earlier, be it as he wills, we shall one day come into possession of the goodly land. Now, if it is sweet to be an heir while you are in childhood, what is it to be an heir when you have arrived at perfect manhood?

Was it not delightful to sing that hymn just now, and to behold the land of pure delight, whose everlasting spring and never-withering flowers are just across the narrow stream of death? Oh you sweet fields! You saints immortal who lie down therein! When shall we be with you and be satisfied? If the mere thinking of heaven ravishes the soul, what must it be to be there, to plunge deep into the stream of blessedness, to dive and find no bottom, to swim and find no shore? To sip of the wine of heaven as we sometimes do makes our hearts so glad that we know not how to express our joy; but what will it be to drink deep and drink again, and sit forever at the table and know that the feast will never be over and the cups will never be empty, and that there will be no worse wine to be brought out at the end, but if possible, better still and better still in infinite progression?

The word *kingdom,* which stands next, indicates the richness of the heritage of saints. It is no petty estate, no charity rooms, no happy corner in obscurity. I heard a good man say he would be content to win a corner behind the door. I shall not be. The Lord says we shall inherit a *kingdom.* We would not be satisfied to inherit less, because less than that would not suit our character. He *hath made us kings and priests unto God* (Revelation 1:6), and we must reign forever and ever, or be as wretched as deposed monarchs. A king without a kingdom would be an unhappy man.

If I were a poor servant, a charity room would be a blessing, for it would unite with my condition and degree; but if I am made by grace a king, I must have a kingdom, or I shall not have attained to a position equal to my nature. He who makes us kings will give us a kingdom to fit the nature which he has bestowed upon us. Beloved, do strive after, more and more, that which the Spirit of God will give you – a kingly heart; do not be among those who are satisfied and contented with the miserable nature of ordinary humanity.

A child's glass bead is all the world is to a truly royal spirit. These glittering diadems are only nursery toys to God's kings; the true jewels are up there; the true treasury wealth looks down upon the stars. Do not limit your soul; be not hampered! Get a kingly heart – ask the King of Kings to give it to you and beg of him a royal spirit. Act royally on earth towards your Lord, and for his sake towards all men. Go about the world not as ordinary men in spirit and action, but as kings and princes of a race superior to the dirt-scrapers who are on their knees, crawling in the mud after yellow earth. Then, when your soul is royal, remember with joy that your future inheritance shall be all that your kingly soul pants after in its most royal moments. It will be a state of unutterable richness and wealth of soul.

According to the word *prepared,* we may conceive it to be a condition of surpassing excellence. It is a *kingdom prepared*, and it has been so long a time prepared, and he who prepares it is so wondrously rich in resources, that we cannot possibly conceive how excellent it must be. If I might so speak, God's common gifts, which he throws away as though they were but nothing, are priceless; but what will be these gifts upon which the infinite mind of God has been set for ages upon ages in order that they may reach the highest degree of excellence?

Long before Christmas chimes were ringing, a mother was so glad to think her boy was coming home, after the first quarter he had been out at school, and right away she began preparing and planning all sorts of joys for him. Well might the holidays be happy when the mother had been contriving to make them so. Now in an infinitely nobler manner the great God has prepared a kingdom for his people; he has thought, "That will please them, and that will bless them, and this other will make them superlatively happy."

He prepared the kingdom to perfection; and then, as if that were not enough, the glorious man Christ Jesus went up from earth to heaven; and you know what he said when he departed – *I go to prepare a place for you* (John 14:2). We know that the infinite God can prepare a place fitting for a finite creature, but the words smile so sweetly at us as we read that Jesus himself, who is a man, and therefore knows our hearts' desires, has had a finger in it; *he* has prepared it too. It is a kingdom prepared for you, upon which the thoughts of God have been set to make it excellent *from the foundation of the world.*

But we must not pause: it is a *kingdom prepared for **you*** (emphasis added). Mark that! I must confess I do not like certain expressions that I hear sometimes, which imply that heaven is prepared for some who will never reach it; prepared for those who will be driven as accursed ones into the place of torment. I know there is a sacred expression that says, "Let no man take thy crown"; but that refers to the crown of ministerial success rather than of eternal glory.

An expression that grated on my ear the other evening from the lips of a certain good man, ran something like this: "There is a heaven prepared for all of you, but if you are not faithful you will not win it. There is a crown in heaven laid up for you, but if you are not faithful it will be without a wearer." I do not believe it; I cannot believe it. That the crown of eternal life which is laid up for the blessed of the Father will ever be given to anybody else or left without a possessor, I do not believe. I dare not conceive of crowns in heaven and nobody to wear them. Do you think that in heaven, when the whole number of saints is complete, you will find a number of unused crowns?

"Ah! what are these for? Where are the heads for these?" "They are in hell!" Then, brother, I have no particular desire to be in heaven, for if all the family of Christ are not there, my soul will be wretched and forlorn because of their sad loss, because I am in union with them all. If one soul that believed in Jesus does not get there, I shall lose respect for the promise and respect for the Master too; he must keep his word to every soul that rests on him.

If your God has gone the length of actually preparing a place for his people and has made provision for them and been disappointed, he is no God to me, for I could not adore a disappointed God. I do not believe in such a God. Such a being would not be God at all. The notion of disappointment in his eternal preparations is not consistent with the Deity. Talk thus of Jupiter and Venus if you please, but the infinite Jehovah is, as far as human speech can dishonor him, dishonored by being mentioned in such a connection. He has prepared a place for *you*. Here is personal election. He has made a distinct ordinance for every one of his people that where he is there shall they be.

Prepared from the foundation of the world. Here is eternal election appearing before men were created, preparing a crown before heads were made to wear it. And so God had before the starry skies began to gleam carried out the decree of election in a measure which, when Christ shall come, shall be perfected to the praise of the glory of his grace, *who worketh all things after the counsel of his own will* (Ephesians 1:11). Our portion, then, is one prepared from all eternity for us according to the election of God's grace, one suitable to the loftiest character to which we can ever attain, which will consist in nearness to Christ, communion with God, and standing forever in a place of dignity and happiness.

And now I have very little time to speak, as I hoped to have spoken this morning about the persons who shall come there.

They are recognizable by a secret and by a public character. Their *name* is *blessed of my Father* – the Father chose them, gave his Son for them, justified them through Christ, preserved them in Christ Jesus, adopted them into the family, and now has accepted them into his own house. Their *nature* you have described in the word *inherit.* None can inherit but sons; they have been born again, and have received the nature of God. *Having escaped the corruption that is in the world through lust,* they have become *partakers of the divine nature* (2 Peter 1:4): they are sons. Their *appointment* is mentioned: *inherit the kingdom prepared for you from the foundation of the world.* Their name is blessed, their nature is that of a child, and their appointment is that of God's decree.

Their doings, their outward doings, these we want to speak a minute upon. They appear to have been distinguished among men for deeds of charity, and these were not in any way associated with ceremonies or outward observances. It is not said that they preached – they did so, some of them; it is not said that they prayed – they must have done so, or they would not have been spiritually alive. The actions which are selected as their type, are actions of charity to the impoverished and forlorn. Why these? I think, because *the general audience assembled around the throne would know how to appreciate this evidence of their newborn nature.*

The King might think more of their prayers than of their charity, but the multitude would not. He speaks so as to gain the verdict of all assembled. Even their enemies could not object to his calling those blessed who had performed these actions; for if there be an action that wins for men the universal consent to their goodness, it is an action by which men would be served. Against this there is no law. I have never heard of a state in which there was a law against clothing the naked and feeding the hungry.

This is humanity at once, when its conscience is so seared that it cannot see its own sinfulness, yet detects the virtuousness of feeding the poor. Doubtless this is one reason why these actions were selected. And again, they may have been chosen as evidences of grace, because, *as actions, they are a wonderful means of separating the hypocrite from the true Christian.* Dr. Gill has an idea, and perhaps he is right, that this is not a picture of the general judgment, but of the judgment of the professing church; and if so, it is all the more reasonable to conclude that these works of mercy are selected as the appropriate discerner between the hypocrite and the sincere. I fear that there are some of you high professing Christians who could not stand the test. "Good praying people" they call you, but what do you give to the Lord? Your religion has not touched your pockets.

This does not apply to some of you, for there are many here of whom I would venture to speak before the bar of God, that I know their substance to be consecrated to the Lord and his poor, and I have sometimes thought that beyond their means they have given both to the poor and to God's cause. But there are others of a very different disposition. Now here I shall give you a little plain English talk which none can fail to understand. You may talk about your religion until you have worn your tongue out, and you may get others to believe you; and you may remain in the church twenty years, and nobody ever detects in you in anything like an inconsistency; but, if it be in your power, and you do nothing to relieve the necessities of the poor members of Christ's body, you will be damned as surely as if you were drunkards or whoremongers.

If you have no care for God's church, then this text applies to you and will as surely sink you to the lowest hell as if you had been common blasphemers. That is very plain English, but it is the plain meaning of my text, and it is at my peril that I flinch from telling you of it. *I was an hungred, and ye gave me* – what? good advice, yes, but *no meat. I was thirsty, and ye gave me* – what? a tract, and *no drink.* I was *naked, and ye* gave me – what? your good wishes, but no clothes. *I was a stranger, and* – you pitied me, but – *ye took me not in.* I was *sick,* and you said you could recommend me a doctor, but *ye visited me not.* I was *in prison;* I, God's servant, a persecuted one, was put in prison for Christ's sake, and you said I should be more cautious, but you did not stand by my side and take a share of the blame, and bear with me reproach for the truth's sake.

You see this is a very terrible winnowing fan to some of you tight-fisted ones whose main object is to get all you can and hold it fast, but it is a fan which frequently must be used. Whoever deceives you or spares you, by the grace of God I will not, but will labor to be more bold than ever in denouncing sin. "Well," says one, "what are those to do who are so poor that they have nothing to give away?" My dear brother, do you notice how beautifully the text takes care of you? It hints that there are some who cannot give bread to the hungry, and clothes to the naked, but what about them? Why, you see they are the persons spoken of as *my brethren,* who receive the blessing of kindness, so that this passage comforts the poor and by no means condemns them.

Certain ones of us honestly give to the poor all we can spare, and then of course everybody comes to such; and when we say, "Really, I cannot give anymore," somebody snarls and says, "You call yourself a Christian?" "Yes, I do; I should not call myself a Christian if I gave away other people's money; I should not call myself a Christian if I gave away what I have not got; I should call myself a thief, pretending to be charitable when I could not pay my debts." I have a very great pity indeed for those people who get into the bankruptcy court, but I do not mean the debtors; I have seldom much sympathy for them, but I have a good deal for the creditors who lose by having trusted dishonest people.

If any man should say, "I will live beyond my means in order to get a good character," my dear brother, you begin wrong; that action is in itself wrong. What you have to give must be that which is your own. "But I shall have to pinch myself," says one, "if I do it." Well, pinch yourself! I do not think there is half the pleasure in doing good until you get to the pinching point. This remark of course applies only to those of us of moderate means, who can soon distribute our charity and get down to the pinch point. When you begin to feel, "Now, I must go without that; now I must curtail these in order to do more good," oh! you cannot tell; it is then when you really can feel, "Now I have not given God merely the cheese parings and candle ends that I could not use, but I have really cut out for my Master a good piece of the loaf. I have not given him the old crusts that were getting moldy, but I have given him a piece of my own daily bread, and I am glad to do it, if I can show my love for Jesus Christ by denying myself."

If you are doing this, if you are thus, out of love for Jesus, feeding the hungry and clothing the naked, then I believe that these are put down as tests, because they are such blessed detectives between the hypocrites and the really godly people. When you read "for" here, you must not understand it to be that their reward is *because* of this, but that they are proved to be God's servants *by* this; and so, while they do not merit it because of these actions, yet these actions show that they were saved by grace, which is evidenced by the fact that Jesus Christ effected such and such works in them. If Christ does not work such things in you, you have no part in him; if you have not produced such works as these, you have not believed in Jesus.

Now somebody says, "Then I intend to give to the poor in the future in order that I may have this reward." Ah, but you are very much mistaken if you do that. The duke of Burgundy was waited upon by a poor man, a very loyal subject, who brought him a very large root which he had grown. He was a very poor man indeed, and every root he grew in his garden was of consequence to him; but merely as a loyal offering he brought to his prince the largest his little garden produced. The prince was so pleased with the man's evident loyalty and affection that he gave him a very large sum. The steward thought, "Well, I see this pays; this man has got fifty pounds for his large root. I think *I* shall give the duke a present." So he bought a horse and he reckoned that he should have in return ten times as much for it as it was worth, and he presented it with that view. The duke, like a wise man, quietly accepted the horse, and gave the greedy steward nothing. That was all. So you say, "Well, here is a Christian man, and he gets rewarded. He has been giving to the poor, helping the Lord's church, and see, he is saved; the thing pays, I shall make a little investment." Yes, but you see the steward did not give the horse out of any idea of loyalty, and kindness, and love for the duke, but out of very great love for himself, and therefore he had no return. And if you perform deeds of charity out of the idea of getting to heaven by them, why, it is yourself whom you are feeding, it is yourself whom you are clothing. All your virtue is not virtue, it is foul selfishness; it smells strong of selfhood, and Christ will never accept it, and you will never hear him say "Thank you" for it.

You served yourself, and no reward is due. You must first come to the Lord Jesus Christ and look to him to save you. You will forever renounce all ideas of doing anything to save yourself; and being saved, you will be able to give to the poor and so on without selfishness mixing with your motive, and you will get a reward of grace for the love token which you have given. It is necessary to believe in Christ in order to be capable of true virtue of the highest order. It is necessary to trust Jesus, and to be yourself fully saved, before there is any value in your feeding the hungry or clothing the naked.

God give you grace to go to my Master wounded yonder, and to rest in the precious atonement which he has made for human sin. And when you have done that, being loved at such a rate, show that you love in return; being purchased so dearly, live for him who bought you, and among the actions by which you prove it, let these gleam and glisten like God-given jewels – the visiting of the sick, the comforting of the needy, the relieving of the distressed, and the helping of the weak. God accept these offerings as they come from gracious souls, and to him be praise evermore. Amen.

Chapter 14

The Final Separation

And before him shall be gathered all nations: and he shall separate them one from another, as a shepherd divideth his sheep from the goats. (Matthew 25:32)

J esus Christ, the man of Nazareth, who is also the Son of God, was crucified, dead, and buried, and the third day he rose again from the dead. After he had showed himself to his disciples for forty days – sometimes to one alone, at other times to two or three together, and on one occasion to over five hundred brethren at once – he ascended into heaven. From Mount Olivet, from the midst of his disciples, he rose into midair, and by and by a cloud received him out of their sight.

That same Jesus who has gone into heaven shall so come in like manner as he was seen to go up into heaven, that is to say, in person, in his own risen body. The same Christ who rose into the skies will in the latter day surely descend again. The time of his coming is not revealed to us – *Of that day and that hour knoweth no man, no, not the angels which are in heaven* (Mark 13:32) – but the time is certainly growing nearer every day, and we cannot tell when the hour shall be. We are told that he will come quickly. It seems a long time since that was said, even eighteen hundred years, but we remember that things which are slow with us may be very quick with the Lord; for *one day is with the Lord as a thousand years, and a thousand years as one day* (2 Peter 3:8).

It is not for [us] to know the times or the seasons (Acts 1:7); they remain hidden in the purpose of God.

For excellent reasons these times and seasons are unrevealed, that we may be always on the watchtower, not knowing at what hour the Lord Jesus may be revealed. To the ungodly world he will come as a thief in the night, and take them unaware; but we, brethren, are not in darkness that that day should overtake us as a thief. Being children of the day, we are taught to be awake, and standing in the clear light, with our loins wrapped, and we ought to be always looking for our Master's appearing. Always are we to be watching, never sleeping.

Our text tells us that as one result of his coming there will be a general judgment. I am not going to try and arrange the other events that will happen at the Lord's coming. It is probably true that at his coming there will be first of all a resurrection and rewarding of his saints, a dividing of the ten cities and the five cities, according to the faithfulness of those who were entrusted with talents; and at the close of that period will come that last tremendous day of which prophets and apostles have spoken.

> The day that many thought should never come.
> That all the wicked wished should never come;
> That all the righteous had expected long;
> Day greatly feared, and yet too little feared
> By him who feared it most.

It will be a day of fear and wrath, a day of destruction of the ungodly, a testing day to all mankind, and a day which shall burn as an oven. We may tremblingly say of it, *Who may abide the day of his coming? and who shall stand when he appeareth? for he is like a refiner's fire, and like fullers' soap* (Malachi 3:2).

At that day when Christ shall come, he shall judge all nations. There will be gathered before him not only the Jews, to whom the law was given, but the Gentiles also; not merely those nations who for many an age have heard the gospel, but those also to whom it shall then have been but lately published, for the kingdom of God must be published throughout all nations as a testimony against them. Everywhere Christ will have been preached, and then from all regions, men shall be summoned to stand before him. Remember, this is not merely all the living nations, but also all the nationalities that have passed away. There shall rise from the dead the hosts that perished before the flood and those also who were drowned amid its awful surges. There, too, shall appear the myriads that followed at the call of Nimrod, the swarms of the sons of Japheth who divided the isles of the Gentiles, and the hordes that marched to battle at the command of the kings of Assyria and Babylon.

The dead of Egypt shall rise from their beds of spices, or from the earth with which their dust has mingled. The tens of thousands shall be there over whom Xerxes wept when he remembered how soon they would all pass away. The Greek and the Persian, these shall rise, and the Roman too, and all the hordes of Huns and Goths that swarmed like bees from the northern hives. They all passed into the unknown land, but they are not lost; they shall each answer to the muster roll in the great day of the Lord. The earth, which is now becoming more and more a graveyard, shall yield up her dead, and the sea itself, transformed into a solid pavement, shall bear upon its bosom the lonely ones who lie asleep today in her gloomy caverns.

All of woman born shall come forth from the prolific womb of the sepulcher – myriads, myriads as countless as the drops of the morning, or as the sands of the seashore. Multitudes, multitudes shall be gathered together in the valley of decision. Their bones shall come together, and breath shall enter their bodies anew, and they shall live once more. As long as it has been that they have slept in the tomb, they shall all rise with one impulse and start up with one thought – *to appear before their judge.*

The great white throne shall be set on high, all pure and lustrous, bright and clear like a sapphire stone, as one vast looking glass in which every man shall see himself and his sins reflected; and on that throne shall sit the Son of Man. That same Jesus who was nailed to the tree and rose to heaven shall sit upon the judgment seat, appointed to determine the cases of all mankind of every age. What an assembly! No imagination can comprehend it. As far as the eye can carry – alas, as far as the eagle's wing can soar – the earth shall be covered with men, like a field with grass in the springtide; and there will they all stand with the judge upon the great white throne as the common center of observation, for *every eye shall see him, and they also which pierced him: and all kindreds of the earth shall wail because of him* (Revelation 1:7). It will be a motley throng, as you may well imagine, but the Shepherd, the Great Shepherd, the judge himself, shall divide them.

That division will be the one work of the judgment day. He will divide them as readily and unerringly as a shepherd divides his sheep from the goats. My business shall be to draw the attention of each one to that division, that each of you may inquire what will be the result of it upon himself. I have thought it over on my own account, and desire to think of it still. I would bid my mind to fly into the future, and see for a moment the pomp of that tremendous day when Christ with clouds shall come; I would anticipate the verdict of that hour, and I would recall the dread alternative of heaven or hell. I pray we may all think about it, and especially you who are unprepared for it, that you may at once fly to him whose blood and righteousness alone can make you hold up your head in that tremendous hour.

Three things we shall speak about: the first is the *division;* the second is *the divider;* and the third is *the rule of the division.*

The first, then, is the division. *Before him shall be gathered all nations: and he shall separate them one from another, as a shepherd divideth his sheep from the goats* (Matthew 25:32).

That is to say, first, *they shall be divided into two parts* – his sheep and the goats. There shall be two positions: he shall put his sheep on the right hand, but the goats on the left. Is there no place for a third party? No, for the simple reason that there will then be no third class; and there will then be none for this other reason – that there never was a third class. I know there are some here even tonight who dare not say they believe in Jesus, but they would not like to be put down among the ungodly; yet I pray you remember that there are but two books, and in one or other of those two your name must stand recorded by the hand of God, for there is no third book. There is the Lamb's Book of Life, and if your name is there, happy are you. If it is not there, your sins still stand recorded in the books which contain the condemning evidence which will seal the death warrants of unbelievers.

Listen to me. There is nowhere in this world any other sort of people beside those who are dead in sin and those who are alive unto God.

There is no state between. A man either lives or is dead; you cannot find a neutral condition. A man may be in a swoon, or he may be asleep, but he is alive; no state is there that is not within the boundary of either life or death. Is not this clear enough? There is no state between being converted and unconverted – between being revived and being dead in sin. There is no condition between being pardoned and having our sins upon us. There is no state between dwelling in darkness and being brought into marvelous light.

One or the other must always be our condition, and this is the great folly of mankind in all times – that they will dream of a middle state and try to loiter in it. It was for this cause that the old prophet, standing on Mount Carmel's brow, said, *How long halt ye between two opinions? if the Lord be God, follow him: but if Baal, then follow him* (1 Kings 18:21). And it is for this reason that we have to constantly call the attention of mankind to the great declaration of the gospel – *He that believeth and is baptized shall be saved; but he that believeth not shall be damned* (Mark 16:16).

God has given to the preacher two hands, so that he may set the people on each side, and deal out the truth to two characters and no more. Be not deceived about it; you are either on the way to heaven or on the road to hell. There is no purgatory or middle condition in the next world. Purgatory is an invention of the pope for the filling of his cellar and his pantry; and no more profitable speculation has ever been set going than the saying of masses and the robbing of fools, under the pretense of altering that state which is fixed forever. Purgatory Pickpurse was the name the first Reformers gave it. You will *go to* heaven or to hell, and you will *remain* in one place or the other; for you have either a character that is fit for heaven or a character that is fit for hell, and there is no character which can be supposed, if we understand the Scriptures correctly, which would be fit for a middle place; neither is there any middle place prepared for it. *He shall separate them one from another, as a shepherd divideth his sheep from the goats: and he shall set the sheep on his right hand, but the goats on the left* (Matthew 25:32-33). The human flock will be divided into two companies.

Observe, next, that *they will be divided readily*. It is not everybody that could divide sheep from goats. I suppose, according to your ordinary judgment of goats, you would very readily be able to tell them from sheep; but one who has traveled in the East, and even in Italy, knows that it takes a somewhat tutored eye to know a certain kind of goat from a certain kind of sheep. They are extremely like each other. The wool of some sheep in a warm climate becomes so like hair, and the hair of a kind of goat is so much like wool, that a traveler scarcely knows which is which; but a shepherd who has lived among them knows the difference well.

So in this world, it is easy enough to tell the sinner from the saint in some cases. You need no great sense to discern the characters of the grossly dishonest, the drunken, the debauched, the Sabbath breaking, and the profane. You know that they have no part among the people of God, for they bear upon their forehead the emblems of the children of the Evil One: the immoral are easily separated from the pure in heart. But inside the church there are a number of persons who have so much about them that looks good, and yet so much that is terribly inconsistent, that we are quite unable to discover which is their true nature.

Thank God we are not called upon to judge them, nor even allowed to do so. The most experienced pastor must scarcely attempt to do so; certainly, if he feels so much trouble about the matter that he takes it to his Lord, and asks for directions as to how to deal with these tares, he will be told to let them grow on until harvest time, lest in rooting up the tares he should also root up the wheat with them. I talked today to a certain good man who labors hard among the poor in the East End. He said, "We have a great number who profess to be converted, but I do not think that much more than one in five actually stays and turns out to be really so. But we have no trouble with them in the church – not such trouble as you would be likely to have with your people, because, among the class of people who go to the tabernacle, there is a feeling that it is right to go to the house of God at least once on the Sabbath, if not twice; and if persons join the church there, they will from habit continue to attend. But the moment a man of the poorest class ceases to be a Christian in heart, he ceases at the same time to attend the public services, because there is no enthusiasm to keep him up to it; and so he follows his own tastes, stops at home and loafs about, and in all probability gets drunk or falls into some other of the common vices of his class, and he is sifted out at once."

In such cases the classes are easily separated. But among a more respectable class of people, who do not drink and who observe the Sabbath day, you will have a number of people who remain in the church, though they have no secret devoutness, no real love for Christ, no private prayer; and therefore there is all the more danger. Now, dear friends, what *we* cannot do, and must not try to do, Jesus Christ will do easily enough. The Shepherd when he comes will soon separate his sheep from the goats. His eye of fire will read each heart; the hypocrites in the church will tremble in a moment, instinctively reading the meaning of that glance, as Christ will by that eye say to them, "What are you doing here among my people?"

Remember, that as the division will be made readily, *it will be made infallibly;* that is to say, there will not be found among the goats one poor trembling sheep left to be driven off with the unclean herd. When Christ says, *Depart from me, ye cursed,* he will not say that to one sincere but feeble soul. Ah no, you may condemn yourself, but if you really have a living faith the Lord will not condemn you. You may often be afraid that he will bid you to depart, but he will not. No lamb of his flock shall be among the goats. The whole company of his redeemed shall be safely gathered into their eternal mansions.

> Lord, those shall bear that day, so dread, so splendid,
>   Whose sins are by thy merits cover'd o'er,
> Who when thy hand of mercy was extended,
>   Believ'd, obey'd, and own'd thy gracious power;
> These, mighty God, shall see without dismay
>   The earth and heaven before them pass away.

The sword cuts the other way too, and therefore be sure of this, that there will be no goat permitted to enter the pastures of the blessed among the sheep; no unconverted graceless person will follow the Great Shepherd to those living fountains above which afford eternal doses of bliss to the purchased flock. Though the sinner may have led a sort of outwardly consistent life for forty or fifty years, though he may have preached the gospel and done many wonderful works, yet Christ will say to him, *I never knew you* (Matthew 7:23).

He will not be able to keep his sheep's clothing on then, or bleat any longer in sheep fashion. Christ will know him under whatever disguise he may wear; he will find him out, and drive him to his own place, so that not a single one of the accursed shall enter into the city with the blessed. It will be an infallible judgment; there is, therefore, good reason that we be prepared for it. There is no bribing or deceiving the judge, and no avoiding his tribunal. Oh, be ready to face that eye which will read you through and through!

That division, when it shall take place, let me further beg you to remember, *will be very keen and sharp.* Think it over, think it over; for some of you may have to ache through it. Two men shall be in the field: one shall be taken and the other left. These were two laborers who worked together, and they had guided the same plow and driven the same oxen; but the one shall be upon the right hand and the other on the left. Two carpenters at the same bench had handled the same cutting tool and the same plane, but one shall be taken and the other left. Two had served in one shop at the same counter with the same goods, and one shall be taken and the other left; they were familiar acquaintances and old shop mates, but one shall rejoice to hear the welcome, *Come,* and the other shall tremble as he receives the dread sentence, *Depart.*

Alas, the division will come closer home still. Two women shall be in one house: the one shall be taken and the other left. Two women shall be grinding at the mill, that is, engaged with the household duties, grinding the morning's breakfast wheat: one shall be taken and the other left. So you may be two servants in the same house, cook and housemaid: one saved and the other lost; two sisters living together under the same roof: one brought into glory and the other cast into shame; two of you may be dwellers under the same roof, eating bread at the same table, drinking from the same cup, and yet one of you shall feast at the eternal banquets and the other shall cry for a drop of water to cool his burning tongue. You would not like to be separated, but separated you must be.

Alas, there will be a separation still more painful yet! Two shall be in one bed, and the one shall be taken and the other left – the husband taken away from the wife, and the wife parted from her husband. Oh, there will be partings, there will be partings; and consequently there will be weeping. There will be weeping at the judgment seat of Christ:

not for the godly, for in them the glory of their Lord will swallow up all other thoughts, but for the Christless, the prayerless, the graceless. Oh, the wailing of the children, and the wailing of the women, and the wailing of the husbands, and the wailing of the fathers when their children are saved, or their parents are saved, or their husbands and wives are saved, and they themselves are cast out forever!

> O there will be mourning
>> Before the judgment seat,
> When this world is burning
>> Beneath Jehovah's feet.

> Friends and kindred then shall part,
>> Shall part to meet no more;
> Wrath consume the rebel's heart,
>> While saints on high adore!

The separation will be agony indeed to the lost. I could scarcely have the heart to bid a man good-bye if I knew that I would never see him again. The worst wish I could entertain concerning the worst enemy I ever had – though I do not know that I have one in the world – would not go so far as to say I wished I might never see him again, for since I hope I shall be where Jesus is, I should like to see him, be he who he may, and see him there among the blessed. But it must not be; it must not be if sinners will not repent of sin, if they will persist in rejecting Jesus Christ.

Except you believe in Jesus, the parting will be keen and cutting, dividing between joints and marrow, tearing asunder marriage ties and bonds of filial or parental affection; slaying all vain hopes forever. O unrepentant souls, I could weep for you! If you are linked in blood relationship with the saints, it will not help you if you die unregenerate! Though you were bone of each other's bone and flesh of each other's flesh, yet must you be separated unless you are one with Christ. I beg you unregenerate ones to lay this to heart at once, and trifle no longer!

That division, dear friends, remember, *will be very wide* as well as very keen; for the division will be such as will be represented in its distance by heaven and by hell, and what a distance is that! The distance between God and devil! Between happiness and misery! Between glory and everlasting contempt! Between infinite joy and boundless sorrow! Between songs and weeping! Between triumphs and wailing, feasting and gnashing of teeth! If the only division would be such as might arise from differences in degrees of glory (if such there be), one might still yearn to have the companionship of our dear ones. But the difference is between heaven and hell, and Christ says of it that *there is a great gulf fixed: so that they which would pass from hence to you cannot; neither can they pass to us, that would come from thence* (Luke 16:26). The distance will be as wide as eternity, the separating gulf will be as deep as the abyss, and as impassable as hell.

And remember, *the separation will be final.* There is no flinging a bridge across that vast abyss. Damned spirits may look down into that dread gulf, into the unutterable blackness of its darkness, but they will never see a hope of crossing to the land of the blessed. The key is lost; they can never come out of the dungeon of despair. "Forever, forever, forever," is written upon the chain which binds the lost spirit. No hope of restoration was ever indulged by a man in hell, and it is idle to dream about it now. Of all figments of the brain it has the least support in Scripture. The lost sinner is forever separated from Jesus and from the disciples of Jesus, however near akin in the flesh those disciples may have been to him. Unalterable is the separation, and eternal.

Beloved, these are such weighty things that while I dwell upon them, I feel far more inclined to sit down and weep than to stand up and speak to you. The theme causes me to feel the weakness of mere words, and in a measure makes me lose the power of expression; for what if any of you should be lost forever? It was a touching thing to me yesterday when I saw a sister in Christ who has been my hearer for many years, and she told me that she was decided for Christ by my saying, when I went away last time, that perhaps I might never address you again, and might find a grave in a foreign land. I felt that it might be so at the time I uttered the words, though I am glad that they have not been fulfilled.

She thought, "Well, he has been preaching to me these many years, and if I die unconverted, I shall never see him again," and then it flashed across her mind: "How much worse to feel that I shall never see the King in his beauty; I shall never see the Savior," and she was thus led by the Holy Spirit to give her heart to Jesus. Perhaps the Lord may use the thought of this separation to move some of you to say, "I will come to Jesus, and I will rest in him." O Lord, my God, grant it may be so, for Jesus' sake.

We have spoken about *the division;* we will now have a few words about *the divider.* **He** *shall separate them one from another* (Matthew 25:32, emphasis added).

Christ Jesus will be the divider of the race of men into two parts; and this I am glad to know, because, first of all, this will be *the occasion of lasting, yes, of eternal joy for all the saints.* No child of God will ever have a doubt in heaven; but it is needful that they begin their bliss with a very strong assurance of divine love, or else, it seems to me, they might have a doubt. Unless God had ordained the method at which the text hints, I could well imagine myself in heaven saying to myself, after I had been there a little while, "Oh, can it be, can it be that I am here? I do remember the sin of such a day, and the shortcomings of such an hour, and my murmurings, and my unbelief, and all my departures from my God; and am I here, after all?"

I could imagine, if there had not been the means used to put an end to such a possibility, my saying, "Surely I am to taste this only for a moment, that I may be driven to my duly deserved punishment after all, that my hell may be made the more terrible because I have seen what heaven is, and that my hunger may grow the more intolerable because I have eaten of the bread of angels." If such a fear were possible, behold the answer to it. "He, the judge, the judge, the judge himself has said, *Come, ye blessed of my Father*" (Matthew 25:34). That judge cannot be mistaken, for he is Jesus the infallible Son of God. God himself has blessed his chosen, and Jesus tells them so in the plainest terms – *Come, ye blessed of my Father, inherit the kingdom prepared for you.*

Since Jesus has decreed his everlasting happiness, the child of God cannot doubt throughout eternity. That voice will sound forever in his ears, sweeter than music of flute or harp or dulcimer. *Come, ye blessed of my Father.* Why, it will be the very basis of the bliss of heaven to think, "Jesus bade me to come. Who shall ask me the question, How earnestly did you come into this place? Did not *he* admit me? Who shall question my right to be here? Did not *he* say, *Come, ye blessed of my*

Father? Do you not see that it is a choice and a comforting fact that we shall not divide ourselves at the end, nor shall an angel do it who might err, but the divider will be Jesus himself, the Son of God; and therefore the glory which he measures out to us will be most surely ours and we may enjoy it without fear.

But then, note on the other hand, that *this will increase the terror of the lost,* that Christ will divide them.

Christ, full of infinite love, would he destroy a sinner unless it must be? He that would have saved Jerusalem and wept because it must be destroyed! The guilty city was resolved to perish, but as her Lord pronounced the sentence, he wept. When I hear of a judge putting on the black cap to condemn a man, I like to read in the papers: "The judge's voice faltered, and he was evidently unable to suppress his emotion as he uttered the sentence of death."

What right-minded man could be otherwise than moved when compelled to deliver his fellow creature to the gallows? But no judge on earth has such compassion for his fellow man as Jesus has for sinners; and when it comes to this that *he* says, "I must do it, I must condemn you," then sinner, it must be so indeed. When incarnate love says, *Depart, ye cursed,* then you must be cursed with an emphasis. You must be infamous beings indeed when he whose lips drop blessings as lilies, drop sweet-smelling myrrh – when *he* calls you so! There must be something very horrible about you that *he* should bid you to *depart;* and, indeed, there is an abominable thing in you, for unbelief in God is the most horrible thing, even in hell. Not to believe that God is love is worthy of the utmost condemnation. You will have to say if you are lost, "I was condemned by the most loving judge that ever sat upon a judgment seat. The Christ that died lifted his pierced hand at the very moment when he said, *Depart, ye cursed!*"

Yet there is something more, though this might be enough. If you should be lost, as God forbid you should be, it will infinitely add to your terror to know that you were condemned by one who is infinitely just. You will feel that the Christ who condemned you was the holiest of men, in whom was no sin, and that, besides, he is pure and perfect God; so that you will not be able to quibble at the sentence. Neither will there be any question about a new trial; your own conscience will make you feel that the decision is final, for it is just; and you will be too well assured of its reality and certainty, for he who will pronounce that sentence is the God of truth. He said, "I am the way and the truth." You chose to not have him for a way, but you will find him to be the truth; and when he pronounces you cursed, cursed you will be beyond all question.

Once more. If he that condemns you is the Christ of God, you will know that he has power to carry out the sentence, for all power is given unto him in heaven and in earth, and the government shall be upon his shoulders; and if he says, "Depart into everlasting fire," into that fire you must go. If he declares that the fire shall never be quenched, depend upon it, that it will burn on forever; and if he decrees that the worm shall never die, that worm will live and gnaw to all eternity, for he who gives forth the sentence is able to make it good. Remember how he said, *Verily I say unto you, . . . Heaven and earth shall pass away, but my words shall not pass away* (Matthew 24:34-35). Firmer than the rocks shall stand the irrevocable decree – *These shall go away into everlasting punishment: but the righteous into life eternal* (Matthew 25:46). My soul trembles while I thus proclaim Jesus as the judge whose awful voice divides the sinners from the saints.

Lend me your ears but for a minute or two longer, while I notice, in the third place, *the rule of the division.* Did you notice where the division is made? It is very wonderful to me – very wonderful indeed! *The great division between the sons of men is Christ.* Here are the sheep; there are the goats. What parts them? Christ! He is the center. There is no great barrier set up, as it were, on that last tremendous day, but he himself is the division. He shall set the sheep on his right hand, and the goats on his left. Now, that which parts us into two portions is our relationship to Jesus Christ. On which side of Christ are you ? I want you to question yourselves about that.

If you are on his right hand you are among his people. If you are not with him you are against him, and so are on his left hand. That which parts the saint and the sinner is Christ; and the moment a sinner comes to Christ he passes over to the other side and is numbered with the saints. This is the real point of separation. Christ stands between the believers and the unbelievers and marks the boundary of each class. When Aaron stood between the living and the dead, swinging the censer full of incense, what separated the dead from the living?

Realize the scene before you answer the question. There they lie! There they lie, I say, stricken with pestilence! The unseen avenger has slain them in heaps. But here are the living, rejoicing and safe. What separates them? The priest standing there with the censer. Even thus our Great High Priest stands at this moment between the living and the dead, while the incense of his merits ascends before God, and makes the most-real dividing wall between dead sinners and those who are alive unto God by Jesus Christ. Christ is the divider; Christ is himself the division.

But what is the rule by which he separates the people? *The rule of the division is, first, actions.* Actions! Did you notice that? He says nothing about words. He dwells upon deeds of mercy. *I was an hungred, and ye gave me meat: I was thirsty, and ye gave me drink: I was . . . naked, and ye clothed me* (Matthew 25:35-36). These are all actions. Now, perhaps you would have liked the judge to have said, "You were accustomed to singing hymns out of 'Our Own Hymnbook.' You were accustomed to talking very sweetly about me and calling me Master and Lord. You were accustomed to sitting at the Communion table." Not a word is said about these things. No, nor is anything said about ceremonial actions.

He does not say, "You used to bow before the pyx (container holding consecrated bread); you reverently stood up at one part of the service, and knelt at another; you walked around the church singing the processional hymn." Nothing is said about these performances, only common actions are noticed. *I was an hungred, and ye gave me meat: I was thirsty, and ye gave me drink;* these are all commonplace matters. Actions will be the great rule of judgment at last. I am not preaching now contrary to the gospel, but only repeating in other words what our Lord himself has said. *So then each one of us will give an account of himself to God* (Romans 14:12); *that every one may receive the things done in his body, according to that he hath done, whether it be good or bad* (2 Corinthians 5:10) is the statement, not of the law, but of the New Testament of our Lord and Savior Jesus Christ. Those that have done evil shall go away into eternal punishment.

Are we, then, saved by our works? By no manner of means. Yet our works are the evidence of our being saved, and grace will bring out this evidence in our lives if we possess them. A magistrate judges by the actions which are proved upon evidence. It is true that he may and will have respect to the motive which urged the actions, but first of all the actions themselves must be before him in evidence; and so here the King mentions the actions that were done.

Let us notice that the actions which were the rule of judgment *were all of them actions about Christ.* I want you carefully to note this. The Lord says, **I** *was an hungred, and ye gave* **me** *meat:* **I** *was thirsty, and ye gave* **me** *drink: . . . I was sick, and ye visited* **me** (emphasis added). This summary is made up of actions about Christ. I will, therefore, very earnestly put this question to you – What actions have you ever done in reference to Jesus? "I am a church member," says one. I will not hear about that just now, because the judge will not say anything about it. I am glad you are an avowed disciple, if you are honestly so; but do your actions prove that you are really so? That is the question.

Have you ever *done* anything for Christ? Have you ever given anything to Christ? Could Christ say to you, *I was an hungred, and ye gave me meat: I was thirsty, and ye gave me drink*? Now, I know some professing Christians of whom I fear that Jesus Christ could not speak thus, for he cannot speak that which is not true. Their pockets are sealed in a completely airtight manner, like tins of Australian meat; even the smell of their money never reaches Christ's poor. Give meat to a hungry man? Not they. Let him go to the church. Give clothes to a naked man? Not they. What do we pay rates for?

The idea of giving anything to another, or doing anything for another, without getting paid for it or praised for it seems to them to be out of all character. Now, selfishness is as much opposed to the spirit of the gospel as the cold of the northern region is to the warmth of the sun. If the sun of Christ's love has shone into your heart you will love others, and you will show your love to others by desiring to do them good in all sorts of ways, and you will do it for the Lord's sake, so that when he comes he will be able to say, **I** *was an hungred, and ye gave* **me** *meat:* **I** *was thirsty, and ye gave* **me** *drink: . . . I was sick, and ye visited* **me; I** *was in prison, and ye came unto* **me.** What have your actions been with regard to Christ? I pray you, brethren and sisters, who are one with me in the profession of allegiance to Christ, judge yourselves by your actions with regard to him, as I also will judge myself.

Now, notice that Christ, as it were, inferentially tells us that *the actions which will be mentioned at the judgment day, as the proof of our being the blessed of the Lord, spring from the grace of God,* for he says, *Come, ye blessed of my Father, inherit the kingdom prepared for you from the foundations of the world* (Matthew 25:34). They fed the hungry, but sovereign grace had first fed *them.* They clothed the naked, but infinite love first clothed *them.* They went to prison, but free grace had first set *them* free from a worse prison. They visited the sick, but the Great Physician in his infinite mercy first came and visited *them.* They evidently had no idea that there was anything meritorious in what they did; they had never dreamed of being rewarded for it.

When they stand before the judgment seat, the bare idea of there being any excellence in what they have done will be new to the saints, for they have formed a very lowly estimate of their own performances, and what they have done seems to them too faulty to be commended. The saints fed the hungry and clothed the naked because it gave them much pleasure to do so. They did it because they could not help doing it; their new nature impelled them to do it. They did it because it was their delight to do good and it was as much their element as water is for a fish or the air is for a bird. They did good for Christ's sake, because it was the sweetest thing in the world to do anything for Jesus.

Why is it that a wife is so kind to her husband? Because it is her duty, you say. All very well, but the real reason is because she loves him so intensely. Why is a mother so careful over her babe? Is there any rule or act of parliament commanding mothers to be fond of their little ones? No, there is no act of parliament; there is an act of God, in the bosom somewhere, passed *nem con* (no one contradicting) in the chamber of the heart, and the mother cannot but be kind. Now, when the Lord puts a new nature into us, and makes us one with Jesus Christ, we cannot help loving his people and seeking the good of our fellow man; and the Lord Jesus Christ will acknowledge this at the last day as an evidence that there was love in the heart, because love was shown by the hand. May God grant that when the judge of all shall come, we may be found renewed in heart and full of love through the power of his Holy Spirit.

"Oh," says one, "I wish I had that renewed heart that would produce such actions." Jesus can give it to you. You will always live for self in some sense or another until you are saved. Even the most philanthropic people who have loved their fellow creatures best, without religion, have generally sought for their esteem, and the verse is true concerning the praise of our fellow creatures –

> The proud, to gain it, toils on toils endure;
> The modest shun it but to make it sure.

But when you receive a new heart you will not live for the praise of your fellow man. Then your charity will be done in secret, and you will not let your left hand know what your right hand does. Then, when you do your kindnesses, it will not be that others may publish abroad the announcement that you have visited the sick and clothed the naked, but your charity's deeds will be done behind the door and in the corner, where none shall know of them but your God, and the grateful recipients of your bounty. You will quietly put into the treasury the two mites that make a farthing, and think yourself unobserved; but One who sits over against the treasury, who knows your heart, will take good note of it. Your Lord will accept what you do because you do it out of love for him; and at the end, while you blush to hear it, he will tell it to the angels and to the listening hosts of earth and heaven, and swing wide the gates of immortal bliss, and let you in, according to the promise of his grace.

God bless you, beloved, for Jesus' sake. Amen.

Chapter 15

What the Farm Laborers Can Do and What They Cannot Do

And he said, So is the kingdom of God, as if a man should cast seed into the ground; and should sleep, and rise night and day, and the seed should spring and grow up, he knoweth not how. For the earth bringeth forth fruit of herself; first the blade, then the ear, after that the full corn in the ear. But when the fruit is brought forth, immediately he putteth in the sickle, because the harvest is come. (Mark 4:26-29)

Last Lord's Day morning our subject was the laborers upon God's farm and their great Master; and then we tried to show how far human agency was necessary in the work of the gospel. We also saw how thoroughly all holy results depend upon God, for *neither is he that planteth any thing, neither he that watereth; but God that giveth the increase* (1 Corinthians 3:7). We have much the same subject this morning, only it goes a little deeper, and yet it more fully shows how far the laborer can go, and how far he cannot go. It shows where man may enter with holy industry, and where no human work can possibly intrude. Our subject on this occasion will mainly be the measure and limit of human instrumentality in the kingdom of grace. If we shall be taught of the Spirit of God, we shall find this Scripture to be full of instruction upon the matter.

It is remarkable that the parable before us is peculiar to Mark. No other Gospel writer has recorded it, but we do not think any the less of it on that account. If it had been told to us four times, we would have been glad to hear the repetition, and would have given it a fourfold attention; as it is told to us but once, we will give the more earnest heed to a voice that speaks once and for all. We are glad that the Holy Spirit led Mark to reserve this pearl out of the many excellent things which our Lord said which have been lost. John tells us that if a record of all the works which Jesus did could have been preserved, they would have made a library so large that scarcely the world itself could have contained all the books. Many of the things that Jesus said floated about, no doubt, for a time, and were gradually forgotten, and we have to be thankful to the Spirit of God for perpetuating this choice parallelism by the hand of his servant Mark. Preserved in the amber of inspiration, this choice instruction is of priceless value.

Here is a lesson for sowers – for the laborers upon the farm of God.

It is a parable for all who are concerned in the kingdom of God. It will be of little value to those who are in the kingdom of darkness, for they are not bidden to sow the good seed: *Unto the wicked God saith, What hast thou to do to declare my statutes?* (Psalm 50:16). But all who are loyal subjects to King Jesus, all who are commissioned to scatter seed for the royal Husbandman will be glad to know how the kingdom advances, glad to know how the harvest is preparing for him whom they serve. Listen, then, you that sow beside all waters, you that with holy diligence seek to fill the gatherings of your God – listen, and may the Spirit of God speak into your ears as you are able to bear it.

We shall, first, learn from our text what we can do and what we cannot do. Let this stand as our first topic.

So is the kingdom of God, as if a man should cast seed into the ground (Mark 4:26). This the gracious worker can do. *And the seed should spring and grow up, he knoweth not how* (Mark 4:27). This is what he cannot do; it belongs to a higher power. Man can neither make the seed spring nor grow up; he is out of the field in that respect, and may go home to *sleep, and rise night and day* (Mark 4:27). Seed once sown is beyond human jurisdiction and is under divine care. Yet before long the worker comes in again: *When the fruit is brought forth, immediately he putteth in the sickle* (Mark 4:29). We can reap in due season, and it is both our duty and our privilege to do so. You see, then, that there is a place for the worker at the beginning, and though there is no room for him in the middle passage, yet another opportunity is given him further on when that which he sowed has actually yielded fruit.

Notice, then, that *we can sow.* Any man who has received the knowledge of the grace of God in his heart can teach others. I include under the term "man" all who know the Lord, be they male or female. We cannot all teach alike, for all have not the same gifts; to one is given one talent, and to another ten. Neither have we all the same opportunities, for one lives in obscurity and another has far-reaching influence. Yet there is not within the family of God an infant hand that may not drop its own tiny seed into the ground. There is not a man among us who needs to stand idle in the marketplace, for work suitable to his strength is waiting for him. There is not a saved woman who is left without a holy task; let her do it and win the approving word. *She hath done what she could* (Mark 14:8).

Something of sacred service is within the reach of everyone's capacity, whether it be the mother in the family, the nurse-girl with the infant, the boy in the school, the workman at the bench, or the nurse at the bedside. Those with the smallest range of opportunities can, nevertheless, do something for Christ and his cause. The precious seed of the Word of God is as small as a grain of mustard seed and may be carried by the feeblest hand where it shall multiply a hundredfold.

We need never quarrel with God because we cannot do everything, if he only permits us to do this one thing; for sowing the good seed is a work which will need all our mind, our strength, our love, and our care. Holy seed sowing may well be adopted as our highest pursuit and be no inferior object for the noblest life that can be led. You will need heavenly teaching so that you may carefully select the wheat and keep it free from the darnel of error. We must even winnow out of it our own thoughts and opinions, for these may not be according to the mind of God. Men are not saved by our word, but by God's Word. We are bound to see that we know the gospel and teach the whole of it. To different men we must, with discretion, bring forward that part of the Word of God which will best bear upon their consciences; for much may depend upon the word being *in season,* and not a chance sentence thrown out at random. We shall have enough to do if we look well to the seed basket, lest, perhaps, we should sow tares as well as wheat, or should cast good seed mischievously, where it can only feed evil birds.

Having selected the seed, we shall have plenty of work if we go forth and sow it over a broad area everywhere, for every day brings its opportunity, and every company furnishes its occasion. *In the morning sow thy seed, and in the evening withhold not thy hand* (Ecclesiastes 11:6). *Sow beside all waters* (Isaiah 32:20). Imitate the sower in the parable, who was not so penny-wise that he would only cast the seed where, according to his judgment, all was good soil, but who, feeling that he had other work for his judgment besides the selecting of the soil, also threw the seed right and left as he went on his way, and denied not a handful even to thorny and rocky soils. You, dear fellow workers, will have enough to do if at all times and in all places, as prudence and zeal suggest, you spread abroad the living Word of the living Lord.

Still, wise sowers discover favorable opportunities for sowing, and gladly seize upon them. There are times when it would clearly be a waste to sow, for the soil could not receive it, because it is not in a suitable condition. After a shower, or before a shower, or at some such time as he that has studied husbandry knows, then is the time to be up and doing. So while we are to work for God always, yet there are seasons when it would be casting pearls before swine to talk of holy things; and there are other times when if we were slothful it would be a shameful waste of promising seasons. Sluggards in the time of plowing and sowing are sluggards indeed, for they not only waste the day, but also throw away the year. If you watch for souls, and use hours of happy advantage, and moments of sacred softening, you will not complain of the scanty space allowed for operation. Even should you never be called to water, or to reap, your office is wide enough if you fulfill the work of the sower.

For as little though it seems to teach the simple truth of the gospel, yet it is essential. How shall men hear without a teacher? The farm never brings forth a harvest without sowing. Weeds will grow without our help, but not so wheat and barley. The human heart is so depraved that it will naturally bring forth evil in abundance, and Satan is quite sure not to let it lie without a sowing of evil seed; but if ever a man's soul is to yield fruit unto God, the seed of truth must be cast into it from without. Servants of God, the seed of the Word is not like thistledown, which is borne by every wind, nor like certain seeds wafted by their own parachutes here, there, and everywhere; but the wheat of the kingdom needs a human hand to sow it, and without such an agent it will not enter into men's hearts, neither can it bring forth fruit to the glory of God.

The preaching of the gospel is the necessity of every age; God grant that our country may never be deprived of it. Even if the Lord should send us a famine of bread and a famine of water, may he never send us a famine of the Word of God. Faith comes by hearing, and how can there be hearing if there is no teaching? Scatter you, scatter you then, the seed of the kingdom, for this is essential to the harvest. The spreading of the gospel is not a thing that you may do or may not do, according to your pleasure, but it is a duty urgently needful, to be neglected at your peril. You can sow the seed and the seed must be sown.

This seed should be sown often, for the times are such that one sowing may not suffice. Sow again and again, For many are the foes of the wheat, and if you do not repeat your sowing, you may never see a harvest. The seed must be sown everywhere, too, for there are no choice corners of the world that you can afford to let alone, in the hope that they will be self-productive. You may not leave the rich and intelligent under the notion that surely the gospel will be found among them, for it is not so; the pride of life leads them away from God.

You may not leave the poor and illiterate, and say, "Surely they will of themselves feel their need of Christ." Not so; they will sink from degradation to degradation unless you uplift them with the gospel. No tribe of man, no peculiar constitution of the human mind may be neglected by us, but everywhere we must preach the Word, in season and out of season. I have heard that Captain Cook, the celebrated circumnavigator, was in one respect an admirable example to us. Wherever he landed, in whatever part of the earth it might be, he took with him a little packet of diverse English seeds, and he was often observed scattering them in suitable places. He would leave the boat and wander up from the shore.

He said nothing to anybody, but quietly scattered English seeds wherever he went, so that he smacked the world with the flowers and herbs of his native land. Imitate him wherever you go; sow spiritual seed in every place that your foot shall tread upon. Some of you will before long be at the seaside, or amidst the mountains of Switzerland, or in some other regions of the earth, in search of variety and beauty; carry the heavenly seeds with you, and be not satisfied unless in every place you let fall a grain or two that may bring forth fruit unto your God. This is what you can do; mind that you do it.

Let us now think of what you cannot do. *You cannot, after the seed has left your hand, cause it to put forth life.* I am sure you cannot make it grow, for you do not know how it grows. The text says, *And the seed should spring and grow up, he knoweth not how* (Mark 4:27). That which is beyond the range of our knowledge is certainly beyond the reach of our power. Can you make a seed germinate? You may place it under circumstances of dampness and heat which will cause it to swell and break forth with a shoot, but the germination itself is beyond you. How is it done? We know not. After the germ has been put forth, can you make it further grow and develop its life into leaf and stem? No; that, too, is out of your power. And when the green, grassy blade has been succeeded by the ear, can you ripen it? It will be ripened, but can *you* do it?

You know you cannot; you can have no finger in the actual process, though you may promote the conditions under which it is produced. Life is a mystery; growth is a mystery; ripening is a mystery, and these three mysteries are as fountains sealed against all intrusion. How comes it that there is within the ripe seed the preparations for another sowing and another growth? What is this vital principle, this secret reproducing energy? Do you know anything about this? The philosopher may say that he can explain life and growth, and immediately he will, according to the ordinary process of philosophy, bamboozle you with terms which are less understandable than the ordinary talk of infants; and then he will say, "There is the whole matter! It is as clear as possible." He cloaks his ignorance with learned jargon, and then calls it wisdom.

To this day it still remains true of the growth of the most common seeds – *He knoweth not how.* The scientific man may talk about chemical combinations and physical permutations, and he may proceed to quote analogies from this and that, but still the growth of the seed remains a secret; it springs *he knoweth not how.* Certainly, this is true of the rise and progress of the Word of God in the heart. It enters the soul and roots itself you know not how. Naturally men hate the Word, but it enters and it changes the heart so that they come to love it, but we know not how. Their whole nature is renewed, so that instead of producing sin it yields repentance, faith, and love, but we know not how. How it is that the Spirit of God deals with the mind of man, how he creates the new heart and the right spirit, how he *hath begotten us again unto a lively hope* (1 Peter 1:3), how we are born of the Spirit, we cannot tell.

The Holy Spirit enters into us; we hear not his voice, we see not his light, we feel not his touch; yet he works an effective work upon us, which we are not long in perceiving. We know that the work of the Spirit is a new creation, a resurrection, a reviving from the dead; but all these words are only covers to our utter ignorance of the mode of his working, with which it is not in our power to meddle. We do not know how he performs his miracles of love, and, not knowing how he works, we may be quite sure that we cannot take the work out of his hands. We cannot create, we cannot revive, we cannot transform, we cannot regenerate, we cannot save.

This work of God having proceeded in the growth of the seed, what next? *We can reap the ripe ears.* After a season God the Holy Spirit uses his servants again. As soon as the living seed has produced first of all the blade of thought, and afterwards the green kernel of conviction, and then faith, which is as a full head of wheat, then the Christian worker comes in for further service, for *he can reap. When the fruit is brought forth, immediately he putteth in the sickle* (Mark 4:29). This is not the reaping of the last great day, for that does not come within the scope of the parable, which evidently relates to a human sower and reaper.

The kind of reaping that the Savior here intends is that which he referred to when he said to his disciples, *Lift up your eyes, and look on the fields; for they are white already to harvest* (John 4:35). After he had been sowing the seed in the hearts of the Samaritans, and it had sprung up so that they began to show faith in him, the Lord Jesus cried, *Look on the fields; for they are white already to harvest* (John 4:35). The apostle says, *One soweth, and another reapeth* (John 4:37). Our Lord said to the disciples, *I sent you to reap that whereon ye bestowed no labour* (John 4:38). Is there not a promise: *In due season we shall reap, if we faint not* (Galatians 6:9)?

Christian workers begin their harvest work by watching carefully to see when men reveal signs of faith in Christ. They are eager to see the blade, delighted to observe the ripening ear. They often hope that men are believers, but they long to be sure of it; and when they judge that at last the fruit of faith is put forth, they begin to encourage, to congratulate, and to comfort. They know that the young believer needs to be housed in the barn of Christian fellowship, so that he may be saved from a thousand perils. No wise farmer leaves the fruit of the field long exposed to the hail that might beat it out, or the mildew that might destroy it, or the birds that might ransack it.

Evidently no believing man should be left outside of the gathering of holy fellowship; he should be carried into the midst of the church with all the joy that attends the bringing home of the sheaves. The worker for Christ watches carefully, and when he discerns that his time has come, he begins at once to fetch in the converts so that they may be cared for by the brotherhood, separated from the world, screened from temptation, and laid up for the Lord. He is diligent to do it at once, because the text says, *Immediately he putteth in the sickle* (Mark 4:29).

He does not wait for months in cold suspicion; he is not afraid that he shall be encouraged too soon when faith is really present. He comes with the word of promise and the smile of brotherly love at once, and he says to the new believer, "Have you confessed your faith? Is not the time come for an open confession? Has not Jesus bidden the believer to be baptized? If you love him, keep his commandments." He does not rest until he has introduced the convert to the communion of the faithful. For our work, beloved, is but half done when men are made disciples and baptized. We have then to encourage, to instruct, to strengthen, to console, and to help in all times of difficulty and danger. What does the Savior say? *Go ye therefore, and teach all nations, baptizing them in the name of the Father, and of the Son, and of the Holy Ghost: teaching them to observe all things whatsoever I commanded you* (Matthew 20:19-20).

The reaper is the man who gathers in the converts, and he fulfills an honorable and useful office. If I preach the gospel today, and some shall be converted, I shall be the sower; but if going home to the respective towns in which you live, you who have dropped in here as strangers shall be received into the churches by your own pastors, and they will be reaping what I have sown. I envy not my brother minister his success in gathering in the converts, but I rejoice with him. The sower and the reaper may well rejoice together, for our work is one, and we labor for one Lord.

Observe, then, the sphere of service. We can introduce the truth to men, but that truth the Lord himself must bless; the living and growing of the Word within the soul is the operation of God alone. When the mystic work of growth is done, we are able to introduce the saved ones into the church. To bring them into the fellowship of the faithful is our work, and we must not fail to do it. For Christ to be formed in men, the hope of glory, is not of our working; that remains with God. But when Jesus Christ is formed in them, to discern the image of the Savior and to say, *Come in, thou blessed of the Lord; wherefore standest thou without?* (Genesis 24:31), this is our duty and delight. To create the divine life is God's, to cherish it is ours. To cause the hidden life to grow in secret is the work of the Lord; to see the uprising and perfecting of that life, and to rejoice in it is the work of the faithful. even as it is written, *When the fruit is brought forth, immediately he putteth in the sickle, because the harvest is come* (Mark 4:29.

This, then, is our first lesson; we see what we can do and what we cannot do.

Our second topic is like unto the first and consists of what we can know and what we cannot know.

First, *what we can know.* We can know when we have sown the good seed of the Word that it will grow, for God has promised that it shall do so. Not every grain in every place will grow, for some will go to the bird, and some to the worm, and some to be scorched by the sun; but as a general rule, God's Word *shall not return unto [him] void, but it shall . . . prosper in the thing whereto [he] sent it* (Isaiah 55:11). This we can know. And we can know that the seed when once it takes root will continue to grow; that it is not a dream or a picture that will disappear, but a thing of force and energy that will advance from a grassy blade to a head of wheat, and under God's blessing will develop to actual salvation, and be as the *full corn in the ear* (Mark 4:28). God helping and blessing it, our work of teaching will not only lead men to thought and conviction, but also to conversion and eternal life.

We also can know, because we are told so, that the reason for this is mainly because there is life in the Word. In the Word of God itself there is life, for it is written, *The word of God is quick, and powerful* (Hebrews 4:12) – that is, it is "living and powerful." It is the incorruptible seed, *which liveth and abideth for ever* (1 Peter 1:23). It is the nature of living seeds to grow, and the reason why the Word of God grows in men's hearts is because it is the living Word of the living God, and where the word of a king is, there is power. We know this because the Scriptures teach us so. Is it not written, *Of his own will begat he us with the word of truth* (James 1:18)?

Moreover, the earth, which is here the model of the man, *bringeth forth fruit of herself* (Mark 4:28). We must mind what we are about in expounding this, for human hearts do not produce faith of themselves; they are as hard rock on which the seed perishes. But it means this – that as the earth under the blessing of the dew and the rain is, by God's secret working upon it, made to take up and embrace the seed, so the heart of man is made ready to receive and embrace the gospel of Jesus Christ within itself. There is something suitable in the earth to the seed that is sown in it, so that the seed is adopted and nourished by the soil. Just so is it by the heart of man when God makes it honest and good ground. Man's awakened heart wants exactly what the Word of God supplies.

Moved by a divine influence, the soul embraces the truth, and is embraced by it, and so the truth lives in the heart, and is invigorated by it. The man's love accepts the love of God; man's faith effected in him by the Spirit of God believes the truth of God; man's hope effected in him by the Spirit of God lays hold upon the things revealed, and so the heavenly seed grows in the soil of the soul. The life comes not from you who preach the Word, but it is placed within the Word that you preach by the Holy Spirit. The life is not in your hand, but in the man himself who is led to take hold upon the truth by the Spirit of God. Salvation comes not from the personal authority of the preacher, but through the personal conviction, personal faith, and personal love of the hearer.

You, the sower, are thus taught by the parable that spiritual life and growth are of God and come by the seed and the soil far more than by you. As far as the truth is concerned, its intrinsic power is the same no matter who preaches it. It is not because such and such a preacher, whom God has blessed, speaks forth the gospel, that therefore it lives in men's hearts. Oh no; it is because of the truth itself, and because of the hearts themselves that receive the truth by the secret working of God's blessed Spirit. So much as this we may know, and is it not enough for all practical purposes?

Still, there is *a something which we cannot know,* a secret into which we cannot pry. I repeat what I have said before, that you cannot look into men's inward parts and see exactly how the truth takes hold upon the heart, or the heart takes hold upon the truth. Many have watched their own feelings until they have become blind with despondency, and others have watched the feelings of the young until they have done them rather harm than good by their rigorous supervision. In God's work there is more room for faith than for sight. The heavenly seed grows secretly. You must bury it out of sight, or there will be no harvest. Even if you keep the seed above ground, and it does sprout, you cannot discover *how* it grows; even though you microscopically watched its swelling and bursting, you could not see the inward vital force that moved the seed.

Behind the veil that conceals the secret working of God in the mysteries of natural life and growth you cannot pry; and as for the divine life in man, it must forever be hidden from all mortal eyes. The result of it you shall be able to see, and something about the way of its development you shall be able to know; but the actual *modus operandi* – the secret and innermost mystery of the new birth – shall not be given to you to perceive. *Thou knowest not what is the way of the spirit* (Ecclesiastes 11:5). His work is done in secret, and you *canst not tell whence [he] cometh, and whither [he] goeth* (John 3:8). "Explain the new birth," says somebody. My answer is: "Experience the new birth, and you shall know what it is."

There are secrets into which we cannot enter, for their light is too bright for mortal eyes to endure. O man, you cannot become omniscient, for you are a creature, and not the Creator. For you there must ever be a region not only unknown but also unknowable. So far shall your knowledge go, but no further; and you may thank God it is so, for thus he leaves room for faith, and gives cause for prayer. Cry mightily unto the Great Worker to do what you cannot attempt to perform, so that, when you see the salvation of men, you may give him all the glory evermore.

Thirdly, our text tells us what we may expect if we work for God, and what we may not expect. According to this parable, we may expect to see fruit. The husbandman casts his seed into the ground, and the seed springs and grows, and he may expect a harvest. I wish I could say a word to stir up the expectations of Christian workers, for I fear that many work without faith. If you have a garden or a field, and you sow seed in it, you would be very greatly surprised and grieved if it did not come up at all; but many Christian people seem quite content to work on, and they never count on a result so much as to look for it expectantly. This is a pitiful kind of working – pulling up empty buckets by the year together. Surely, I must see a result for my labor and be glad, or else, failing to see it, I must be ready to break my heart if I be a true servant of the great Master. We ought to expect results; if we had expected more, we should have seen more, but a lack of expectation has been a great cause of failure in God's workers.

But we may not expect to see all the seed that we sow spring up the moment we sow it. Sometimes, glory be to God, we have but to deliver the Word, and immediately men are converted. The reaper overtakes the sower in such instances, but it is not always so. Some sowers have been diligent for years upon certain plots of ground, and apparently all has been in vain, until at the end the harvest has come, a harvest which, speaking after the manner of men, would never have been reaped if they had not persevered to the end. This world, as I believe, is to be converted to Christ, but not today, nor tomorrow, and perhaps not for many an age. But the sowing of the centuries is not being lost; it is all working on towards the grand ultimatum.

A crop of mushrooms may soon be produced, but a forest of oaks will not reward the planter until generations of his children have disintegrated into the dust. It is ours to sow, and to hope for quick reaping; but still we ought to remember that *the husbandman waiteth for the precious fruit of the earth, and hath long patience for it, until he receive the early and latter rain* (James 5:7), and so must we. We are to expect results, but not to be discouraged if we do not see them today or tomorrow.

We are also to expect to see the good seed grow, but not always after our fashion. We are nearly all of us like children, for still there are not many fathers, and like children we are apt to be impatient. Your little boy sowed mustard and cress yesterday in his little garden. This afternoon Master Johnny will be turning over the ground to see if the seed is growing. There is no probability that his mustard and cress will come to anything, for he will not let it alone long enough for it to grow.

So it is with hasty workers: they think they must see the result of the gospel immediately, or else they will cease, and distrust the blessed Word. Although the people may have taken the Word into their minds and may be considering it, certain preachers are in such a hurry that they will allow no time for thought, no space for counting the cost, no opportunity for men to consider their ways and turn to the Lord with full purpose of heart. All other seeds take time to grow, but the seed of the Word must grow before the speaker's eyes like magic, or he thinks nothing has been done. Such good brethren are so eager to produce blade and ear there and then, that they roast their seed in the fire of fanaticism, and it never lives at all. They make men think that they are converted, and thus effectively hinder them from coming to a saving knowledge of the truth.

I am solemnly convinced that some men are prevented from being saved by being told that they are saved already, and by being puffed up with a notion of perfection when they are not even broken in heart. Perhaps if such people had been taught to look for something deeper, they might not have been satisfied with receiving seed on stony ground; but now they are content with that which comes of seed sown on unbroken rocks, and they exhibit a rapid development and an equally rapid decline and fall. Let us believingly expect to see the seed grow, but let us look to see it advance after the manner of the preacher – firstly, secondly, thirdly – *first the blade, then the ear, after that the full corn in the ear* (Mark 4:28).

You are in a hurry, my brother, but it would be better to exhibit the patience of principle than the heat of passion. Let all men be in a hurry to be saved, but let those who are preaching the truth be content to see men convinced of sin, delivered from self-confidence, enlightened as to the grace of God, and thus led by sure steps to faith. Some of the best Christians do not know the exact point at which they were converted; it was a gradual process, from green blade to ripe ear, and they cannot tell exactly when the actual fruit of faith was formed in them.

Some of the most thoughtful minds are not jerked all of a sudden into religion, but are brought gradually into light, even as the noon of day approaches by degrees.

With many there is at first nothing but a little blade, and you cannot tell whether it is not grass and grass only; their feeling looks like a natural emotion caused by the fear of hell, and this might lead to nothing effective. Then follows a little belief, so formed as to be like the wheat-ear of faith, and yet it may be only a notion. It takes time with such persons before they show the full wheat of assured faith in Jesus. Growth is often, if not generally, gradual, and shall we wish to alter God's method of working? We may expect the seed to grow, but every soil is not equally sharp and speedy, and we must not demand of God that he should work uniformly at the same rate of speed.

We may expect also to see the seed ripen. Our work will lead up by God's grace to real faith in those he has worked upon by his Word and Spirit, but we must not expect to see it perfect at the beginning. How many mistakes have been made here. Here is a young person under impression, and some good, sound brother talks with that young person and asks profound questions. He shakes his experienced head and knits his furrowed brows. He goes into the wheat field to see how the crops are prospering, and though it is early in the year, he laments that he cannot see a head of wheat; indeed, he perceives nothing but mere grass. "I cannot see a trace of wheat," says he. No, brother, of course you cannot, for you will not be satisfied with the blade as an evidence of life, but must insist upon seeing everything at full-growth at once.

If you had looked for the blade you would have found it, and it would have encouraged you. For my own part, I am glad even to perceive a faint desire, a feeble longing, a degree of uneasiness, or a measure of weariness of sin, or a craving after mercy. Will it not be wise for you also to allow things to begin at the beginning, and to be satisfied with their being small at the beginning? See the blade of desire, and then watch for more. Soon you shall see a little more than desire; for there shall be conviction and resolve, and after that a feeble faith, small as a mustard seed, but bound to grow. Do not despise the day of small things.

Do not examine the newborn babe about Calvinism in its different shades, to see whether he is sound after your idea of soundness;

chances are ten to one that he is a long way off of sound, and you will only worry the dear heart by introducing difficult questions. Speak to him about his being a sinner, and Christ a Savior, and you will in this way water him, so that his grace in the ear will become the full head of wheat. It may be that there is not much that looks like wheat about him yet, but by and by you shall say, "Wheat! ah, that it is, if I know wheat. This man is a true head of wheat, and gladly will I place him among my Master's sheaves." If you crush the blades, where will the heads come from? If you cut off the green heads, where will the ripe ones be? Expect grace in your converts, but do not look to see glory in them just yet. It is enough if you see heaven begun; do not look to see it complete in them here below.

Expect then, brethren – for you may expect it – to see a harvest, but do not expect to find every seed springing up. "There," says one, "that is a discouraging word." It may be so, but it is a true word. There is an old worldly proverb that says, "Blessed are those who expect nothing, for they shall never be disappointed." I do not believe in that proverb, but I believe in a moderate form of it: "Blessed are those who do not expect what is unreasonable, for they will not get it." If you young people who begin to work for God expect that every word you speak will be useful to all who hear it, it will not happen, and you will grow discouraged; therefore, I would raise your expectation as high as truth permits, and no higher.

I would have you climb to the top of the ladder; but if I encourage you to go any higher, you will soon be going down the other side, under the notion that you are ascending. I never like to see a man expecting what he will not obtain. Now, I know that some of our seed will fall among thorns, and some in stony places, and I do not despair when it happens to be so. I do not expect when I preach the gospel that everybody who hears it will receive it, because I know it will be a savor of life unto life to some, and of death unto death to others. I pull the net in, hauling away with all my might; but I know that when it comes to shore it will contain some strange things that are not fish, which will have to be thrown away, and I am heartily glad that there will also be in it a cheering number of good fishes.

The results of our ministry in these days will be mixed, even as they were when Paul preached, and some believed and some believed not.

We must be prepared for that, and yet I bid you to let your expectations be very large, for you may have sixty or a hundredfold of fruit from the seed if God be with you, and that will abundantly repay you, even if the crows and the worms should eat their share of the grain.

The last topic is this: what sleep workers may take, and what they may not take; for it is said of this sowing man that he sleeps and rises night and day, and the seed springs and grows up, but *he knoweth not how* (Mark 4:27). They say a farmer's trade is a good one because it is going on while he is in bed and asleep; and surely ours is a good trade, too, when we serve our Master by sowing good seed, for it is growing even while we are asleep.

But how may a good workman for Christ lawfully go to sleep? I answer, first, that he may sleep the sleep of restfulness born of confidence. You are afraid the kingdom of Christ will not come, are you? Who asked you to tremble for the ark of the Lord? Are you afraid for the infinite Jehovah that his purposes will fail? Shame on you! Your anxiety dishonors your God. You degrade him by a suspicion of his failing. Shall the Omnipotent be defeated? You had better sleep than wake to play the part of Uzzah.

Rest patiently, for God's will shall be done, and his kingdom will come, and his chosen will be saved, and Christ *shall see of the travail of his soul.* Take the sweet sleep that God gives to his beloved, the sleep of perfect confidence, such as Jesus slept in the back part of the ship when it was tossed with a tempest. The cause of God never was in jeopardy, and never will be; the seed sown is insured by omnipotence and must produce its harvest. In patience possess your soul, and wait until the harvest comes; for the pleasure of the Lord must prosper in the hands of Jesus.

Also take that sleep that leads to a happy waking of joyful expectancy. Get up in the morning and feel that the Lord is ruling all things for the accomplishment of his own purpose. Look for it. If you do not sleep, you certainly will not wake up in the morning refreshed and ready for more work. If it were possible for you to sit up all night and eat the bread of carefulness, you would be unfit to attend to the service that your Master appoints for the morning; therefore, take your rest and be at peace, and work with calm dignity, for the matter is safe in the Lord's hands.

Take your rest because you have consciously resigned the work into God's hands. After you have spoken the Word, resort to God in prayer, and commit it into God's hand, and then do not fret about it. It cannot be in better keeping – leave it there.

But do not sleep the sleep of unwatchfulness. The farmer sows his seed, but he does not therefore forget it. He has to mend his fences to keep the cattle out; it may be that he has to drive away birds, remove weeds, or prevent floods. While he is not sitting down to watch the growth, he has plenty else to do. He never sleeps the sleep of indifference or even of inaction, for each season has its demand upon him. He has sown one field, but he has another to sow. He has sown, but he also has to reap; and if reaping is done, he has something else to do. He is never done, for in one part or other of the farm he is needed. His sleep is but an interlude that gives him strength to continue in his occupations. Consider that the parable teaches us that we do not have to intrude into the domain of God; but with regard to the secret working of truth upon man's mind, we are to take our rest, and go on our way, serving our day and generation according to the will of God.

I want you, dear brethren and sisters, to come to that point this morning. "Lord, this is your work. Lord, you can do your own work. Lord, do your own work – we beg and implore you to do it. Lord, help us to do *our* work, both at the beginning of the chapter and at the end of the chapter, confident that you will not fail in the middle of the chapter, but that you will do your work. Help us to exercise faith in you, and to go about our labor in the confidence that you are with us, and that we are workers together with you."

Up, brethren, to the mountain, to the brow of Carmel this afternoon, up there and pray that God will send a shower of heavenly rain by his Spirit. Up, Elijah; put your head between your knees and cry until you are certain that the cloud, though it be little at first as a man's hand, will cover all the earth and water the land with blessing. Up and pray that God would sweep away all the doubts which, like locusts, devour the church today, and all love of sin and all rejection of Christ, so that at this hour, even at this hour, God may glorify himself by the feeble hand of his sower while he scatters the seed. I beg your prayers, my dear and faithful friends, this afternoon and this evening, that the Word of the Lord may be divinely victorious. I stand back that God may work, and then come forward that God may work through me; and to him be praise forever. Amen!

Chapter 16

The Choice of a Leader

And he spake a parable unto them, Can the blind lead the blind? shall they not both fall into the ditch? The disciple is not above his master: but every one that is perfect shall be as his Master. (Luke 6:39-40)

Man can hardly be retained in the place of wisdom, even if brought there. Truth lies between two extremes, and man, like a pendulum, swings either too much this way or that. He abides not long in one place, but tosses from side to side; never, except by divine grace, finding rest in the middle point of wisdom at all. Two extremes exist in reference to the pilgrimage and scholarship of life. Some assert that man needs no guide whatever. Is he not a noble creature, gifted with high intelligence? Can he not reason and judge, and understand and discern? He can surely find his own way without direction from outside of himself.

As a learner, why does he need a teacher? He can instruct himself. Is he not possessed of science? Has he not already found out many inventions? Such self-sufficient boasters will not, therefore, stoop to sit at the feet of a master, or follow the track of a guide, and consequently, they frequently become erratic, peculiar, lawless, and unreasonable in their modes of thought, and even of action. Into the mazes of infidelity and atheism such pilgrims wander; into foolishness and strong delusion such teachers of themselves conduct their own minds.

This scheme is dangerous, but its opposite pole is not less so. Deliver a man from rationalism, and he often swings into superstition, and says, "I see that I need a guide; I will take the one nearest at hand." Finding a guide constituted by this authority or that, the man who has ceased to use his judgment surrenders himself at once to his leadership, and reckons that to question is to be guilty of wicked unbelief. Without considering whether the guide be a seeing man or blind, or the teacher be an instructed and qualified instructor, the naive yield themselves up to priests or leaders, and are misled. Weary of thinking, they beg others to think for them, and there they leave the matter.

This is the religion of a great many, and they find much peace in it: the peace of slumbering stupidity. They meet with a church that claims to be revered for antiquity, and then they believe whatever that church chooses to teach; they consider that they have no right any longer to judge or to use their understandings. They hang conscience and reason in a sling, as if they were broken arms, no longer usable, and they give themselves up to be wheeled about like invalids in the chairs of tradition and dogmatism. They do not dare to question – that would spoil the whole thing. They shut their eyes and let other people see for them; no, they shut their eyes to be guided by blind men. They give up thinking, to be directed by those who have also given up thinking, who have long ago shut their eyes and opened their mouths to take in whatever a supreme council or a pope may please to put into them.

Between these two extremes there is a narrow path of right, and happy is he who finds it, namely, the honestly and sincerely judging who the leader and teacher should be, the discovery that a leader has been appointed in the person of the Lord Jesus, and a teacher in the divine Spirit, and then a complete, willing, and believing submission of the whole man to this infallible guidance. Happy is that man who neither in the pride of intellect determines to be a guide to himself, and so to be guide to a fool, nor in the idleness of superstition surrenders himself up to be guided by his fellow man, calling him priest, or pope, or minister, or what you will; but who, having found that God has sent his Son into this world of ours to be the captain of salvation, who shall bring many sons into glory, follows where his commander leads the way, and having seen this same Jesus appointed to be the prophet of his people, delights to sit at his feet and receive his words – reason, affection, contemplation, and will, all finding perfect rest in him. He with his eyes open follows the All-seeing One, and with his mind illuminated becomes a disciple of the eternal Light.

It is clear that the most important thing, if we are agreed that we need a guide, is to examine the claims of those who aspire to the office. Some take a guide because, as I have said before, he is appointed by authority; he happens to be the minister of the church, or the family minister, and he is at once accepted without consideration. He would be a very foolish person who would, in climbing the mountains of Switzerland, take a guide merely because he professed to be one, and carried the usual certificates, if upon looking at him it was clear that the man was stone-blind. Would you say that does not matter because he says he is appointed by authority? Would you go to the top of Mont Blanc with him? If so, he would soon conduct you into a crevasse, and there would be an end to your folly.

Yet multitudes resolve to take their religion by prescription, feeling confident that what is patronized by the great, and established and endowed by the nation, must of course be right. Whether the guide can see or not seems to be a trifle, but he must have been properly ordained and duly inducted; if that be settled, the unthinking many ask no more. For my part, I like to look at my guide's eyes; I like to know whether he has ever traveled the country, and whether he has had experience on the way; and if he cannot satisfy me on those points, then I look elsewhere to one who is all sight, and has had all experience, even the Lord Jesus. His authority I cannot question; I take for granted all that he teaches me. I am glad to be a seeing man following a seeing leader, and I endeavor to be an intelligent scholar learning from a wise and sympathetic teacher.

Our text has much wisdom about it as to this matter; for, first, *it announces to us a great general principle,* as a warning, namely, that a disciple does not get above his Master, but becomes like him. Secondly, *it gives a special application* of the great general principle to Christ, that as we are perfected we shall become like him, even as in the case of all other disciples who grow like their masters. After these points, I shall try to use the text for the encouragement of those who desire Christ as their Master, by saying that *we may put the fact mentioned in the text to a practical test.*

Let us take the great general principle as a warning.

Several truths are involved in the text, and these all illustrate the main point. It is evident that *the disciple is generally drawn to the master who is most like himself* – the blind man is led by the blind. It is not merely that birds of a feather flock together, and therefore men of kindred minds form association with each other, but there is also about us all a natural tendency to admire our own image, and to be willing to submit to any who are superior to us, and yet are of our type. A teacher who does not shock our prejudices but shows a sympathy with our tastes, we are at home with at once.

The priest is like the people because the people are pleased to have him so. It is true of teachers as of idols: *They that make them are like unto them* (Psalm 115:8). If the blind man only could see, he would not choose a blind man to be his guide; but since he cannot see, he meets with one who talks as blind men talk, who judges things as they are in the dark, and who does not know what sighted men know, and therefore never reminds the blind man of his infirmity, and at once he says, "This is my ideal of a man; he is exactly the leader I require, and I will commit myself to him."

So the blind man takes the blind man to be his guide, and this is the reason why error has been so popular. No error would live if it did not chime in with some evil propensity of human nature, if it did not gratify some error in man to which it is compatible. Idolatry is a prevailing sin because man is alienated from God who is a spirit, and in his carnal folly demands a god whom his senses can understand. When you hear of crowds going over to Roman Catholicism, do not wonder at it. Roman Catholicism is the religion of depraved human nature put into shape by the devil, and therefore it is no marvel that the nations are fascinated by it, for what they love and what the god of this world sweetens to their tooth must go down with them. Roman Catholicism and other forms of sacramentalism are a soft bed for idle limbs; and as surely as a lazy man lies down, so surely does a superstitious man take to these systems.

Give a superstitious man the information contained in the Bible, and a pair of scissors to cut his coat according to his shape, and Roman Catholicism in some shape or other will be the religion that he will cut out for himself; consequently, it is popular. You cannot at first understand how the blind man who sets up for a guide could expect to find clients; neither would he, only there are so many other blind people around who know nothing about his blindness, and are sure to come to him. Take care that you are not so blind yourself as to follow their example.

Young man, take care who it is you choose for a guide. Your tendencies will be to select a wrong one, because your tendencies themselves are wrong. Pray that you may begin correctly the journey of life, having grace infused into your hearts, that you may choose the Christ of God who is *the way, the truth, and the life* (John 14:6). O Lord, let no soul here be so blind as to choose blind atheism, blind skepticism, or blind superstition to be his leader, but do take the blind by the hand and lead them by a way that they know not and by paths which they have not seen. Do these things unto them, and do not forsake them.

Having chosen his tutor, the student gradually becomes more and more like his Master, or, having taken his guide, the tendency is to tread more closely in his footsteps, and obey his rules more fully every day. We must all be conscious that we imitate those whom we admire. Love has a strange influence over our nature, to mold it into the form beloved. A true disciple is like clay on the wheel, and his Master fashions him after his own image. We may be scarcely conscious of it, but we are most surely being conformed to the likeness of those to whose influence we submit ourselves.

Whoever then your Master may be, dear friend, you are changing into his image. If you choose to be led by the follower of pleasure, you will become more and more frivolous; if you admire the slave of greed, you will become greedy; if you feel the sway of the idol of corruption, you will grow corrupt yourself. If a man who despises the Word of God becomes your hero, you will before long despise it too. While you are gazing upon him with admiration, a kind of photography is going on, and you, like a sensitive plate, receive his image. I charge you, therefore, to be careful who becomes your guide.

And observe, *the pupil does not go beyond the tutor,* nor does the man who submits to be led go beyond his guide. Such a case is very rarely found; indeed, I may say never found, for when the one who is led goes beyond his leader, he is not in truth led any longer; rarely enough does it ever come to that. Men, if they outstrip their leaders, generally do so in the wrong direction. They seldom exaggerate their virtues, those they frequently omit, but they usually exaggerate peculiarities, follies, failings, and faults. It is said that in the court of Richard III, because the king was round-shouldered, the courtiers gradually became hump-backed, and we have seen a whole country idiotic enough, not in the last century, but in this century, to have almost all its women limping because a popular princess was afflicted with a temporary lameness.

It is the way of mankind; they imitate each other as if by instinct, and this is the only excuse I know of for Darwin's theory of our having descended from the ape. Imitativeness is well developed in us, but if left to itself it works with a bias the wrong way, and the imitation is most forcible in the direction of deformity and defect. In music, and painting, and poetry, and literature, men of a school seldom excel their master, or, if they do, they leave him; but the habit is to perpetuate the master's mannerisms and weaknesses. It is even more so in the art of living. Young men, in the task of choosing a master for your faith, I beg you to be careful to have none but the best, for you will not excel, but rather fall behind the master you follow. If you are choosing a leader, choose one who knows the road, for if he has made some blunders you will make ten times as many, and in all probability, you will exaggerate each one of his mistakes.

The most solemn truth remains to be noted. *When a man chooses a bad leader for his soul, at the end of all bad leadership there is a ditch.* A man teaches error which he declares he has drawn from Scripture, and he backs it up with texts perverted and abused. If you follow that error, and take its teacher for a leader, you may for a time be very pleased with yourself for knowing more than the poor plain people who keep to the good old way; but, mark my word, there is a ditch at the end of the error. You do not see it yet, but there it is, and into it you will fall if you continue to follow your leader. At the end of error there is often a moral ditch, and men go down, down, down; they scarce know why, until presently, having imbibed doctrinal error, their moral principles are poisoned, and like drunken men they find themselves rolling in the mire of sin.

At other times the ditch beyond a lesser error may be an altogether damnable doctrine. The first mistake was comparatively trifling, but, as it placed the mind on an inclined plane, the man descended almost as a matter of course, and almost before he knew it, he found himself given over to a strong delusion to believe a lie. The blind man and his guide, whatever else they miss, will be sure to find the ditch; they need no sight to obtain an abundant entrance into that. Alas! to fall into the ditch is easy, but how shall they be recovered? I would earnestly implore especially professing Christians, when novelties of doctrine come up, to be very cautious as to how they give heed to them. I bid you to remember the ditch. A small turn of the switch on the railway is the means of taking the train to the far east or to the far west: the first turn is very little indeed, but the points arrived at are remote.

There are new errors that have lately come up that your fathers knew not, with which some are mightily busy, and I have noticed when men have fallen into them that their usefulness ceased. I have seen ministers go only a little way in speculative theories, and gradually glide from latitudinarianism into Socinianism or atheism. Into these ditches thousands fall. Others are precipitated into an equally horrible pit, namely, the holding nominally of all the doctrines in theory and none of them in fact. Men hold truths nowadays with the bowels taken out of them, and the very life and meaning torn away. There are members and ministers of evangelical denominations who do not believe evangelical doctrine, or if they do believe it, they attach but little importance to it; their sermons are essays on philosophy, tinged with the gospel. They put a quarter of a grain of gospel into an Atlantic Ocean of talk, and poor souls are drenched with words to no profit.

God save us from ever leaving the old gospel, or losing its spirit, and the solid comfort that it brings; yet into the ditch of lifeless profession and philosophical dreaming we may soon fall if we commit ourselves to wrong leaderships. All this should prevent us, as I think, from taking any man whatever as our leader, for if we trust any mere man, though he may be right in ninety-nine points out of the hundred, he is wrong somewhere, and our tendency will be to be more influenced by his one wrong point than by any one of his right ones. Depend upon it in matters of religion, that the ancient curse is abundantly verified: *Cursed be the man that trusteth in man, and maketh flesh his arm* (Jeremiah 17:5).

There is one whom you may follow implicitly, and one only. There is one whom you may trust without reserve, and only one – the Man Christ Jesus, the Son of God. But if you do not wish to be led into errors of heart and practice, then beware of men, and follow none but Jesus, and follow no footsteps but the footsteps of that flock that follows at his heel. You will do best not even to follow the sheep, but to follow the Shepherd only, and to do that even if you walk alone. May the Holy Spirit be given to you to lead you into all truth. Thus much upon the great principle; let it act as a warning.

Its special application to our Lord Jesus Christ is our encouragement. If we have the Lord Jesus Christ as our leader, we certainly cannot go beyond our leader, but we shall be privileged to grow more and more like him, and we shall be perfected according to our text, as our leader is.

First, *this is what we might have expected.* We see ordinarily, as we have said, that the disciple grows like his Master, but with such a Master the process becomes more sure. With such a Master, of whom these lips cannot speak well enough, a Master the latchets of whose shoes I am not worthy to untie, it may well come to pass that we are melted down with love and poured out into the mold of obedience. He is the Creator; can he not create in us his image? From such a one as he is we confidently expect it.

For, observe, the teaching itself is such that it must have power over hearts that yield to it. His doctrine is almighty love; all his teaching is divine, and yet so broken down to human capacity that it exactly suits the man who has taken the yoke of Christ upon him, and is determined to learn of him. Other masters teach us crooked and doubtful lessons, and when learned too often, the best wisdom is to unlearn them; but with our Lord the teaching is most sure, most heavenly, most potent, and we feel within ourselves that it is so true, so noble, so grand, that it comes to us with authority, and not as the word of man.

If I knew only what Jesus teaches, I would conclude that a teacher who gives forth such doctrines and such precepts must influence his disciples; but it is not in his teaching alone that his influence lies; the most potent charm is *himself.* When he spoke here below they said, *Never man spake like this man* (John 7:46), and the reason was because "never man lived like this man." His word was with power, but then he himself was the Word. If you view the precepts of Christ as embodied in his life, they glow with beauty and flash with power. You can bear from such a teacher what you could not have endured from anybody else, for his character gives him a right to speak.

Many of his precepts would have seemed perfectly preposterous had they first fallen from the lips of fallible men, for their hearers would have cried out, *Physician, heal thyself* (Luke 4:23). Coming from him they come naturally as good fruit from a good tree; they are the necessary out-gushings of such a nature and such a life. Who can help being persuaded when the arguments live before our eyes? We are overpowered by the grandeur of the Redeemer's goodness, by the splendor of his love, and by the infinity of his self-sacrifice. Jesus commands our faith by the revelation of himself, and by that same manifestation he conforms us to himself. Was there ever such a life as his? Was there ever such a death? Was there ever such an altogether lovely person as his? Was there ever such perfection as his? In life he was so outspoken and yet so gentle, so courageous and yet so kind, so unflinching and yet so tender, wearing his heart upon his sleeve in the transparency of truth, but prudent and guarding himself with infallible wisdom; a match for all, however they might attack him, and yet apparently never on his guard at all, but he was as a child among them, the holy child Jesus.

Oh, if you sit at Jesus' feet you will not only learn of him, and his teaching will have power over you, but you will also learn *him,* for he himself is his own best lesson. Never did eyes look up into those dear eyes of Jesus, which *are as the eyes of doves by the rivers of water, washed with milk, and fitly set* (Song of Solomon 5:12), but they were themselves cleansed and purified until they became *like the fishpools in Heshbon, by the gate of Bathrabbim* (Song of Solomon 7:4). Who could bear the Lord Jesus on his heart, like a cluster of myrrh, and not be perfumed by his presence? Who could be with him and not be like him?

We feel quite sure that the disciples will grow like their Master in the case of Jesus, because he inspires them with an intense love for himself, which flames forth in enthusiasm for him. Get a teacher whom all the scholars love and admire, and they will soon learn. Make them enthusiastic for him, and no lesson will be too hard. This our dear and blessed Lord, of whom these lips cannot speak as they should, has done. We admire, we love, no, we adore him; he is our God, our all in all, and therefore we yearn to be molded at his will. Live for him? Yes, we find it to be our joy, *for the love of Christ constraineth us* (2 Corinthians 5:14). Die for him? Alas, his saints in all ages have rejoiced to lay down their lives for him. Full of fervor and fired with enthusiasm, they have suffered losses and reproaches for his name's sake. If the teacher inspires such enthusiasm, doubtless he will shape the disciples in his likeness.

Best of all, our Great Teacher has a spirit with him, a mighty Spirit, God himself, the Holy Spirit, and when he teaches, he teaches not with words alone, but with a power which goes beyond the ear into the heart itself. Other teachers, except as they follow Christ, must depend upon the charms of eloquence, or the force of argument; but our Lord, though most eloquent of all, for his lips are like lilies dropping sweet-smelling myrrh, though full of arguments, for his is the wisdom of God, relies upon the energy which he felt when he said, *The Spirit of the Lord God is upon me; because the Lord hath anointed me* (Isaiah 61:1).

The divine Spirit casts a light into the soul, of such a brilliance that things not seen stand out in clearest evidence, and things hoped for are grasped in their very substance. With that light there comes also life to feel, power to realize, and discernment to judge, and so the soul is led into all truth, and the scholar receives the lessons of his Lord in their life and energy. Who else can give this Spirit? By what other teacher can the Holy Spirit be breathed into us? Who would not sit at the feet of a Master so transcendently above all others in possessing such an infinite gift? I would to God while I am speaking thus, that some present here would say, "Willingly would I commit myself to that Great Teacher." Remember, beloved, if you want him to be your Master, he equally longs for you to be his disciple.

I think I have now shown that it was to be expected that with such a Master, the disciple should become like him. Now let me observe that *this was virtually promised*. It is promised to us in effect in the great decree of predestination: *For whom he did foreknow, he also did predestinate to be conformed to the image of his Son* (Romans 8:29). This is the great purpose of God, that Christ may be the firstborn among many brethren, and that the brethren may be a company in whose faces the Lord will discern the image of the Only Begotten. What God predestinates we may confidently expect.

It is promised to us in the very name of Jesus Christ, for that name is *Jesus: for he shall save his people from their sins* (Matthew 1:21). But saving men from their sins is the bringing of them back into a condition of purity and holiness. This, indeed, is the salvation that we preach, not the mere forgiveness of sin, as some think, but also the conquering of sin, the driving-out of sin, the making of men to be like the Lord Jesus by the Spirit of God. The very name of Jesus tells us that he means to make his disciples free from sin as he is.

We know also that this was our Lord's object, for the design of Christ's life is clearly seen in his last prayer when he prayed, *Sanctify them through thy truth: thy word is truth. And for their sakes I sanctify myself, that they also might be sanctified through the truth* (John 17:17, 19). You can see that his one object is to make his people holy as he is holy, to keep them from evil even as he was kept, and to make them conquerors over sin even as he conquered. All his life long he labored at this with the twelve and with others who followed him, and his last prayer breathes this: *I pray not that thou shouldest take them out of the world, but that thou shouldest keep them from the evil* (John 17:15).

Everywhere this is seen to be true. The relationships which he assumes suppose it, for brethren are like their brother, and friends are like their friend. The metaphors that he uses imply the same thing, for the ingrafted branch drinks in the nature of the stem, the spouse grows like her husband, and the members of the body are of the same nature as the head. The mystical Christ is not like the image of the Babylonian monarch's dream with head of gold and feet of clay, but Christ is one throughout – the grace which dwells in the head, transforming the whole body. It is our delightful expectation that *we shall be like him; for we shall see him as he is* (1 John 3:2), and then shall we be satisfied, for we shall wake up in his likeness.

Well, brethren, what we might have expected, and what God has thus virtually promised, *has been actually seen,* for the disciples have been like their Lord, and this is where I want to lay the most stress. Have not the disciples been like their Lord in points of character? It would be very absurd for me to say that the Old Testament saints were disciples of Christ in a literal sense, and yet in spirit they all were so, for the gospel is the same in all ages, and it is the same light *which lighteth every man that cometh into the world* (John 1:9). The inner teaching of the Spirit was the same to Abel and to Noah as it was to John and Paul, and while apostles looked back to Jesus and were enlightened, patriarchs looked forward and had light too.

Now each of the saints in the olden time had some likeness to the Lord Jesus Christ. Think of a few of them, and you will see some of his beauties. Abel reveals his righteousness, and Enoch his walking with God. Job shows his patience, and Abraham his faith; Moses his meekness, and Samuel his power of intercession. Daniel is like him in his integrity, and Jeremiah in his weeping. Like drops of morning dew, all these reflected the light of the Sun of Righteousness. In the New Testament we see the transforming power of his teaching in many instances. Peter and John were like their Master, for we read that when their enemies *saw the boldness of Peter and John, and perceived that they were unlearned and ignorant men, they marvelled; and they took knowledge of them, that they had been with Jesus* (Acts 4:13). The likeness was so striking that they were obliged to confess it.

Take John alone, for a minute, and who can read his epistles without saying, "Even thus his Master spoke"? John was far behind his Lord, but yet how marvelously like him! You have smiled at your children sometimes when you have seen your own ways repeated in them. You have beheld your own peculiarities as in a looking glass. Almost unconsciously they have been yourself in miniature. So was it evidently with John. If it be true, as tradition says, that he was carried into the assembly when he was too old to walk, and was accustomed to saying to them, "Little children, love one another; little children, love one another," it was so like our Lord Jesus Christ that you might have thought the Master had returned to earth.

As for Paul, in many aspects he is the counterpart of his Lord, and as I read that strange passage in Romans that staggers some, where he says, *I could wish that myself were accursed from Christ for my brethren, my kinsmen according to the flesh* (Romans 9:3), I am led to say, "Herein he resembles that Blessed One who was actually made a curse for us, as it is written, *Cursed is every one that hangeth on a tree*" (Galatians 3:13). Now, all the saints of God more or less, according as they have fully been disciples of Jesus, display his characteristics. I cannot stop this morning to tell you what characteristics I see in you that are like my Lord; I rejoice that I do know brothers and sisters here of whom I have often said to myself, "I can see their Master in them." I wish I could say so of all of you, but still I am glad to see in so many the points of true likeness to Jesus, the family characteristics that mark all the children of God. There are little touches of their Father in all the heirs of salvation, which make us feel that they belong to the same family as Jesus; they could not have learned those ways, they must have been imparted by a birth from above.

It is a very noteworthy thing that those who are disciples of Christ even become like him as to their life story. Going back to the old saints as being really disciples of the doctrine of the Redeemer, there is Melchizedek bringing forth bread and wine to refresh Abraham – would you not have thought it was Christ himself? There is Isaac gently submitting to his father while he draws the knife to slay him – could you not have said that it was Jesus? There is Joseph making himself known to his brethren, and ruling all Egypt for their good – might we not have thought that it was our Lord come on earth before his time in order to bless his chosen ones?

Yonder is David coming back with Goliath's head, while all the maidens of Israel rejoice around him – could you not have thought it was our Lord returning from Edom with dyed garments from Bozrah? The saints are types of him because they are of the same type as he is. As for the disciples after Christ came, you will often find them in positions which set forth Jesus Christ most evidently. See Stephen boldly declaring the gospel until his enemies stone him. Have you not read of his Master many times: "They would have stoned him, but he transported himself out of their sight"? Look at Paul at Lystra. They are about to sacrifice to him: it makes you think of days when the crowd cried "Hosanna, Hosanna."

Lo, the apostle rebukes the throng, and now they are stoning him, and it recalls to your memory the time when the crowd shouted, "Crucify him, crucify him! Away with such a fellow from the earth!" Read the story of Paul in the shipwreck, when he says to the captain of the ship, and to the officer of the troops, *Be of good cheer: for there shall be no loss of any man's life among you* (Acts 27:22). You might almost have thought it was the Savior himself saying to the winds and waves, *Peace, be still* (Mark 4:39); there was so much of his Master in him. Indeed Christ is in all his members; his life is written out again in their lives.

Beloved, I could mention many saints of modern times in whose lives we may see Jesus. That poor woman who dropped into the treasury her two mites, which were all her living; is she not very like him who gave up all for us and became poor that we through his poverty might be rich? Others are like the woman who broke the alabaster box of precious ointment, to give her best things to her Lord. Do they not remind you of the lover of our souls, who broke the precious alabaster box of his body and filled all earth and heaven with the perfume? Everyone who gives up self for God's glory is Jesus in miniature. Look at John Howard going about among the dungeons of Europe, spying out poor prisoners to do them good. Is not that Christ over again, with glad tidings for the captives? Or John Williams landing at Erromango, with his life in his hand, to convert cannibals; was not that laying down his life for the sheep?

Now, dear friend, do you think if we had your life before us we could make out anything like Jesus Christ in it? If you are his disciple, it will be so. There will be in your biography as your children will read it – for they will read it better than anybody else – as your wife will read it, as those you work with will read it, something that looks as if it were extracted from the life of Jesus. Students in Christ's college must be like their Tutor, and they are. I dare say the brother is present here of whom I am about to speak, and if so, he will be sorry to hear me tell the story, and would stop my mouth if he could; I will, however, be bold to go on.

I know a house painter who was working with other men over the top of the Great Northern Railway, at a great height. One of his fellow workmen had been drinking very heavily and was unsteady on the lofty scaffold. He said to himself, "That man will never get down alive," and rather than he should perish, he actually offered to carry him down on his back. I believe it would have been death to them both if the attempt had been made, but he cheerfully offered.

He said, "My soul is safe; I am a Christian. I am afraid you will be killed, and if you are, your soul will be lost. I will carry you down if you will only keep quiet." The man rejected the kind offer, though persuaded again and again, and alas, in trying to descend he fell into the middle of the railway, from a dreadful height, and was taken up dead. When I heard of my good brother, a humble member of the church doing that, I thought, "There is our Master, revealed in his disciple." Our life is a painting, and if we are in Christ's studio there will be traces of his hand, and men will exclaim, "That was no common painter; that stroke, that line, is just the line that the great Master used to make; I am sure he has put in those touches." O brethren, we need none of us wish to be originals; let us plagiarize Christ, and that will be the grandest originality. God help us in this.

Now I was going to say, but time has fled, that Christ's disciples grow like him in their struggles and in their temptations. They are met by Satan as Christ was; they are tested by the world as Christ was; they are attacked by Sadducean unbelief and Pharisaic superstition as Christ was; they have to go through the same fight, and, blessed be God, they win the same victories. Christ's disciples overcome sin; by their Master's help they rise above doubt, they vanquish the world, and they stand in purity and faith. By and by they shall be like him in their rewards. *To him that overcometh,* says he, *will I grant to sit with me in my throne, even as I also overcame, and am set down with my Father in his throne* (Revelation 3:21).

It is a beautiful subject, if I had the power to work it out, the way in which the disciple of Jesus thus by sure steps becomes perfected into the image of Christ, until the likeness is so near and so close that even the blurry eyes of this wicked world in the dim atmosphere of its ignorance cannot help seeing that the man is like the Master.

Now, lastly, we will dwell for two or three minutes upon this encouraging fact, that we may put all this to the test this morning if we will. Brethren and sisters, if you are not disciples of Jesus Christ, remember that he will receive you. He will receive you though you have been to other masters, and learned a great deal under them, all of which you will have to unlearn. It is a very easy thing to take a man and teach him if his mind is clear and clean, but you have learned a great deal that you will have to forget.

O you of forty, fifty, or sixty years old, what a world of mischief there is in you that will have to come out. Well, my Master will take you for pupils, though you have been with other masters all this while; and, though you do not know even the basic principles of what he is going to teach, he will take you. My Lord Jesus keeps an ABC school; he begins with the infants. What a mercy it is that he takes such poor, stupid heads as ours, who know nothing except what we ought not to know. And I will add, if you have but very little capacity, or none at all, it does not matter.

> He takes the fool and makes him know
> The wonders of his dying love.

Not many great men, not many mighty are chosen; but God has chosen the poor of this world, and things that are not and things that are despised, yes, and weak things and foolish things, has God chosen. Come to him; for if you are incapable, he is not, and his capacity will soon overcome your incapacity. You say, "I cannot learn." Ah, but you do not know how well he can teach, for he can teach so well that even those who think they cannot learn are soon instructed in his school.

Do not stand back, dear friend, because you cannot pay the fee, for my Master's is a free school; he takes nothing from us, but he gives everything to us. The only admission ticket that you need is simply to be willing to be taught, to be conscious that you need teaching and guiding, and to submit yourself to his guidance and instruction. Are you willing to do so? "Oh," say you, "I shall grieve him until he gives me up." Well, I have often thought so. I do not wonder that you are troubled with that thought; it has often come across me when I see what little progress I have made after being so many years in his school. If I had any human master, he would have been out of patience with me long ago, but the Lord Jesus Christ never gives up a scholar; having once commenced to teach, he continues his divine lessons until they are fully learned, and the more difficult it is for him to teach, the more honor it will be when he gets all his scholars educated for the skies.

He will not tolerate a defeat in this matter; he will overcome ignorance, and sin, and hardness of heart, and infirmity, and incapacity, until he shall have instructed us in the lesson of heaven, and made us fit to be partakers of the inheritance of the saints in light. Come, dear brethren and sisters, you who are scholars of Christ, let us sit at his feet, let us follow in his ways more closely than ever. And you, dear friends, who as yet are not in his school, he says to you, *Whoso is simple, let him turn in hither: as for him that wanteth understanding, . . . Come, eat of my bread, and drink of the wine which I have mingled* (Proverbs 9:4-5). May the Lord Jesus incline your hearts to learn of him, for His name's sake. Amen.

Charles H. Spurgeon
– A Brief Biography

Charles Haddon Spurgeon was born on June 19, 1834, in Kelvedon, Essex, England. He was one of seventeen children in his family (nine of whom died in infancy). His father and grandfather were Nonconformist ministers in England. Due to economic difficulties, eighteen-month-old Charles was sent to live with his grandfather, who helped teach Charles the ways of God. Later in life, Charles remembered looking at the pictures in *Pilgrim's Progress* and in *Foxe's Book of Martyrs* as a young boy.

Charles did not have much of a formal education and never went to college. He read much throughout his life though, especially books by Puritan authors.

Even with godly parents and grandparents, young Charles resisted giving in to God. It was not until he was fifteen years old that he was born again. He was on his way to his usual church, but when a heavy snowstorm prevented him from getting there, he turned in at a little Primitive Methodist chapel. Though there were only about fifteen people in attendance, the preacher spoke from Isaiah 45:22: *Look unto me, and be ye saved, all the ends of the earth.* Charles Spurgeon's eyes were opened and the Lord converted his soul.

He began attending a Baptist church and teaching Sunday school. He soon preached his first sermon, and then when he was sixteen years old, he became the pastor of a small Baptist church in Cambridge. The church soon grew to over four hundred people, and Charles Spurgeon, at the age of nineteen, moved on to become the pastor of the New Park Street Church in London. The church grew from a few hundred attenders to a few thousand. They built an addition to the church, but still needed more room to accommodate the congregation. The Metropolitan Tabernacle was built in London in 1861, seating more than 5,000 people. Pastor Spurgeon preached the simple message of the cross, and thereby attracted many people who wanted to hear God's Word preached in the power of the Holy Spirit.

On January 9, 1856, Charles married Susannah Thompson. They had twin boys, Charles and Thomas. Charles and Susannah loved each other deeply, even amidst the difficulties and troubles that they faced in life, including health problems. They helped each other spiritually, and often together read the writings of Jonathan Edwards, Richard Baxter, and other Puritan writers.

Charles Spurgeon was a friend of all Christians, but he stood firmly on the Scriptures, and it didn't please all who heard him. Spurgeon believed in and preached on the sovereignty of God, heaven and hell, repentance, revival, holiness, salvation through Jesus Christ alone, and the infallibility and necessity of the Word of God. He spoke against worldliness and hypocrisy among Christians, and against Roman Catholicism, ritualism, and modernism.

One of the biggest controversies in his life was known as the "Down-Grade Controversy." Charles Spurgeon believed that some pastors of his time were "down-grading" the faith by compromising with the world or the new ideas of the age. He said that some pastors were denying the inspiration of the Bible, salvation by faith alone, and the truth of the Bible in other areas, such as creation. Many pastors who believed what Spurgeon condemned were not happy about this, and Spurgeon eventually resigned from the Baptist Union.

Despite some difficulties, Spurgeon became known as the "Prince of Preachers." He opposed slavery, started a pastors' college, opened an orphanage, led in helping feed and clothe the poor, had a book fund for pastors who could not afford books, and more.

Charles Spurgeon remains one of the most published preachers in history. His sermons were printed each week (even in the newspapers), and then the sermons for the year were re-issued as a book at the end of the year. The first six volumes, from 1855-1860, are known as *The Park Street Pulpit*, while the next fifty-seven volumes, from 1861-1917 (his sermons continued to be published long after his death), are known as *The Metropolitan Tabernacle Pulpit*. He also oversaw a monthly magazine-type publication called *The Sword and the Trowel,* and Spurgeon wrote many books, including *Lectures to My Students, All of Grace, Around the Wicket Gate, Advice for Seekers, John Ploughman's Talks, The Soul Winner, Words of Counsel for Christian Workers, Cheque Book of the Bank of Faith, Morning and Evening*, his autobiography, and more, including some commentaries, such as his twenty-year study on the Psalms – *The Treasury of David.*

Charles Spurgeon often preached ten times a week, preaching to an estimated ten million people during his lifetime. He usually preached from only one page of notes, and often from just an outline. He read about six books each week. During his lifetime, he had read *The Pilgrim's Progress* through more than one hundred times. When he died, his personal library consisted of more than 12,000 books. However, the Bible always remained the most important book to him.

Spurgeon was able to do what he did in the power of God's Holy Spirit because he followed his own advice – he met with God every morning before meeting with others, and he continued in communion with God throughout the day.

Charles Spurgeon suffered from gout, rheumatism, and some depression, among other health problems. He often went to Menton, France, to recuperate and rest. He preached his final sermon at the Metropolitan Tabernacle on June 7, 1891, and died in France on January 31, 1892, at the age of fifty-seven. He was buried in Norwood Cemetery in London.

Charles Haddon Spurgeon lived a life devoted to God. His sermons and writings continue to influence Christians all over the world.

Other Similar Titles

Life in Christ (Vol. 1 - 12),
by Charles H. Spurgeon

Men who were led by the hand or groped their way along the wall to reach Jesus were touched by his finger and went home without a guide, rejoicing that Jesus Christ had opened their eyes. Jesus is still able to perform such miracles. And, with the power of the Holy Spirit, his Word will be expounded and we'll watch for the signs to follow, expecting to see them at once. Why shouldn't those who read this be blessed with the light of heaven? This is my heart's inmost desire.

– Charles H. Spurgeon

Available where books are sold.

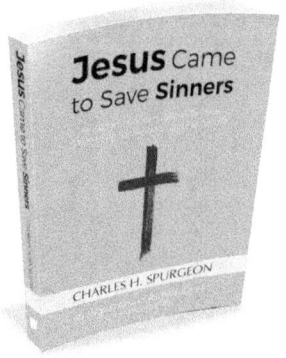

Jesus Came to Save Sinners, by Charles H. Spurgeon

This is a heart-level conversation with you, the reader. Every excuse, reason, and roadblock for not coming to Christ is examined and duly dealt with. If you think you may be too bad, or if perhaps you really are bad and you sin either openly or behind closed doors, you will discover that life in Christ is for you too. You can reject the message of salvation by faith, or you can choose to live a life of sin after professing faith in Christ, but you cannot change the truth as it is, either for yourself or for others. As such, it behooves you and your family to embrace truth, claim it for your own, and be genuinely set free for now and eternity. Come and embrace this free gift of God, and live a victorious life for Him.

Available where books are sold.

Words of Warning,
by Charles H. Spurgeon

This book, *Words of Warning,* is an analysis of people and the gospel of Christ. Under inspiration of the Holy Spirit, Charles H. Spurgeon sheds light on the many ways people may refuse to come to Christ, but he also shines a brilliant light on how we can be saved. Unsaved or wavering individuals will be convicted, and if they allow it, they will be led to Christ. Sincere Christians will be happy and blessed as they consider the great salvation with which they have been saved.

Available where books are sold.

According to Promise,
by Charles H. Spurgeon

The first part of this book is meant to be a sieve to separate the chaff from the wheat. Use it on your own soul. It may be the most profitable and beneficial work you have ever done. He who looked into his accounts and found that his business was losing money was saved from bankruptcy.

The second part of this book examines God's promises to His children. The promises of God not only exceed all precedent, but they also exceed all imitation. No one has been able to compete with God in the language of liberality. The promises of God are as much above all other promises as the heavens are above the earth.

Available where books are sold.

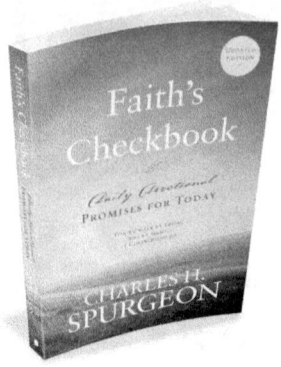

Faith's Checkbook, by Charles H. Spurgeon

Faith's Checkbook is a one-year devotional meant to encourage you to take God at His Word – to take hold of God's promises by faith. Each day you will be presented with a specific promise from the Bible, along with accompanying exhortation by Charles Spurgeon.

This is your "spiritual checkbook," if you will. God's bank account of provision is ample, and it cannot be overdrawn. Every situation you might face is equally met with a promise that, if accepted, will sufficiently see you through.

"God has given no promise that He will not redeem. He does not offer hope that He will not fulfill. To help my brethren believe this, I have prepared this little volume."
    – Charles H. Spurgeon

***Morning by Morning,* by Charles H. Spurgeon**

Charles H. Spurgeon's devotionals *Morning by Morning* and *Evening by Evening* have inspired, encouraged, and challenged Christians for generations. Spurgeon, with his masterful hand, carefully selected his text from throughout the Bible and covered a broad range of topics, in order to present a well-balanced and fruitful daily devotional for readers both young and old.

Now updated into more-modern English for today's readers, and again separated into two volumes as originally published, with morning devotionals in one volume and evening devotionals in the second. We chose a 11-point font for the sake of legibility, and formatted the devotionals so each fits on a single page.

Available where books are sold.